Agile Service Management
with Scrum
Researched

Agile Service Management with Scrum Researched

On the way to a healthy balance between
the dynamics of developing and
the stability of managing
the information provision

Bart de Best

Edited by
Louis van Hemmen

Colophon

More information about this and other publications can be obtained from:
Leonon Media
(0)572 - 851 104

Common questions: info@leonon.nl
Sales questions: verkoop@leonon.nl
Manuscripts / author: redactie@leonon.nl

© 2018 Leonon Media

Cover design: Eric Coenders, IanusWeb, Nijmegen
Production: Printforce B.V., Alphen aan den Rijn

Title: Agile Service Management with Scrum Researched
Sub title: On the way to a healthy balance between the dynamics
             of developing and the stability of managing the
             information provision
Date: 17 August 2018
Author: Bart de Best
Publisher: Leonon Media
ISBN13:   978-94-92618-17-7

TRADEMARK NOTICES

ArchiMate® and TOGAF® are registered trademarks of The Open Group.
ASL® and BiSL® are registered trademarks of ASL BiSL Foundation.
COBIT® is a registered trademark of the Information Systems Audit and Control Association
   (ISACA) / IT Governance Institute (ITGI).
ITIL® and PRINCE2® are registered trademarks of Axelos Limited.
Scaled Agile Framework® and SAFe® are registered trademarks of Scaled Agile, Inc.

You must learn from the mistakes of others. You can't possibly live long enough to make them all yourself.

Sam Levensen

Table of Contents

Figures

Tables

Appendices

Preface

Recently, my book 'Agile Service Management with Scrum' has been published. In this book, a number of risks were identified for each service management process. These risks have to be managed in order to ensure the agreed service norms. Per risk is also indicated how they could be managed within Agile Scrum. The question is whether these risks are also recognized in reality and how they are controlled.

In order to find an answer, I conducted a survey at ten organisations to look at how they deal with these risks. This is done by discussing all risks one by one in an on-site visit. This took an average of three to four hours per organisation. During that visit, the collaboration between the development and service management processes was also outlined. In this book, all participating organisations are described briefly. In addition, I asked these organisations to participate in a maturity research for the Scrum development process and the change management process. Finally, I asked for a self-assessment regarding the implementation of Scrum.

All results are anonymized and cannot be traced back to an individual organisation. I would like to thank all the people who have contributed to this book to thank them for their contribution and energy to make this book what it is: A treasure trove of information to help Agile Scrum system development and service management work together successfully.

In particular, I would like to thank the following reviewers and editors of this book for their great contribution to this book and the fine cooperation!

- J.A.E. (Jane) ten Have   APG-AM
- dr. L. (Louis) van Hemmen   BitAll b.v.
- F.J. (Fred) Ros RE RA   Auditdienst Rijk, Ministerie van Financiën

I wish you a lot of pleasure when reading this book. If you have questions or comments, please do not hesitate to contact me.

A lot of time has been spent to make this book as complete and consistent as possible. If you find any shortcomings, I would appreciate it if you inform me. These items can then be processed in the next edition.

Bart de Best, Zoetermeer.

bartb@dbmetrics.nl

1 Introduction

- This book describes how ten organisations deal with the risks described in the book "Agile Service Management with Scrum." [Best 2018].
- The study included both a maturity study of the Scrum process and the change management process. In addition to the maturity scores of these processes, the answers to the research questions have also been published in this book.
- All ten organisations cooperated open by indicating how they deal with the identified risks. The countermeasures appointed by the organisations are numbered according to the case number in Chapter 7. This allows a certain type of organisation to review how such an organisation deals with the identified risks.

This chapter outlines the background of this research (1.1), the purpose of the research (1.2) and the target group (1.3). Paragraph 1.4 describes the structure of this book. This chapter concludes with the reading guide in section 1.5.

1.1 Background

In ten organisations, an investigation has been performed into how they manage the risks recognized by management within their Scrum process. This book describes the results of this research. The risks and possible countermeasures are published in the book 'Agile Service Management with Scrum' [Best 2018]. In this book, these countermeasures are repeated only summarily because the intended purpose of this book is to find out how other organisations deal with these issues.

In order to participate in the investigation, the ten organisations had to comply to only two preconditions. The first is that they in the past have introduced a service management organisation that used the best practices of Information Technology Infrastructure Library (ITIL). Secondly, they use now an Agile development process based on Scrum or Kanban.

1.2 Purpose research

The purpose of the research is to find out what best practices organisations apply in reality in controlling the risks that are recognized by service management. One of the derived purposes is to determine the extent to which service management processes have been adjusted to match the Scrum development process.

1.3 Target audience research

The research focuses on the widest possible spread of organisations across the market segments. In total, four market segments are represented in the research: healthcare institutions, government agencies, software producers and financial institutions.

1.4 Target audience book

The target audience of this book includes all parties involved in the use of an Agile system development approach. The Service Level Agreement (SLA) norms of information systems can only be achieved if there is good cooperation between all involved parties involved. These parties are customers (user organisation), suppliers (external and internal project staff) and administrators (functional management, application management and infrastructure management).

Next to process owners, process managers, staff of functional-, application- and infrastructure management processes and developers such as product owners, scrum masters, architects, designers, programmers, testers, etcetera, this book is well suited to give other interested parties an impression picture of the importance of structurally combining best practices of service management and agile system development.

For example, line managers, program managers, information managers, business analysts, steering group members, business process owners, mandators and the like, each of them have their own role in establishing and managing the provision of information.

Finally, there is also a target group that does not develop or manage but determines whether what is in production meets the required framework of norms. This target group includes quality managers and Information Technology (IT) auditors. They can use the book as a framework to identify the risks to be investigated based on risk acceptance or risk management.

1.5 Structure

This book starts with a summary in Chapter 2. Next in chapter 3, an impression is given of the maturity of the Scrum development processes and the change management processes of the casus organisations. Before the risk management is elaborated in Chapter 5, it is indicated in Chapter 4 what the casus organisation is currently applying from the Scrum or Kanban ideas. In chapter 6, a conclusion of the applicability after implementation of the Agile method is given for each service management process. In order to be able to put the answers in a particular context, a brief description of each case organisation is given in Chapter 7. This also gives a good insight into the diversity of applying and embedding of the Agile development process.

1.5.1 Chapter 2, Summary

To get an understanding of the results of the research, a summary is included in Chapter 2. The topics relate to the maturity of the Agile development processes and the change management process. It is also indicated which aspects of Agile are applied.

Based on the content of Chapter 5, which describes the risk management, a classification has been given of the extent to which the case organisations control the risks. The measure here is the indicated solution direction. Of course, this assessment is arbitrary because the solution is not exhaustive and risk management is also a matter of probability * impact as well as the risk appetite of the organisations. Nevertheless, this table provides an insight into the degree of risk management at the service management process level and at individual risk levels. However, this overview does not say anything about the risk management ability of the case organisation itself. Finally, this chapter summarizes the extent to which management processes have been made Agile.

1.5.2 Chapter 3, Process maturity

The degree to which risks are managed depends on the maturity of the Agile development processes. Therefore, chapter 3 summarizes the assessment results of the Agile processes of the case organisations. As a reference framework, a self-assessment has been used as listed in Annex A. This self-assessment is based on the UK Office of Government Commerce (OGC) self-assessment for ITIL v2 processes. By using the same format of levels and types of questions for the Agile development process, it is possible to estimate the maturity level in a short period of time. A second advantage is that the maturity of the development process is comparable with the maturity of the service management processes.

This chapter also reflects the maturity of the change management process. The maturity of this process has been included because the Agile development process shows a major overlap with that of the change management process. The self-assessment of the change management process is included in Annex B.

For the sake of readability and clarity, the assessment questions are not all included in Chapter 3, but only the key words are included. The answers to the questions give a good indication of how certain aspects of the Agile development process and the change management process can be shaped.

1.5.3 Chapter 4, Agile application

No case organisation uses Scrum and / or Kanban in the same way. In order to gain insight, a self-assessment has been prepared with questions about the use of this Agile approach.

The questions relate to the terminology used, the process implementation, the governance implementation and the used tools used.

1.5.4   Chapter 5, Agile risk control
All casus organisations have been visited individually, so the risk list could be walked through interactively. Most organisations have chosen one of the development teams as a reference. It was often too difficult to give a complete picture of all the teams of one casus organisation because of the size and the people needed to interview. Therefore, the answers of a case organisation should be considered from the above perspective.

1.5.5   Chapter 6, Agile service management
In addition to best practices in the area of risk control, it is important to determine the effect of Agile way of working on the service management processes. Implicitly, in the research attention has also been paid to this aspect. Therefore, in Chapter 6, an overview is provided to demonstrate the observed effect of the use of the Agile way of working on the service management process implementation and application.

1.5.6   Chapter 7, Case organisations
The answers to many questions are only valuable when placed in the context of the case organisation. Of course, all participating organisations want to remain anonymous, even how well the scores are. Therefore, the case organisations are described in general terms and the case organisations are identified with a number. Therefore, it is possible to relate a large part of the answers within a context of the applicable case organisation. By applying this structure in the book, all answers for one organisation can be walked through, for example a care organisation. Also, the answers can be compared to the software development organisations.

1.5.7   Appendices
The appendices contain some important information that helps you further to understand the issue of managing information systems, generated by Agile system development processes.

Appendix	Subject	Description
A	Assessment Scrum development process	This appendix contains a number of questions that help you to determine how mature your Scrum development process is.
B	Assessment Change Management	This appendix contains a number of questions that help you to determine how mature your change management process is.
C	Literature	In this book, references are included as: [AUTO YEAR]. In this appendix provides, the author, the title and the ISBN number of these references.
D	Glossary	Only the most important concepts are explained in this annex.
E	Abbreviations	In the Information Communication Technology (ICT) there are many abbreviations. In order to keep this book readable to anyone, it has been chosen to make use of them. The first time an abbreviation is used, it will be spelled in full, except for the embedded concepts such as ICT.
F	Tools	This research lists many tools. This appendix lists the tools including the shortened names, full names, and the websites where more information about this product can be found.
G	Use of tools	This appendix describes the use of tools at the casus organisations.
H	Websites	A summary of the relevant websites that contain additional information about acceptance criteria or related topics.

Appendix	Subject	Description
		This reference is recorded as [http Name].
I	Index	Index of the most important concepts in this book.

Table 1-1, Appendices.

1.6 Reading guidelines

The number of abbreviations is kept limited. However, there are terms that come back and forth again. In order to promote readability, these are abbreviated. In addition, common abbreviations are used, but they are spelled in full. Appendix D and Appendix E explain the terms and abbreviations used.

In case Business Information Services Library (BiSL), Application Services Library (ASL) and ITIL are mentioned, it relates to the most recent version of these models, unless otherwise specified.
Tools often have long names and abbreviated names. In this book, at the first time the product is named, the long name is used with the short name in parentheses. In this book, only the shortened name is mentioned. Appendix F gives an overview of the tools.

The references to publications on the Internet are listed in Appendix H. In the text of this book is referred to Appendix H using the following format [http Name]. This includes "http" for the reference to Appendix H and "Name" for the subject.

2 Summary

Message:
- The research is best represented by the financial institutions. It was much easier to find candidates here than in industry or care.
- It appears that nine out of ten organisations that are using Scrum for their information system development are still using a change management process. This process seems to have high maturity.
- The maturity of the development process is generally much lower than that of the change management process. This may be due to the short period that the organisations use Scrum.
- The use of Scrum in the case organisations is very different. Not all terms are used.
- The degree to which the risks are managed is also very diverse. Each organisation has found its own way of managing risks.

Reading guideline:
This chapter describes in section 2.1 from which sectors the case organisations are represented, as well as the distribution level. Section 2.2 summarizes the maturity of the organisations' Scrum process. Section 2.3 compares the maturity of the change management processes. The extent to which Scrum is applied, differs per organisation. Paragraph 2.4 gives a summary of this. The most important part of the research focuses on the degree of risk management. A summary of this control is included in section 2.5. The summary of the impact of working with an Agile development process is described in section 2.6. Paragraph 2.7 finalizes this chapter with a conclusion.

2.1 Case organisations

Ten organisations participated in the research. Figure 2-1 shows the division of case organisations per industry. The financial institutions are best represented (40%), followed by software producers (30%). The government institutions (20%) and healthcare institutions (10%) scored the lowest. It is remarkable that it was very difficult to interest organisations in the manufacturing industry for this research.

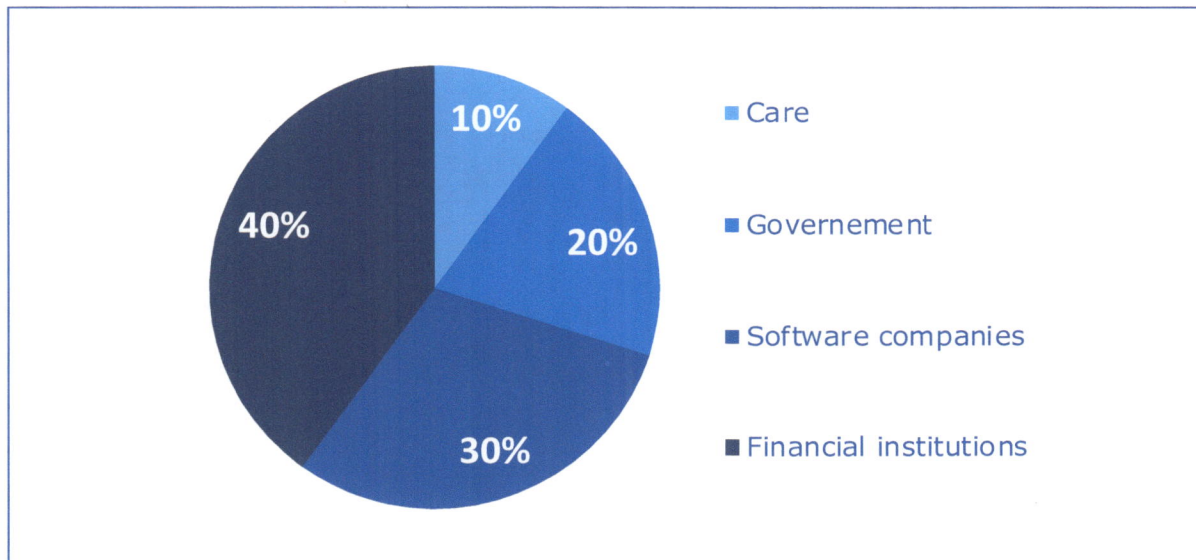

Figure 2-1, Distribution of case organisations per industry.

Important to know is that many casus organisations work with more than one Scrum team. Also, these Scrum teams often differ greatly in terms of composition and work area. Therefore, most case organisations have decided to answer the questions from the perspective of one Scrum team.

However, the entire lifecycle of a change has been taken into account. So, those questions that fall outside of the Scrum team, such as those about the service desk and software roll-out, are often also answered.

2.2 Maturity Agile development process

The maturity of the Agile development process is shown in Figure 2-2. A green cell indicates that a level has been reached. A red cell indicates that a level has not been reached. A yellow cell is an achieved level. However, the yellow cells do not count towards the adult level because a lower level is not reached. The years on the X-axis of Figure 2-2 indicate how long a casus organisation already applies an Agile development process.

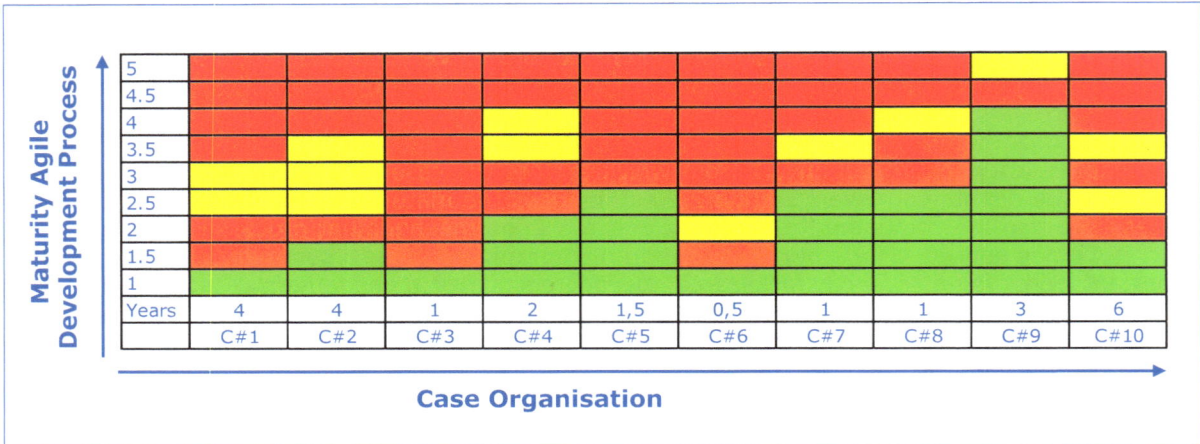

Figure 2-2, Maturity of the Agile development process.

2.3 Maturity change management

With the advent of the Agile development process, it is the question of what role the change management process still plays. To establish this, all casus organisations have been asked to complete a self-assessment of the change management process. A grey cell column means that the process has been replaced by the Scrum process. The results are shown in Figure 2-3.

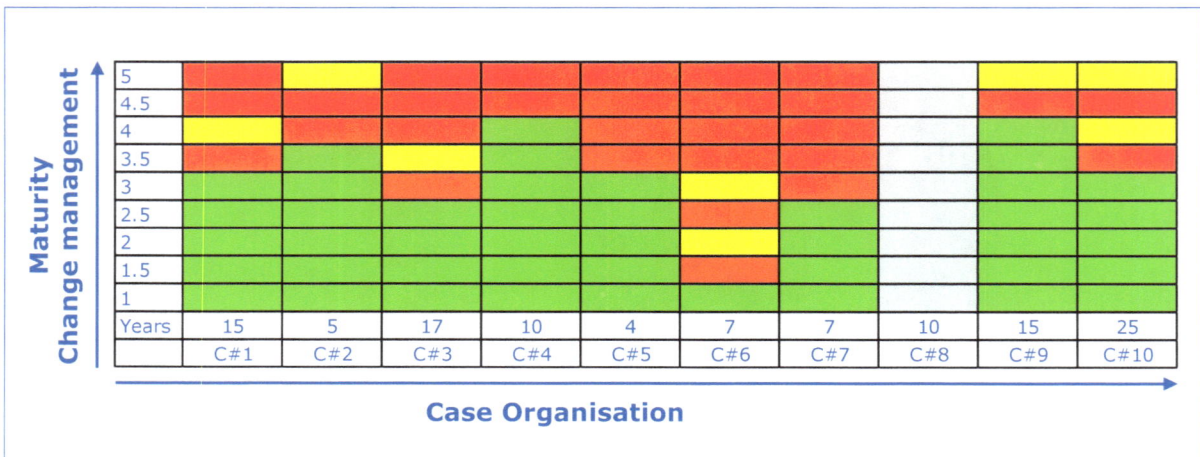

Figure 2-3, Maturity change management process.

It is clearly visible that the change management process still plays a prominent role in most organisations. Only in one organisation, the change process does not control the Agile development process. It also appears that the maturity of the change management process is quite high in relation to the Agile development process.

2.4 Application Agile

Table 2-1 summarizes the scope of the Agile development process in the relevant case organisations. The numbers in this table represent the number of case organisations, which indicates that a part of the organisation is involved in the Agile development process. The user organisation appears to be not involved in the development process at all. This is because information management represents the user organisation. Infrastructure is hardly involved in the Agile development process.

Level of steering	User organisation	Information Management	Application management	Infrastructure management
Strategical steering	-	1	3	1
Tactical steering	-	4	5	1
Operational steering	-	2	7	-
Innovation steering	-	5	10	1

Table 2-1, Scope of the Agile development process.

The focus is on innovative management from application management, supported by information management. The tactical control has a reasonable contribution. This is mainly because of the planning of the change and planning of people and resources. Striking is also the involvement of the operational management of application management. This is because many organisations use Scrum and / or Kanban in conjunction with Development & Operations (DevOps).

2.5 Risk control

Table 2-2 gives an overview of the risks per service management process and its control in the case organisations. The risks are only provided with an ID (ID) in this table. Chapter 5 gives a complete description of these risks. The risks that are controlled by the development team are shown in green. If 'N/A' is indicated, then this means that the risk does not apply to the case organisation. If the 'N/R' is indicated, this means that no research has been carried out on this risk. The colouring of this rating of risk management is only an indication. There is no mathematical formula used that leads to an unambiguous result.

Risk	O#1	O#2	O#3	O#4	O#5	O#6	O#7	O#8	O#9	O#10
Service Portfolio Management										
Is the alignment with the business enabled?										
SPM-R01	Yes	Yes	Yes	Yes	Partly	Yes	Yes	No	Yes	Yes
Are patch works prevented?										
SPM-R02	Yes	Yes	Yes	Yes	N/A	Yes	Yes	No	Yes	Yes
Demand Management										
Has the future use of the software been analysed?										
DEM-R01	No	Yes	Yes	Yes	N/A	Partly	Yes	No	Partly	Yes
Is unmanaged growth of service levels and norms prevented?										
DEM-R02	N/A	Partly	Yes	Yes	Yes	Yes	N/A	No	Partly	No
Financial Management for ICT Services										
Is there a cost control?										
FIN-R01	No	Yes	N/A	Yes	Yes	Yes	Yes	Yes	Yes	Yes
Is the economic value of the software monitored?										

Risk	O#1	O#2	O#3	O#4	O#5	O#6	O#7	O#8	O#9	O#10
FIN-R02	Partly	Yes	Yes	Yes	Yes	Yes	Yes	Yes	Yes	Yes

Service level management

Does the product owner determine the non-functional requirements for the SLA?

SLM-R01	N/A	Yes	No	Yes	No	No	Yes	No	Yes	N/A

Is it guaranteed that the mutual expectations are not out of order?

SLM-R02	N/A	Yes	No	No	No	Yes	Yes	No	Yes	N/A

Is compliance with the SLAs guaranteed?

SLM-R03	N/A	Partly	No	No	No	No	No	No	No	N/A

Is the attention of non-functional requirements guaranteed?

SLM-R04	N/A	Yes	Partly	Yes	No	Yes	Yes	Yes	Partly	Partly

Is the customer's management of quality guaranteed?

SLM-R05	N/A	No	Partly	Yes	No	No	Yes	Partly	No	Yes

Has the risk and impact analysis of non-functional requirements been guaranteed?

SLM-R06	N/A	Yes	No	Yes	N/A	Yes	Yes	No	Yes	Yes

Is the time-to-market managed?

SLM-R07	N/A	Yes	Yes	Yes	Yes	Yes	Yes	Yes	Yes	Yes

Supplier management

Is fragmentation of purchase prevented?

SUP-R01	Yes	Yes	Partly	Yes	Yes	N/A	Yes	No	Yes	Yes

Is the integration of tools across Scrum teams guaranteed?

SUP-R02	N/A	N/A	Partly	Yes	Yes	N/A	N/A	N/A	Yes	Yes

Information Security Management

Is loss of information prevented?

ISM-R01	Yes	Yes	Yes	Yes	Partly	Partly	N/A	Yes	Yes	Yes

Is the integrity of information monitored?

ISM-R02	Yes	Yes	Yes	Yes	No	Partly	Yes	Yes	Yes	Yes

Is the confidentiality of the information monitored?

ISM-R03	Yes	Yes	Yes	Yes	No	Yes	N/A	Yes	Yes	Yes

Availability Management

Is unavailability of the application prevented?

AVI-R01	Yes	Yes	N/A	Yes	No	Yes	Yes	Yes	Yes	No

Is unreliability of the application prevented?

AVI-R02	Yes	Yes	Yes	Yes	Yes	Yes	Yes	Yes	Yes	Yes

Is the software's maintainability guaranteed?

AVI-R03	Yes	Yes	Partly	Yes	Yes	Yes	Yes	Yes	Yes	Yes

Is contractibility guaranteed?

AVI-R04	N/A	N/A	N/A	N/A	N/A	Yes	N/A	Yes	N/A	N/A

Is the resilience of the application guaranteed?

AVI-R05	Yes	Yes	Yes	Yes	Yes	No	Yes	Yes	No	Yes

Risk	O#1	O#2	O#3	O#4	O#5	O#6	O#7	O#8	O#9	O#10
Capacity Management										
Are 'panic' purchases prevented?										
CAP-R01	Yes	Yes	N/A	Yes	No	N/A	Yes	No	N/A	N/A
Is the performance of the application guaranteed?										
CAP-R02	Yes	Yes	Yes	Yes	Yes	Yes	Partly	Yes	Yes	Yes
Is the innovation of used technology deployed?										
CAP-R03	Yes	Yes	N/A	Yes	Yes	Yes	No	Yes	Yes	Yes
IT Service Continuity Management										
Is the contingency provision arranged?										
ITSCM-R01	Yes	Yes	Yes	N/A	N/A	No	Partly	Yes	Yes	Yes
Change Management										
Are the tooling standardization and Standard, Rules & Guidelines used to prevent incidents?										
CHM-R01	Yes	Yes	Yes	Yes	Yes	Yes	Yes	Yes	Yes	Yes
Is tracking performed in the development process?										
CHM-R02	N/A	Yes	Yes	Yes	Yes	Yes	Yes	Yes	Yes	Yes
Are there any measures to prevent delays in decision making?										
CHM-R03	Yes	No	Yes	Yes	N/A	No	Partly	Yes	Partly	Yes
Are risk management methods used to ensure the quality of the software?										
CHM-R04	Yes	No	Yes	Yes	No	No	Yes	No	No	Yes
Is there any evidence regarding the authorization of software modification?										
CHM-R05	N/A	Yes	Yes	Yes	Yes	Yes	N/A	No	N/A	Yes
Has an escalation path been pre-defined for conflicting priorities?										
CHM-R06	Yes	Yes	Yes	Yes	Yes	Yes	Yes	Yes	Yes	Yes
Service Asset & Configuration Management										
Is the quality of the CMDB secured by the development process?										
SACM-R01	Yes	Yes	Partly	Yes	Yes	No	No	No	Yes	No
Is there a verification of the quality of the Software CMDB (S-CMDB)?										
SACM-R02	Yes	Yes	No	Yes	Yes	No	Yes	No	Yes	Partly
Service Validation and Testing										
Are test strategies performed?										
SVT-R01	Yes	Yes	Partly	No	Yes	No	Yes	No	Yes	N/A
Are coverage analyses performed?										
SVT-R02	Yes	Yes	Yes	Yes	Partly	No	Yes	No	Yes	Yes
Is the efficiency of testing guaranteed?										
SVT-R03	Yes	No	No	No	Yes	Yes	Yes	No	Yes	Yes
Are recurring incidents prevented?										
SVT-R04	No	Yes	Yes	Yes	Yes	Partly	Yes	Yes	Yes	Partly
Are regression tests performed to prevent escaped defects?										
SVT-R05	Yes	Yes	No	Yes	Yes	Partly	Yes	Yes	Yes	Yes

Risk	O#1	O#2	O#3	O#4	O#5	O#6	O#7	O#8	O#9	O#10
Release and Deployment Management										
Is delay of continuous integration and continuous delivery prevented?										
RDM-01	Yes	No	No	Partly	Partly	Partly	Partly	Partly	Yes	Partly
Is the integrity of objects in the DTAP street secured?										
RDM-02	No	Yes	No	N/R	Yes	No	Yes	No	Yes	Yes
Is disturbance of the development process by LCM changes prevented?										
RDM-03	Yes	Yes	Yes	Yes	Yes	Yes	N/A	Yes	Yes	Yes
Are delays in the DTAP street adequate prevented?										
RDM-04	Yes	Yes	Yes	Yes	Yes	Yes	Yes	Yes	Yes	Yes
Are manual tasks reduced?										
RDM-05	Yes	Yes	No	Partly	Yes	Partly	Partly	Partly	Partly	Partly
Is over-writing of object in the production environment prevented?										
RDM-06	Yes	Yes	Yes	Yes	N/A	Yes	Yes	Yes	Yes	Yes
Event Management										
Has consideration been given to exceptions during the design and realization of the software?										
EVT-R01	Partly	No	Partly	No	Partly	No	No	Partly	Yes	Yes
Is event filtering enabled by measures in the software?										
EVT-R02	Yes	Partly	No	No	No	No	Yes	No	Yes	Partly
Is event correlation supported by measures in the software?										
EVT-R03	No	Partly	No	No	No	No	No	Yes	Yes	No
Incident Management										
Is incident matching simplified by measures in the software?										
ICM-R01	No	No	No	No	N/A	N/A	Yes	No	Yes	Yes
Is routing simplified by measures in the software?										
ICM-R02	No	No	Partly	No	N/A	N/A	Yes	No	No	No
Is prioritization simplified by measures in the software?										
ICM-R03	No	No	Yes	No	Yes	No	Yes	No	Yes	No
Are heterogeneous incidents prevented through software measures?										
ICM-R04	N/A	N/A	No	No	N/A	N/A	Yes	N/A	Yes	No
Does the DoD have a check whether the service desk is informed about new service requests?										
RFQ-R01	N/A	N/A	Yes	N/A	No	Partly	Yes	No	No	Yes
Does the development team perform Pareto analyses or recurring analyses to find problems?										
Problem Management										
PBM-R01	N/A	N/A	Partly	N/A	Yes	Yes	No	No	N/A	Yes
Is proactive problem management supported by measures in the software?										
PBM-R02	No	No	No	Yes	No	No	No	No	No	No

Table 2-2, Risk control.

2.6 Agile service management

Figure 2-4 gives an overview of the number of case organisations that give substance to the subject areas of project management, service management and Agile system development.

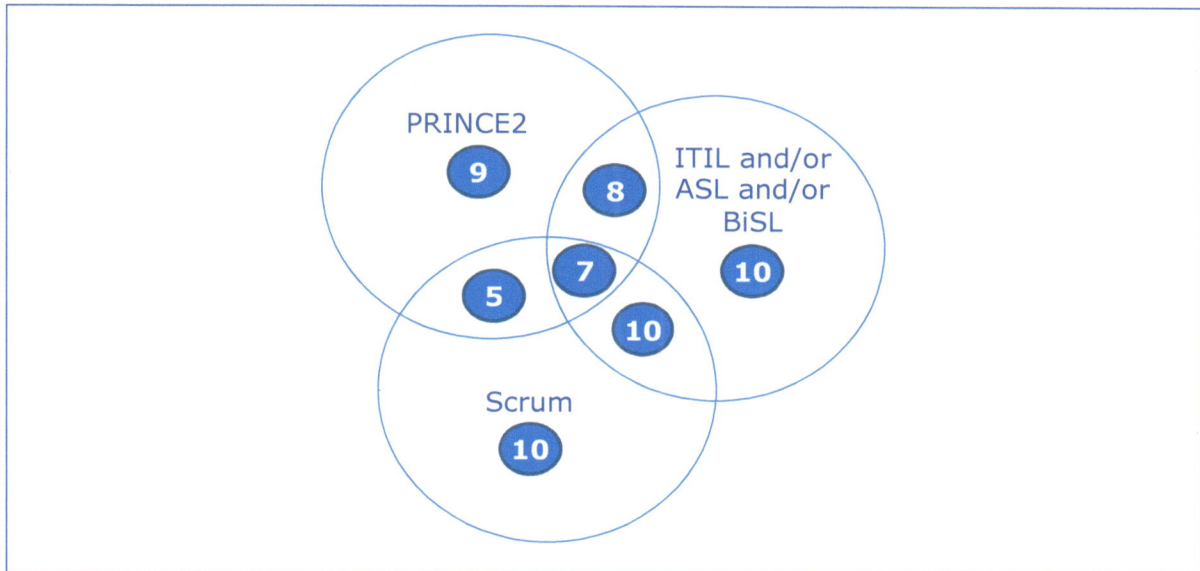

Figure 2-4, Number of case organisations versus discipline.

This figure is compiled based on the outcome of the interviews with the case organisations. Chapter 6 contains more information on the content of these disciplines as well as the interface between these disciplines.

When implementing an Agile development process, often the existing project management and service management best practices are not discarded. This is partly due to the transition phases of the change from Waterfall to Agile. But this also takes place because certain projects are not suitable to develop in an Agile manner. Furthermore, service management is still widely used in the case organisations. However, it is striking that the interface between Waterfall project management and Agile system development is the poorest represented.

2.7 Conclusion

The results of the research show that there are a number of focus areas where more emphasis should be placed on.

The first focus area is the service level management process. It turns out that many organisations do not properly define the responsibility of this process. This means that quality management is also deplorable. Often, the product owner is not involved in the preparation and agreement of the SLA. It is then often that for the architects draw up an SLA with the service level manager. The input comes mostly from the service management organisation and not from the business itself.

A second cluster of attention is that of controlling the change. The risk and impact analysis are often not structured. There are few specific acceptance criteria prescribed to the development team in relation to the risks. The relationship with configuration management is also primarily a service management and not a development issue. As a result, the focus of testing and the maturity of regression tests is not in order. Most worrying is that there are currently not many organisations that have laid the basis for the automation of continuous integration and continuous delivery based on automated regression testing.

The last cluster of attention that should be highlighted is that of the measures in the program to support event management and incident management. This is very important, in combination with the lack of attention to service level management.

3 Process maturity

Message:
- The maturity of the Agile development process is still under development. There are many improvements to be made.
- The maturity of the Scrum development process is not in line with the number of years that the organisation uses Scrum.

Reading guideline:
The first paragraph gives the assessment results of the Agile development process. The second paragraph describes the change management process.

3.1 Agile development process

All case organisations have scored the Agile development process based on the assessment as included in Appendix A.

3.1.1 Maturity

The maturity of the Agile development process is shown in Figure 3-1. It is clear that the Agile development process is not as mature as the change management process.

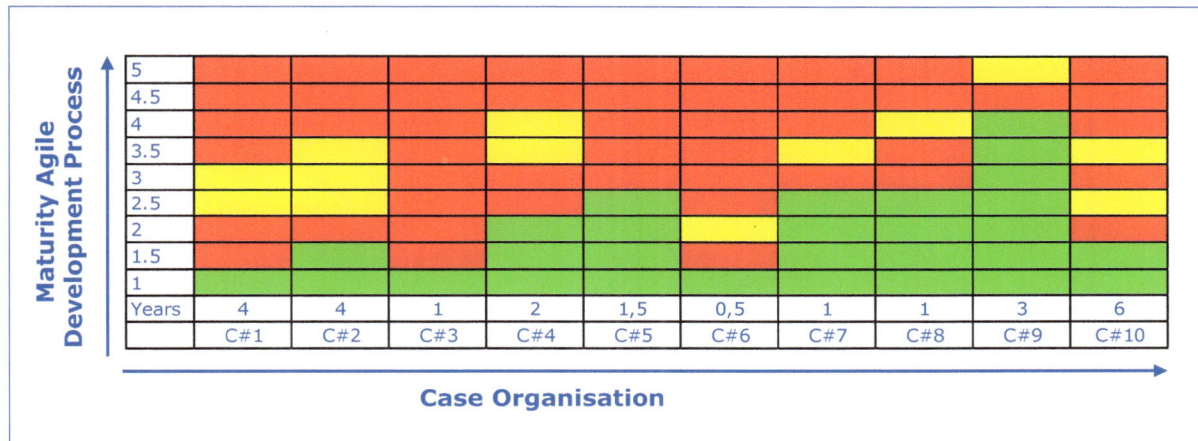

Figure 3-1, Maturity of the Agile development process.

Each organisation has answered per level a set of questions. All mandatory questions must be answered with a 'Yes' and a minimum number of optional questions. Only then is a level reached and coloured green. This does not mean that there are no improvement points for the green cells. A red cell indicates that the level has not been reached. A yellow cell indicates that a level has been reached but not counted for the maturity score because a lower level is not reached. However, a yellow cell indicates a potentially faster maturity of the process.

3.1.2 Explanation

In addition to the scores, a number of case organisations have also completed the following specific questionnaire. The comments are included in this section per subject. The assessment is based on a Scrum development process. Where necessary, the case organisations have replaced Scrum with Kanban or Scrumban. In some cases, two or more case organisations have given the same answers. In that case, the answer given in parentheses is how many case organisations have given this answer.

Q#	Subject / Remarks
Q1.0/1	Which teams? • Several Agile teams have been set up.

Q#	Subject / Remarks
	• One development team has been set up. • One team with two processes has been set up. • A number of Scrum teams have been set up.
Q1.0/1	Which type of application service? • From front-end to various back-office applications. • Business application. • Our Scrum team mainly build end-user applications. • Specific service, the Enterprise Service Bus (ESB). • Content Management System (CMS) + Interfaces + BizTalk. • Components about SharePoint websites.
Q1.0/2	Customer Identification: • The business is divided into business departments. The teams are connected to the business department. • External customers are served. • We have external customer groups, these are executive, service and commercial agencies. • There are both internal and external customers. • Internal customer groups. • The customer group is organisation wide because it is a shared service. Is the product owner the contact point? • Yes. • The service level manager is the point of contact for all customers and in this case also part of the Scrum team The product owner is the contact point for the completion of the customer's requirements (descriptive), the prioritization and the acceptance. • All products are assigned to a product owner. • All customers are assigned to a product owner. • The customers are represented by a product owner. • The customers are assigned to one product owner. Where are the provisioned services described in: • There is no service catalogue. • The services are described in the product catalogue. • The service catalogue has not yet been completed.
Q1.0/3	Interface with the customers: • The service desk is used as interface with the customer. • The product owner is the interface with the customer. • The product owner takes care for all interfaces with the outside world. • The service desk and the product owner are the interface (mentioned twice). • The product owner and the service desk. • The interface is known by the product owner and the service desk etcetera. Basically, the customer can deal directly with the Scrum masters (obviously not with the developers). When it comes to incidents and the like, then the service management organisation is to be contacted. When it comes to priorities (and create new features, etcetera), then the product owner is contacted (and then through design before it reaches the component factory). What is the customer allowed to request through this interface? • The customer may report features, stories and incidents.

Q#	Subject / Remarks
	• Incidents can be reported by everyone via the service desk. The rest is dealt with by the product owner. • The product owner is the contact point for the completion of the customer's requirements (descriptive), the prioritization and the acceptance. • The customer may request anything. • Customers can report incidents and service requests. • The service desk report Request for Change (RFC) in the form of epics via the product owner and in addition, incidents that come from the customer. • Features and stories. Incidents not, this can be done via the service management organisation that submits a change request based on a bug.

Table 3-1, Q1.0 Explanation with Scrum-assessment.

Q#	Subject / Remarks
Q1.5/1	Are the goals and benefits spread in the organisation, what is the evidence that this is the case: • The benefits are known at the workplace, but not at the senior management level. • Initiative from the workplace is embraced by management and distributed as standard within all business departments. • Yes, this is evident from Scrum's choice. The advantage is that the customer gets the changes faster and can give feedback faster. Also, not everything needs to be known at the beginning of the process / project. And the customer is given the opportunity to describe his wishes by means of progressive insight. Due to the nature of the work, the project was difficult to plan and through plans within the sprints, it was possible to ensure that the required adjustments were made for the deadlines. • The Scrum process is widely supported. In the management team, the Scrum project is regularly discussed. The Scrum demos are well-attended by all echelons of the organisation. • The benefits are partly spread in the organisation. This is evidenced by the reorganisation that was shaped on the basis of Scrum and Kanban. • Scrum is being used by more and more projects and has been declared de facto standard by the organisation for new development projects. The Agile Scrum approach has been explained in presentations and workshops to, among others, the management. A working group has translated this into Agile policy. In June 2014, this policy was established by the Board of Directors with the agreement of all divisions. This is the formal side. The informal side is that management actively calls for an agile approach when launching new projects and for information sessions to get better informed. • (Increasingly) wide-scale adoption.
Q1.5/2	Who controls the product backlog: • The backlog is controlled by the product owner (mentioned three times). • The product owner controls the backlog. • The priority of the backlog is discussed by the product owner in management calls (with stakeholders). Backlog control and reliability of the planning: • Story points and a burndown chart are used. • Reliability of backlog planning differs from team to team. This is getting more and more managed. • The reliability of the planning on the backlog is moderate. • There is no business backlog and planning. We are making effort in this area.

Q#	Subject / Remarks
	• Not all teams are in the same phase. Most teams collect metrics. ○ Number of realized stories per sprint per team. ○ Number of tasks, completed tasks per sprint. • This reliability of the planning of objects in the product backlog is also implicit evidenced by the control of the development process by using a Definition of Ready (DoR) (tollgate), velocity (story points), demo (added value and refining) and during the retrospective (control process). • The throughput time per sprint is three weeks. The reliability of the planning is related to the predictability of team velocity versus the global planning of the epics / user stories. • The reliability of the backlog management is completed by checking whether Product Backlog Item (PBI) complies with the DoR.
Q1.5/3	Agreements about measurability of the process: • There are agreements about the throughput time. • There are agreements about the sprint throughput time, not the number of user stories. • There are agreements about the throughput time and the amount of story points. • There are agreements about the amount of points. • There are agreements about the standard two-week throughput time and the number of operations that will be completed. Method of control and reporting: • The manner of steering and reporting on the agreements about the throughput time and amount of story points vary from team to team. Teams use burndown charts. Work is being done to equalize the sprint length. • There is a weekly report. • At the end of each sprint in the retrospective the number of points that have been achieved is inventoried. • Management on throughput time and number of operations.

Table 3-2, Q1.5 Explanation with Scrum-assessment.

Q#	Subject / Remarks
Q2.0/1	Assignment responsibilities: • Most teams have a product owner who fulfils the role of product manager. Most teams also have a Scrum master / foreman. The tasks, responsibilities and authorities of these roles are not recorded in functions. • The tasks, responsibilities and powers of these roles are described. • This is not very clearly described. • These are described in the Scrum handbook. The product owner is always a representative of the business. • The product owner is the service delivery manager who coordinates with the stakeholders. We do not use the product manager role. The Scrum master role is often related to team manager role. The Scrum master and product owner role are not described. The Scrum masters are a kind of delegated product owner. They are responsible for facilitating and adjusting the team if necessary. The product owner determines the content of the product backlog and the priority.
Q2.0/2	Scope development process determination: • The scope has been determined. • It is clearly agreed which products will be developed by the Scrum team. • From collecting requirements until implementation. • The scope has been determined.

Q#	Subject / Remarks
	• The services that are delivered are in accordance with the standard Scrum method. • The scope are the SharePoint components. Which services have been recognized: • "Project management (Scrum), incident management and change management. • The Scrum team currently has two services: developing new software and maintaining the software developed by the Scrum team. • The scope of the Scrum is also determined by the part of the product portfolio for which it is responsible. • Development and maintenance services have been recognized. • The services concern the construction of the components, no maintenance is carried out, but corrective changes are provided at the request of maintenance.
Q2.0/3	Mechanisms for monitoring product / sprint backlog lead time: • There is steering on the sprint backlog. • All teams switch to standard integrated tooling for backlog management, which means that the monitoring of the product backlog is ensured. At many teams incident also end up on the sprint backlog. • A daily stand-up and Jira is used. • We use Jira and the product owner is responsible for monitoring the backlog. • We monitor the duration of an item in the sprint backlog. There is no control on the lead time of the product backlog items, but there is control on the business case. • We manage based on the retrospective, demo, review and Scrum or Scrum. • The lead time is monitored on the basis of a burndown chart. The product owner reviews the results.
Q2.0/4	Review of the applicability and the authorization of features: • This takes place outside the Scrum team. • This depends on the team. • The product owner is the central point of contact for requests and determines which requests are picked up and in which order. • This takes place through a central body in which business and IT meet weekly. • The product owner collects all requests from both internal and external customers and compiles the product backlog. • This is done by the product owner. • There is a verification of the product owner, all feature requests are verified. To this end, a testing is carried out in the preparation phase by, among others, the product group manager (suitability regarding product portfolio), architect (suitability with regard to IT policy) and Change Advisory Board (CAB) (overall suitability and prioritization based on business value). The product owner is always in the lead. • The authorization is determined by the product owner. The design team checks whether it fits within the context of SharePoint. Deviations are captured in the design process by the solution architect, possibly in collaboration with a domain architect.
Q2.0/5	Presence of procedures for handling feature requests: • This takes place on the basis of the change management process. • Registration in standard integrated tooling for backlog management. A method has been agreed that applies to all teams. • The features are handled like a small waterfall. • From the moment a feature as a user story is in the backlog (and therefore in Jira), it is followed until it is implemented or rejected. • The features must follow the phase of the development process. • This is described in a Standard Operating Procedure (SOP).

Q#	Subject / Remarks
Q2.0/6	Process improvement mechanisms: • The teams are expected to improve continuously, the method used for this is the retrospective. • The retrospective is used for this. • During the retrospective, each team member indicates what went well and what went less well, which are ranked, and the most important ones are discussed and how they can be strengthened / improved. • A spider web chart is also made of Focus / Proficiency / Work Pressure / Quality / Test Environment / Cooperation. • Retrospective meeting by the Business owner, development team and Scrum master. • Retrospective meeting by the Scrum team, periodic team-transcending evaluations, quality gates (including specific reviews) and assigned quality managers (customer + supplier). • The Scrum master organizes a retrospective. • The product owner is not present. • The product owner is present at the sprint review (demo). Who controls the improvement: • The Scrum master steers once per sprint. • The team is responsible for its own development. The retrospective is not yet actively monitored. • The Scrum master steers once per sprint. • The Scrum master steers on the improvement points of retrospective and the spider web graph. The spider web chart is followed in time and viewed on trends. • Retrospective, here the Scrum master steers. • Retrospective, the Scrum master directs this.

Q2.0/7	Mechanism for continuous integration, regression testing and continuous delivery:
	• Continuous integration is in use, regression testing is set up, a baseline is used.
	• A pilot is being started for continuous integration and continuous delivery. Regression testing is a reason for the transition to standard integrated tooling in which automated testing / regression testing and continuous integration / continuous delivery are possible, in order to make regression testing part of the larger picture.
	• We use Apache Subversion for code repository, we have Jenkins for automatic nightly builds and nightly tests.
	• Yes, we carry out the following steps:
	    ○ automated build;
	    ○ automated release;
	    ○ partially automated acceptance test;
	    ○ no automatic regression;
	    ○ continuous integration / no continuous delivery.
	• Continuous integration and regression tests, but still no continuous delivery.
	• There is a set of tools (out of the box and custom).
	
	Development - Test - Acceptance - Production (DTAP) mechanism:
	• There is an DTAP environment in use, using Subversion / #define and WinMerge / Jenkins / SonarQube.
	• In the DTAP environment we use automated deployments and automatic regression tests using scenarios.

Q#	Subject / Remarks
	• We have a test environment where the last build runs daily, the acceptance and production environment are currently not applicable for the Scrum team and for automated regression testing we use Twist. Flow definition: • The flow is defined, but not automated. • The flow is defined. • The flow definition is part of the build process and at a later stage also of the release management process.

Table 3-3, Q2.0 Explanations for Scrum assessment.

Q#	Subject / Remarks
Q2.5/1	Capturing requirements: • A start architecture is used. • This differs from team to team: many teams use user stories to define the requirements including the acceptance criteria, while other teams still have a traditional list of requirements, which are linked to the stories that give substance to them.Jira contains the acceptance criteria per user story. Capturing requirements: • There are requirements in the format of the user stories. Based on usefulness and necessity, functional designs, technical designs, mock ups, wire frames (design drawing of the Graphical User Interface (GUI)) and process flows are composed. • The check is done by the development team and the product owner. • Yes, these are administered in Team Foundation Server (TFS) and the user stories refer to the documentation Software Architecture Design (SAD), Technical Design (TD) & Detailed Design Document (DDDs). Control delivered deliverables based on (non) functional requirements: • Architecture and maintenance control. • The product owners check the delivery on functional requirements. • There is a test of compliance with the acceptance criteria by testing them, with the occasional manual link between the test case and the user story. • The functional designs, the technical designs, the mock ups, the wire frames and the process flows are part of the acceptance. • The check is done by the analyst, the Scrum master and the product owner.
Q2.5/2	Re-use (non) functional requirements and determine the impact on the basis of the existing requirements: • A new start architecture is being created for new requirements, but this is maintained in a different document. • This is part of our development on Capability Maturity Model Integration (CMMi) maturity. • Together with the product owner, the Scrum team determines the impact of a feature based on existing requirements. • The documentation is being used, but new tasks are coming up in the development process, including new user stories and test cases. • The impact is predetermined via an impact analysis on technology (including the non-functional requirements) and afterwards through testing in the acceptance phase (e.g. load / stress / performance tests).

Q#	Subject / Remarks
	• The impact is determined by design (technical designer / solution architect), and if necessary a new feature / user story is created and existing documentation (TO, SAD & DDD) is re-used and updated (versioning).
Q2.5/3	**Usage regression tests:** • Manual regression tests are done, but there is no test set of test cases that is being reused. **Relationship between requirements on the one hand and acceptance criteria and test cases on the other:** • The relationship between requirements on the one hand and acceptance criteria and test cases on the other is registered in standard integrated tooling for backlog management and automated testing. • We do define feature / stories but no acceptance criteria. There is sometimes a recording of tests. For each feature, a lifecycle is run which starts with the story and ends with the test results. The product owner and testers assess the results of the (acceptance) tests. • Each requirement / user story is built by the Scrum team and tested by another member of the Scrum team after the item in Jira is marked as ready for testing. • Yes, a relationship is being established between requirements, acceptance criteria and test cases. • The results are recorded in an in-house developed test tool, in which test cases / scenarios are archived (with an increment, a zero measurement is therefore possible at all times). The requirements are described in the DDD. No link between the DDD and the test tool. Logical Test Case (LTC) documents link the DDD with the test tool. **Definition of Done (DoD) check on requirements:** • The teams must determine whether the requirements of the DoD have been met. • There is a check in the DoD on the (acceptance) tests. • No, in the DoD this does not come back explicitly - whether all tests have been carried out properly. • Yes, this is done by the system tester and this is included as a check in the DoD. • Being tested is part of the DoD.

Table 3-4, Q2.5 Explanations for Scrum assessment.

Q#	Subject / Remarks
Q3.0/1	**Usage of acceptance tests:** • All forms of acceptance tests (Functional Acceptance Test (FAT), User Acceptance Test (UAT) and Performance Stress Test (PST)) are used (PST if applicable / useful). • We use a FAT and a UAT. • We use a FAT, UAT and PST. • FAT, UAT, PAT, performance, load / stress testing and security testing. • Yes, every component has to be tested by the stakeholders We use a FAT, UAT and PST. **Control on acceptance tests:** • The acceptance test gives the business a handhold to say 'Yes' before transferring to production.

Q#	Subject / Remarks
	• This is certainly being steered. Based on the Product Risk Analysis (PRA), it is determined in advance which tests are to be carried out with which depth in the acceptance phase, for example through a master test plan, various detail plans and overall via release management and quality gates. • That is controlled by the test manager.
Q3.0/2	Definition, recording and maintenance of the service provision of the Scrum team: • This is not yet black and white, but this is present in the form of dashboard reports. • For this purpose, MS Excel is used in combination with TFS and the ReportServer.
Q3.0/3	Registration services and products in a Configuration Management DataBase (CMDB): • The building blocks are registered in the CMDB. • Yes, management is responsible for this.

Table 3-5, Q3.0 Explanations for Scrum assessment.

Q#	Subject / Remarks
Q3.5/1	Documentation standards and quality criteria: • There is a DoD at release level. • There is a DoD on release, feature and sprint level. • There is a DoD on sprint and release level. In addition, underlying industry norms and standards apply. • The DoD says something about a feature and a story, but nothing about a sprint (for example regression test based on unchanged functionality), or a release. • DoD is only applied at feature level and not at sprint and release level.
Q3.5/2	Training Scrum team members: • The teams are all offered the same standard training courses. • The product owner is not trained, the Scrum master is. The product owner is also Scrum master. Not everyone has been trained at Scrum / Kanban foundation level. • Among others Scrum certified (scrum.org) and Certified Agile Tester training.

Q3.5/3	Specific, Measurable, Acceptable, Realistic and Time-bound (SMART) goals for development process:
	• We recognize two goals: the functional and the performance goal. We do not recognize the maturity goal. The velocity is controlled. The velocity is based on story points but also on hours. We also use a control on Car types. This means that we classify the report by type of input: feature / story / issue / etcetera.
	• Yes, Key Performance Indicator (KPIs) have been established and are being reported on. Improvement points are determined during the retrospective.
	  o The functional goal is determined by the product choice: SharePoint and the development service.
	  o The quality goal is determined by the velocity. (Velocity is measured on the basis of operations, the focus factor is also used (hours that contribute to sprint goal / other matters)).
	  o The maturity level for the entire development street is aimed at maturity level CMMi-3.
	  o Under an operation we mean a method, which can be called from the outside, on a component. Specifically, we know the following types of operations: Web API operations (called from the portal), Domain operations (called from Web API or other domain components) and adapter operations (called from a parent domain component).

Q3.5/4	Supporting tools: • Standard integrated tooling, we look at it in a pilot.

Q#	Subject / Remarks
	• Jenkins / SonarQube / Nexus, we do regression tests with a self-built test framework, Selenium and Twist. • Continuous integration by a supplier with the tool: Octopus Deploy and Bamboo. • Subversion / #define include WinMerge / Jenkins / SonarQube. • Continuous delivery tool: Microsoft Release Manager (MRM), for continuous integration: TFS and for regression testing: Microsoft Test Management (MTM) and Custom tooling.

Table 3-6, Q3.5 Explanations for Scrum assessment.

Q#	Subject / Remarks
Q4.0/1	Which service norms are recognized: • Actual performance. • We use standards with respect to velocity and the budget. The progress report is based on the velocity. • In our own term "OPS "and in function points (Gartner). Reporting method: • Reports on hours and progress reports to steering committee (report on steering group meeting or to steering group meeting). • High Light Reporting - which is derived from a burn down chart. • The various burn-down charts per sprint, and there is also reporting by aggregating from user stories to themes. • Every week, the Scrum master reports to the manager development. The development manager reports per sprint to the business with regard to the defined change assignment and planned release. • Reports based on Dashboard in TFS. • The product owner, the product manager and the development manager are responsible for what work is done by the Scrum team. The product manager and the development manager are member of the management team and take care of the internal communication. Measures service deviations: • In the Change Advisory Board (CAB), the service deviations are discussed in order to correct them. • Service norm deviations are mitigated through operational management. May the product owner initiate organisational changes: • In terms of organisational changes, the product owner can scale, and the factory model itself is anchored at senior management level. • The product owner can initiate organisational changes in consultation with the product manager, but he cannot do this alone.
Q4.0/2	Management information on trends in velocity and service level shortcomings: • Velocity is, service level shortcomings are not (mentioned twice). • Via dashboards that have been recorded in MS Excel. In addition, waste is tracked. • Every week in the Scrum demo the number of realized story points is presented to the entire company.
Q4.0/3	Management information about the growth of the product backlog: • Management is informed at the moment that the backlog becomes too small. • The backlog is discussed weekly.

Q#	Subject / Remarks
Q4.0/4	Management information about the realization of the number of features, the releases and the roadmap: • The product owner, the product manager and the development manager are responsible for what the Scrum team is working on and they present the status of the work of the Scrum team and the roadmap in the Management Team (MT) meeting. • Yes, there is a product roadmap on parts. • Yes, every week through the previously named dashboard.

Table 3-7, Q4.0 Explanations for Scrum assessment.

Q#	Subject / Remarks
Q4.5/1	Relation product owner with service level manager and availability manager: • The product owner supplies the non-functionalities. Availability management is a role. The process has been recognized. Availability is part of the SLA. The web application is monitored for availability, the product owner has a role to compile the SLA. • We do not know a service level manager and 2.
Q4.5/2	Relation product owner with capacity management and financial management: • For new services, the product owner consults these processes and for existing services they do not apply. Although the norms may change, but that has not yet been recognized. • The development manager is responsible for support & maintenance and the service levels. He is closely involved in the Scrum development process.
Q4.5/3	Central risk and impact analysis for heterogeneous features through a change management process: • Does not apply.

Table 3-8, Q4.5 Explanations for Scrum assessment.

Q#	Subject / Remarks
Q5.0/1	Control the connection of Scrum team activities performed to the needs of the business: • This is done in the demo. • A UAT is being carried out. • This is the responsibility of the product owner. • The Scrum team does not do this with the end user. The product owner and other internal stakeholders examine with the customer in special organized sessions, whether the deliveries meet the expectations. • We give shape to this check on the basis of the demo, the presence of the business at the stand up, plus in the interim reviews. • Functional acceptance tests are performed by the users before going to production. After or during the promotion to production, product verification tests will also take place.
Q5.0/2	User satisfaction check: • Through demos. • During testing and in the retrospective and in the steering committee. • During the demo at the end of the sprint and during extra sessions. • In the sprint demo. • After every sprint a sprint review will take place for the stakeholders. In addition, the satisfaction of the product owner is explicitly tested by the development team at the end of each sprint.

Q#	Subject / Remarks
	• We control multiple axes. Through acceptance tests within release management. But also, through sprint demos.
Q5.0/3	Monitoring customer satisfaction trend: • Periodic measurement Business satisfaction. • Through Net Promoter Score measurements (Lean). • We do not.
Q5.0/4	Use Customer Satisfaction Survey information in service improvement agenda: • Customer satisfaction surveys are used. • Through continuous improvement program (based on Lean). • We do not.
Q5.0/5	Monitoring perception of the customer: • Customer satisfaction surveys. • Service meetings takes place regularly. • During the demo at the end of the sprint and during extra sessions. • We have a formal meeting on mutual service provision. • We have (among other things) weekly release consultations with the most important stakeholders (customer). In this way the perception of the customer is 'measured' and sometimes the question is asked whether what has been delivered is also what the customer expected.

Table 3-9, Q5.0 Explanations for Scrum assessment.

3.2 Change management

3.2.1 Maturity

All case organisations have completed the self-assessment of the change management process as included in Appendix B. It is clear that the change management process at most organisations has not made room for the Agile development process. Both have a right to exist. The maturity per case organisation is shown Figure 3-2.

A set of questions has been answered per organisation per level. All mandatory questions must be answered with a 'yes' and a minimum number of optional questions. Only then is a level achieved and coloured green. This does not mean that there are no points for improvement for the green cells. A red cell indicates that the level has not been reached. A grey cell means that this process is no longer recognized but is shaped within the development process.

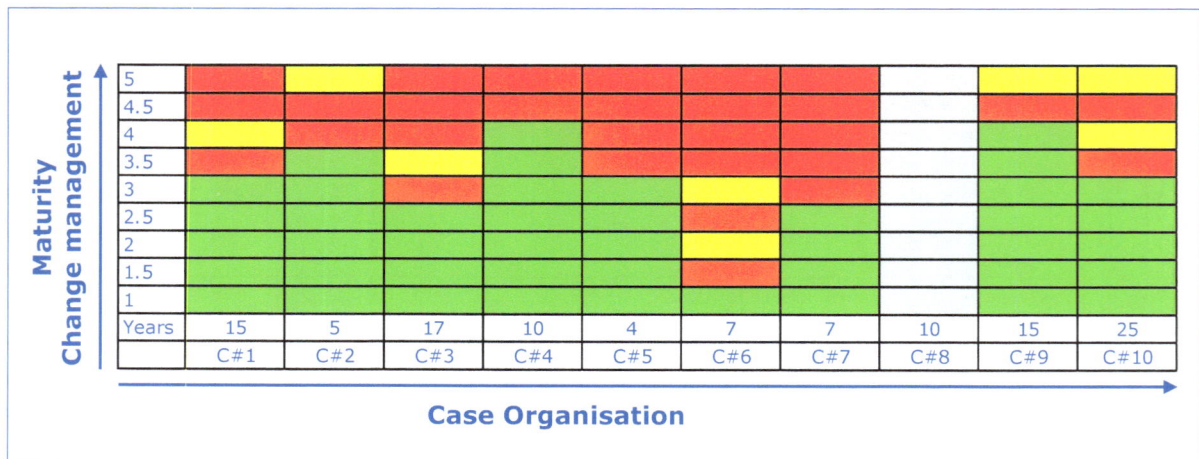

Figure 3-2, Maturity change management process.

A yellow cell indicates that a level has been achieved but that it does not count for the maturity score because a lower level has not been achieved. However, a yellow cell indicates a possible rapid maturation of the process.

3.2.2 Explanation

In addition to the scores, a number of case organisations have also completed the specific questions below. The comments per topic are included in this section. Also, not all questions are included in their entirety but only the subjects. It is instructive to look at the explanation per question of the assessment because it indicates how the change management process is structured and how it interacts with the Scrum development process.

Q#	Subject / Remarks
Q1.0/1	**Registration RFCs, RFC investigations, RFC schedules:** • Changes are recorded in the IBM Tivoli Service Management Suite. • Standard integrated tooling for backlog management and planning is used for this. • RFCs are recorded in documents and the change management system. • Service desk application and an Application Lifecycle Management application. • For smaller RFCs in Jira, for larger on an internal Wiki page. • In a change management system, including TOPdesk and the Portfolio portal (RFC, status / meta-info, all related documents such as impact analyses, etcetera). • These are registered in the Hewlett-Packard (HP) Service Manager tool.
Q1.0/2	**Granted activities to specific individuals or functional areas:** • A job manager has been appointed. • Change management activities are planned and executed. The assignment of the work within the management team depends on the expertise and availability of individuals. • The activities are assigned to the Agile teams. Schedules are approved by CAB in consultation with product owners. • The product manager and delegates within consulting and the development team. • Business and IT release manager, product group manager and product owner. **Implementation activities:** • The following activities are carried out: Impact analysis, design, estimation, development, test, review, delivery. • Example activities are: intake and registration of RFCs, assessing RFC, etcetera. • The product manager is responsible for gathering requirements from external and internal customers. The product manager keeps a list of these requirements, discusses them with the development department, after which these requirements are entered on the Wiki or in Jira. • All activities are carried out: risk & impact, planning, realization and testing.
Q1.0/3	**Procedure for registration RFC:** • Procedures of the IBM Tivoli Service Management Suite. • Procedures from standard integrated tooling for backlog management and planning. An RFC goes through various stages (intake, impact, approval, prioritization, realization / test, implementation, deregistration). • This is specified in the Dossier Agreements & Procedures (DAP). • There is one way to register RFCs. • For small matters to existing applications: create an issue in Jira, for larger cases (e.g. new application) send an e-mail to the product manager. • Sign in change signal (change signal is the used synonym for RFC in the business). • According to the ITIL process.

Table 3-10, Q1.5 Explanations for change management assessment.

Q#	Subject / Remarks
Q1.5/1	Goals and benefits: • Every employee is obliged to be ITIL certified. In addition, workshops on the change management process are also provided. Check for illegal changes: • Compliance (illegal changes) is guaranteed by the application manager, who can check this in production. • Changes may only be implemented after approval of the CAB, which includes checking the correct steps. • Documentation would be out of step, documentation describes how the applications function and test this as well. In the case of an 'illegal' change, the documentation would be out of step. By the way, there is a good chance that the test team would also find out because a regression test goes wrong. • There are no illegal changes. All received requests must be registered and assessed before they are processed. Various (quality) gates and reviews have been defined where checks are performed among other things on scope in order to prevent illegal changes. • Illegal changes are signalled by monitoring. As soon as a service or the like goes down, the Monitoring and Control Center (MCC) will respond to them. They will check whether there is an RFC to which the change is related. The question is whether you can prevent it (a change can also be the renaming of a file; this level of changes is not monitored).
Q1.5/2	Scope change management process: • The scope of the change management process is limited to the service provided by the Scrum team. • All changes are dealt with by the CAB. • The change management process is aimed at managing changes in production. There is no choice for a Scrum approach. But a team does or does not use Scrum. • The scope of the change management process is defined in the SLA, but there remain grey areas. • The Scope is wider than the Configuration Items (CIs) defined in the CMDB. CIs are subdivided into components, and the objects that can be modified are identified for each component. These objects are defined in the application lifecycle management tool and not in the CMDB. • All changes to the applications offered by our organisation in the market fall within the scope of the change management process. Sprint demos fall outside process and this sometimes causes problems. The scope of the change management process is defined for products. • The scope has been defined at various levels. On logical places in the process, different change types are recognized, such as ICT and non-ICT related changes, changes arising from incident management / problem management, etcetera. • The scope is determined on the basis of a subset of the portfolios (application and infrastructure), and a distinction is made between types of changes: infrastructural, applicative etcetera.
Q1.5/3	Quality criteria for notifying and registering changes: • Within the IBM Tivoli Service Management Suite, we ensure that the applicant, the impact, the priority, the throughput time and the downtime are known." The relationship with other releases is known. • The ticket format determines what needs to be filled in. • The tooling and template enforces a few things such as the functional description, the impact, the estimate, the status and the agreement are recorded.

Q#	Subject / Remarks
	• In addition to the usual attributes, the relations to CI, business service and release train must also be registered. • The minimum that has to be registered is the desired feature, and there are no standards for getting the description as complete as possible. • Among other things, the following attributes are registered: reason, target group, product / service affected, components involved, expected result, date of receipt. Matters are structured by, among other things, form change signal (mandatory / non-mandatory fields) and registration system (idem). • Parties or CI's which are affected. The impact of the change is determined on the basis of a number of mandatory questions, etcetera. Agreements must be added.

Table 3-11, Q1.5 Explanations for change management assessment.

Q#	Subject / Remarks

Q2.0/1	Assignment responsibilities:
	• The usual roles have been recognized and assigned.
	• The mandator submits RFCs to the service coordinator who assigns their execution to the team.
	• Various roles have been defined and described.
	• Tooling is implemented role-based.
	• The different responsibilities are divided per role:
	  o The product manager has ultimate responsibility for all changes in the products (applications).
	  o Each application has a product owner, who is technically responsible for the application.
	  o The lead architect takes care of the overall architecture of how all applications fit together.
	  o The development manager is responsible for the development process and the planning.
	• Everybody is allowed to submit change signals. The product group manager is allowed to assess and reject change signals. The business release manager may record change signals, the CAB may prioritize change signals, the management team may decide, etcetera.
	• There are change domain experts, they provide information to the change requesters / owners. The requester / owner creates the change, the change coordinator and change manager assess the change after which it goes to the CAB.

Q2.0/2	Following procedures for initiating changes: • Happens through the service desk. • Audits check whether everything has been implemented according to the rules. • Compliance with the procedures and work instructions for initiating changes is guaranteed. If the procedures are not adhered to, then the change will not be processed. • Changes are only picked up if they are in Jira. • Through a described process. • By marking this in the tool as mandatory (otherwise the change cannot be taken to the next phase) In addition, the change coordinator looks at and assesses all changes.
Q2.0/3	Approve, verify and plan procedures: • Yes, they are defined and executed.

Q#	Subject / Remarks
	• All RFCs are listed in Jira per product (application). Each application has a 'product owner' who is responsible for keeping an eye on the RFCs and understanding them. The product owner then consults with the product manager which RFCs are implemented per release. The planning is done in consultation with the development manager. • Through a described process. • Yes, in accordance with the procedures defined by ITIL.
Q2.0/4	**Execution of business and technical impact analysis:** • Business analysis is always executed, the technical analysis only if there is a reason to do so. • When establishing the RFCs, both a business and a technical impact analysis are executed, for which tools have been developed. Results of the impact analysis must be indicated in the RFC definition. • Not for small, clear changes. • In general, technical impact analyses are always carried out, but business impact analyses are rare, this is a big loss. • Always a (global) business analysis, in which it is determined whether there is also an ICT / technical component in the change, and if so, then a technical impact analysis is also carried out (including for cohesion and dependencies) before the change is actually realized. • The HP Service Manager Tool determines the impact on the basis of the relevant CIs and a number of mandatory questions.
Q2.0/5	**Adequate progress monitoring of RFCs:** • This is the responsibility of the team itself. • Takes place through the CAB and release boards, as well as within the agile teams. • Frequent random sampling is carried out from the CAB. • The progress of RFCs is monitored by the product owner. • Via status updates in TOPdesk and Portfolio portal over the entire lifecycle of the change - Adequate release management. • From Change Management, (automated) e-mails are sent when changes 'stay on' in a phase for a certain duration.
Q2.0/6	**Successful implementation of RFCs:** • Frequent random sampling is carried out from the CAB. • The test team is responsible for confirming that an RFC has been successfully implemented. The product owner is ultimately responsible. • Various Sign-Off moments were included in the process, including during (pre) implementation.
Q2.0/7	**Confirmation / review successful implementation of an RFC by change management:** • The usual controls. • Changes are not always reviewed. • Confirmation always takes place because this is part of the process. Review of successful RFC takes place for larger changes, not for small ones. Review is not (yet) a standard part of the agile change management process. • Yes, every RFC related to an application and every application has a product owner. The product owners are responsible for reviewing their RFCs. They can choose the procedure themselves for how they want to do this. • We have agreed on a quality-gates process that checks the individual and total set of changes at release level. • Yes, a Post Implementation Review (PIR) can be requested from change management, mainly in the event of unsuccessful changes or changes that have exceeded the throughput time limits.

Q#	Subject / Remarks
Q2.0/8	Are sufficient Change Management reports produced: • Ad hoc progress reports, monthly overview in service level reports. • No change management reports are produced. • On various levels and at various moments in the process reporting takes place, based on the 'Just enough & just in time' principle. • Various lists are reported including successfully completed changes, changes that have been rejected, etcetera. I am not a recipient of this myself, so I do not know exactly which ones.

Table 3-12, Q2.0 Explanations for change management assessment.

Q#	Subject / Remarks
Q2.5/1	Central initiation RFCs: • The channels are defined. • Service coordinator coordinates the changes. • No, RFCs can be submitted by various agile teams, as well as portfolio management. • Via standard integrated tooling for backlog management and planning. • Yes, it has been determined which channels can submit RFCs, which is arranged in Jira. • There are no other legal channels than the agreed channels (functional RFCs respectively technically initiated RFCs). • The channels are defined and recorded. In practice this means that all changes are verified via a change coordinator before processing the changes.
Q2.5/2	Central planning and priority determination RFC: • Prioritized per business unit. • Yes, changes are saved in the change management system. • RFCs are prioritized by the product owners and put on the list for "inclusion in the next release", which is then scheduled by the various development team leads and the development manager. • They are planned and agreed in conformity. The priority is defined by the CAB. Communication to service desk • This does not go through the service desk. • If it is necessary. • The service desk has access but does not play a role in the change management process. • We do not have an IT service desk, support is provided by developers. Developers are aware of all RFCs. • Technical changes are passed on to the ICT service desk and functional changes are passed on to the business desk. Central planning is, among others, organized via a CAB and release management. • The changes are not passed on to the service desk but to the Monitoring & Control Center.
Q2.5/3	Current status RFC: • The tool does not enforce the updating of the current status, but the process does. • Administrative steps are sometimes carried out at once. • RFC status is kept on the customer portal and in the ad hoc progress report. The status is not always up-to-date. • Standard requests are made via IT Service Management (Mexon). Customer requests go through another tool and another process. • The changes are up-to-date. The history of the latest changes is visible.

Q#	Subject / Remarks
	Flow control: • The flow control is performed ad hoc by the service coordinator. • There is a report from the teams to the business. • The flow of the change is known: Yes, the change goes through a number of phases. Only the responsible person can adjust these phases. Which statuses: • The following statuses are recognized: registered, submitted (Scrum starts), CAB approved, Change Decision Board (CDB), approved and deployed. • The following statuses are recognized: backlog prioritization, approval of impact, prioritization of realization and implementation. • The following statuses are used towards customers: for approval, adjustment desired, postponed, expired, approved and realized. Internally, we often use the following statuses as well: in progress, to be tested, testing, to be reviewed and reviewing. • RFCs must pass tollgates. If the status is not correctly defined, then an RFC cannot pass the tollgate. • Statuses: accepted, approved, build, ready to deploy, ready to production, deployed. • At the end of each release, the RFCs have the right status. The product owners are responsible for keeping Jira up to date. By the end of a release the test team checks all RFCs in that release in order to see if they are correctly implemented. • The product owners are responsible for the flow control. • The following statuses are recognized: To do, in progress, resolved and done. • The tool is leading when dealing with the changes in the process and is therefore kept up-to-date on a daily basis. Deviations are reported immediately.
Q2.5/4	Registration and analysis of failed RFCs: • No. • The registration and analysis of the failure of an RFC takes place on the basis of incidents following a change. • A failure is recorded either as status information (for example 'rejected'), as finding (for example test failure), incident (based on root-cause linked to the change) or as review finding. • Yes, the Change Management will then ask for a PIR. Consequences: • No. • Caused incidents are also linked to the change in question. • We do not do that.
Q2.5/5	Review original needs: • Yes, through a FAT and a UAT. • Is often seen as part of the acceptance test. • During sprints, demos are given to the business. User Acceptance Test (UAT) takes place before promotion to production. • In the process of development through the tests and sprint reviews. In the acceptance process at the FAT / UAT against the defined requirements. • We do not do that.

Table 3-13, Q2.5 Explanations for change management assessment.

Q#	Subject / Remarks
Q3.0/1	Maintain formal change records: • HP Quality Center and IT Service Management (Mexon). • The formal change records are the issues in Jira. These are maintained by the product owners. • Both in TOPdesk and the portfolio portal up to and including implementation. • Yes, via HP Service Manager.
Q3.0/2	Arrangement planning RFCs: • Is done by the agile teams. Dependencies between teams are managed separately. • Is performed by consultation between business and IT. • For every release, a plan is made of the agreed (and therefore approved) RFCs. • At release level. • There are (online) change calendars of both the internal service organisation and the external service providers in which all changes are mentioned.
Q3.0/3	Create standard reports: • Yes, comes from the tooling. • Among other, sprint reports. • Various lists are reported including successfully completed changes. Changes that have been rejected, etcetera. I am not a recipient of this myself, so I do not know exactly which ones.
Q3.0/4	Standards regarding RFC documentation with regard to risk and impact analysis and planning etcetera: • A risk analysis is performed on the interfaces. • A risk analysis is carried out, for example in case of changes to interfaces, and there is support by the tooling for this. • Standards include scenarios, etcetera. In addition, the impact analysis is integrated in the HP Service Manager tool. • RFC template contains the impact, the risk analysis only incidental and ad hoc. • There is a complete set of prescribed documents that must be used depending on the nature / size of the change.

Table 3-14, Q3.0 Explanations for change management assessment.

Q#	Subject / Remarks
Q3.5/1	Standards quality criteria for documentation RFCs: • Changes within change management are standardized. There are criteria for documentation. • There is an RFC form that needs to be filled in. Mandatory fields must be filled in. There is no checklist. • Among other things for the purpose of functional requirements and non-functional requirements (such as International Standardization Organisation (ISO) 25010). • Yes, scenarios, installation manuals, etcetera (if the change in question requires this, for example a change involving several people in the realization of the change, etcetera). In addition, the agreements are formally laid down in the change (e.g. uploading e-mail with agreements for example). • Not applicable.
Q3.5/2	Training responsibilities: • ITIL foundation and ITIL practitioner are mandatory. • We are actively working on the implementation of responsibilities through explanation, instruction, etcetera.

Q#	Subject / Remarks
	• People are adequately instructed to fill in their role. (To my knowledge) there are no separate training courses on the business side, but on the ICT side separate training courses (IT service management training at all levels). • All employees are (mandatory) ITIL v3 certified. Change management ITIL practitioner. • Not applicable.
Q3.5/3	Established and reviewed process goals: • There is a quality goal and a functional goal, but not a maturity goal (mentioned twice). • There are KPIs mentioned and (integral) ISO certification at level 9001: 20xx is mentioned. • Reduction in number of incidents etcetera. Aim to achieve CMMi level 3. • Not applicable.
Q3.5/4	Used tools: • IBM Tivoli Service Management Suite. • HP Service Manager. • Yes, Jira for administration, Wiki for description and (technical) design and Microsoft Project for planning. • Business: TOPdesk ICT: Omnitracker.

Table 3-15, Q3.5 Explanations for change management assessment.

Q#	Subject / Remarks
Q4.0/1	Management information about RFCs: • The RFCs are presented to an administrative body. • For this purpose, a portfolio portal has been set up with all relevant information per RFC. • Yes, this is communicated weekly and discussed with the (affected) change coordinators. • Not applicable.
Q4.0/2	Management information about the planning: • Is provided to the customer. • For each release a planning is made and with this planning it is indicated which RFCs are included in the release. • Occurs through weekly change coordinators meeting.
Q4.0/3	Management information about numbers of RFCs: • This is reported to an administrative body. • Yes, this is reported to an administrative body. • With reports that can be retrieved from the HP Service Manager system. • Not applicable.
Q4.0/4	Management information about successful RFCs: • Yes, this is reported to an administrative body. • With reports that can be retrieved from the HP Service Manager System. • Not applicable.
Q4.0/5	Management information about throughput time per category: • Not applicable.
Q4.0/6	Information about delays: • With reports that can be retrieved from the HP Service Manager system. • Not applicable.

Q#	Subject / Remarks
Q4.0/7	Number of RFCs initiated from problem management: • No, we do not know any problem records. • The chain of incident, problem and change management is covered and this is also reported by service management. • With reports that can be retrieved from the HP Service Manager system.

Table 3-16, Q4.0 Explanations for change management assessment.

Q#	Subject / Remarks
Q4.5/1	People who are interested in meetings: • At the moment this has been arranged for a large part but is still being further developed. • The product manager regularly consults with customers and internal stakeholders where change requests are discussed and recorded. • Not so much with 'interested parties' Only with stakeholders / related people (Change Coordinators Meeting, CAB, etcetera) This only takes place with stakeholders / related people.
Q4.5/2	CFM: Progress RFCs: • Progress is monitored with IBM Rational ClearCase (ClearCase), or another SCCM package. • At the moment this has been organised for a large part, but still being further developed. • No, we do not know configuration management. • Yes, towards the configuration coordinator, who updates the CMDB.
Q4.5/3	Configuration Management: Impact of RFC on CIs: • The CMDB is used for the impact (lifecycle management information). • At the moment this has been organised for a large part, but still being further developed. • Yes. • Not applicable
Q4.5/4	Problem management: Information exchange with problem management: • Partly organised. • We do not know problem management. • Yes, these are usually also initiated from problem management.
Q4.5/5	Problem management: Problem escalation reports: • Partly organised. • Yes, via problem coordinator. • Not applicable.
Q4.5/6	Problem management: Obtaining problem information: • Partly organised. • Yes, via problem coordinator. • Not applicable.
Q4.5/7	Service desk: Information about RFC progress to service desk: • There is exchange with the service desk, in a number of areas this can be expanded. • Yes, the service desk has access to the RFCs and progress. • Not applicable, the service desk is staffed by developers.
Q4.5/8	Service desk: Announcement of planning at the service desk: • There is exchange with the service desk, in a number of areas this can be expanded.

Q#	Subject / Remarks
	• Not applicable, the service desk is staffed by developers. • General, for information.
Q4.5/9	Service desk: Impact analysis RFC on service desk support levels: • In case the decision trees have to be modified, they will be modified. Also, other service norms will be passed on. • There is exchange with the service desk, in a number of areas this can be expanded. • Changes do not (usually) apply to service levels, where the service levels are adjusted. • Not applicable.
Q4.5/10	Service desk: Information about related incidents: • Yes. • There is exchange with the service desk, in a number of areas this can be expanded. • Not applicable, the service desk is staffed by developers. • If problems occur / have occurred.
Q4.5/11	Release & deployment management: Information about change implementations: • Yes, via tooling. • Release management is the extension of change management and falls within the same team. • Change management and release management are the same group of people: the product manager, the product owners and the development manager. • Structurally arranged (consultation and products). • For example, if there are conflicting changes (addressed to release managers).
Q4.5/12	Release & deployment management: Announcement / planning releases: • Yes, via tooling. • Release management is organized per department, but there is exchange with change management. • Change Management and release management are the same group of people: the product manager, the product owners and the development manager. • Structurally arranged (consultation and products). • Yes, for information by e-mail (addressed to release managers).
Q4.5/13	Service level management: RFC-planning: • Change management and service level management are the same group of people within our organisation: the product manager, the product owners and the development manager. • Structurally arranged (consultation and products).
Q4.5/14	Service level management: Impact RFC on SLA: • Change Management and service level management are the same group of people within our organisation: the product manager, the product owners and the development manager.
Q4.5/15	IT service continuity management: Announcing RFC planning: • Not applicable.
Q4.5/16	IT service continuity management: Impact analysis on the contingency plan: • Not applicable.
Q4.5/17	Capacity management: Influence of RFC on performance & capacity: -

Table 3-17, Q4.5 Explanations for change management assessment.

Q#	Subject / Remarks
Q5.0/1	Support business need: • Acceptance tests and service consultation. • Yes, the product manager checks regularly whether the changes in the most recent releases match expectations. • Through a Post Implementation Review (PIR).
Q5.0/2	Customer satisfaction verification: • Yes, the product manager regularly tests customer satisfaction on an individual basis. • Yes, this is part of the PIR.
Q5.0/3	Trend analysis customer satisfaction: • We have conducted surveys in the past, but have not done so for too long. • Yes, this also concerns a KPI about which is reported (Dashboard in MS Excel).
Q5.0/4	Quality improvement agenda: • Yes, by defining points of improvement / actions based on outcome PIR. • Not applicable.
Q5.0/5	Satisfaction perception: • Yes, through a Post Implementation Review (PIR) we ask what the customer expected (apart from the agreements). • Perception has been interpreted as customer satisfaction, regardless of whether the norms have been met. • Not applicable.

Table 3-18, Q5.0 Explanations for change management assessment.

4 Agile application

Message:
- Most case organisations show equal use of Agile terms.
- The shaping of Agile development processes takes place both bottom-up and top-down.
- The Caluwé blue and Caluwé green change strategy is often used in the establishment.
- Unanimous applied terms are 'daily Scrum', DoD, product backlog, product owner, Scrum master, sprint backlog, sprint planning, sprint retrospective, sprint review, user story and velocity.

Reading guideline:
This chapter discusses the use of Agile terms in section 4.1. Section 4.2 provides an overview of how the case organisations have given substance to the Agile development process. Subsequently, section 4.3 shows how guidance is given to this development process. Finally, section 4.4 indicates which tools have been used by the case organisations.

4.1 Agile terminology

In Table 4-1 the Agile terms are recorded, most of which are used within Scrum such as 'Daily Scrum' and 'Feature'. Other terms are not known within Scrum but within the Agile world such as 'Theme' and 'Product manager'. The table below indicates which terms the case organisations use. This may be within the context of the development team as well as outside, as long it plays a role in delivering an Agile deliverable. The value "ST" in Table 4-1 means "sometimes"

Term	O#1	O#2	O#3	O#4	O#5	O#6	O#7	O#8	O#9	O#10
Affinity estimation	No	No	No	No	No	Yes	No	No	No	No
Burndown chart	Yes	Yes	No	Yes	Yes	Yes	No	Yes	Yes	Yes
Continuous integration	Yes	Yes	No	Yes	Yes	Yes	Yes	No	No	Yes
Continuous delivery	Yes	No	No	Yes	Yes	Yes	No	No	Yes	Yes
Daily Scrum	Yes	Yes	Yes	Yes	Yes	Yes	Yes	Yes	Yes	Yes
Definition of Done	Yes	Yes	Yes	Yes	Yes	Yes	Yes	Yes	Yes	Yes
Development Team	Yes	Yes	Yes	Yes	Yes	Yes	No	Yes	Yes	Yes
Epic	No	No	Yes	Yes	No	Yes	No	Yes	No	No
Escaped defects	No	No	No	No	Yes	No	No	No	No	No
Estimation	Yes	Yes	No	Yes	Yes	Yes	Yes	Yes	Yes	Yes
Feature	Yes	Yes	Yes	Yes	Yes	Yes	No	Yes	Yes	Yes
Ideal Hours / Ideal days	No	No	No	No	No	Yes	No	No	No	No
Impediment	Yes	Yes	Yes	Yes	Yes	Yes	No	Yes	Yes	Yes
Niko-Niko chart	No	No	No	No	No	No	No	No	No	No
Osmotic communication	No	Yes	No	No	No	Yes	No	No	No	No
Planning poker	Yes	Yes	No	Yes	Yes	Yes	Yes	Yes	No	Yes
Planning onion	Yes	No	No	No	No	No	No	No	No	No
Policies	No	Yes	No	Yes	No	Yes	No	Yes	Yes	No
Product backlog	Yes	Yes	Yes	Yes	Yes	Yes	Yes	Yes	Yes	Yes
Product manager	No	No	No	Yes	Yes	No	Yes	No	No	No

Term	O#1	O#2	O#3	O#4	O#5	O#6	O#7	O#8	O#9	O#10
Product owner	Yes	Yes	Yes	Yes	Yes	Yes	Yes	Yes	Yes	Yes
Product portfolio	Yes	No	Yes	Yes	Yes	Yes	Yes	No	Yes	Yes
Product roadmap	Yes	Y/N	Yes	Yes	Yes	Yes	Yes	No	No	Yes
Radiators	No	No	No	No	No	Yes	No	No	No	No
Regression testing	Yes	Yes	No	Yes	Yes	Yes	Nee	Yes	Yes	Yes
Refactoring	Yes	Yes	No	Yes	Yes	Yes	Yes	Yes	Yes	Yes
Refining	Yes	Yes	No	Yes	Yes	Yes	Nee	Yes	Yes	Nee
Release planning	Yes	Yes	Yes	Yes	Yes	Yes	Yes	No	Yes	Yes
Scrum of Scrums	No	No	Yes	Yes	No	No	No	No	Yes	Yes
Scrum master	Yes	Yes	Yes	Yes	Yes	Yes	Yes	Yes	Yes	Yes
Sprint backlog	Yes	Yes	Yes	Yes	Yes	Yes	Yes	Yes	Yes	Yes
Sprint planning	Yes	Yes	Yes	Yes	Yes	Yes	Yes	Yes	Yes	Yes
Sprint retrospective	ST	Yes	Yes	Yes	Yes	Yes	Yes	Yes	Yes	Yes
Story point	Yes	Yes	Nee	Yes	Yes	Yes	Yes	Yes	Yes	Yes
Sprint Review	Yes	Yes	Yes	Yes	Yes	Yes	Yes	Yes	Yes	Yes
Theme	No	No	Yes	No	No	Yes	No	No	No	Yes
Triangulation	No	Yes	No	No	No	No	No	No	No	No
User story	Yes	Y/N	Yes	Yes	Yes	Yes	Yes	Yes	Yes	Yes
Velocity	ST	Yes	Yes	Yes	Yes	Yes	Yes	Yes	Yes	Yes
Work In Progress (WIP)	ST	Yes	No	Yes	No	Yes	No	Yes	Yes	Yes
Workspace	No	Yes	No	No	No	Yes	No	No	Yes	No

Table 4-1, Usage Agile / Scrum terms.

4.2 Agile development process establishment

There are many ways to shape the Agile development process. This section provides a number of characteristics and describes which choices the case organisations have made for the establishment.

4.2.1   Level of commitment for Agile

The initiative for setting up an Agile development process can be initiated by the management (top down) or by the work floor (bottom up).

OO.1	At what level is commitment given for Scrum and / or Kanban?
O#1	The initiation is given substance from bottom-up. We now look at how senior management can give guidance to this organisational shaping.
O#2	The commitment came from bottom up. Up to IT management level there is now commitment.
O#3	The commitment is on C-level.
O#4	Management board / board of directors.
O#5	Management board / management team.
O#6	Operational management.
O#7	Management team level.
O#8	Management board and management level.

OO.1	At what level is commitment given for Scrum and / or Kanban?
O#9	Management board level.
O#10	Management board level. Scrum and Kanban started as an experiment in the department (with the approval of the management board). This has spread over several departments and has been embraced by management board as standard methods.

Table 4-2, Level of commitment for Scrum.

4.2.2 Demotivators for applying Scrum

When introducing Scrum there are often discussions about why to change over to this method. This can be different for each case organisation.

O#	What have been your reasons for not giving substance to Scrum?
O#1	Producing more and more of the same is possible with Scrum, but making something new does not work with Scrum.
O#2	The resistance was that the project leaders thought they were losing control. They thought that no more plans would be made.
O#3	Employees have had doubts about the innovation of the application delivery because it cannot be properly chopped in sprints. There is a DevOps implementation for the run-organisation, but for the innovation it is mainly a project approach.
O#4	None.
O#5	None.
O#6	Sprint rhythm and not being able to deliver a "potentially shippable product".
O#7	Too dynamic, too unplanned, too big team to work on a relatively small application, no analysis & design beforehand.
O#8	None.
O#9	None.
O#10	None.

Table 4-3, Demotivators for applying Scrum.

4.2.3 Motivators for applying Scrum

Each case organisation has another specific reason for the introduction of Scrum. There are also general reasons mentioned.

O#	Why did you choose Scrum?
O#1	There was a need for more insight into what exactly is happening. The planning was not always clear. It is important that we can change faster and smoother.
O#2	The business case was: • Quality of software development and the reliability of the delivery of software development. • Quality began to decline with production disruptions as a result. • Team is extended and set up with Scrum. • Relations with maintainers have been strengthened.
O#3	The predictability of delivery by means of short sprints, involvement of the business partner and the reduction of the overhead.
O#4	Best suitable development approach for effective realization of the business objectives in the e-service provisioning domain.
O#5	To be able to develop faster and to better respond to customer needs.

O#	Why did you choose Scrum?
O#6	Functional developments of which the scope was not yet clear, in combination with the elimination of the 'technical debt'.
O#7	This method fits best with the applications that need to be developed.
O#8	• Short time to market. • Transparency. • Better stakeholder management.
O#9	It provides the organisation with the required agility, predictability and insight. By tightly aligning Scrum teams, the factory model is also well scalable.
O#10	Our organisation has opted for Scrum in order to gain more flexibility, predictability, efficiency and effectiveness.

Table 4-4, Motivators for applying Scrum.

4.2.4 Critical Success Factors for applying Scrum

Every change is accompanied by the identification of risks and countermeasures to prevent failure. The countermeasures of these risks are called critical success factors. By controlling these, it is possible to obtain faster a successful development process. The following Critical Success Factors (CSFs) have been recognized and used by the case organisations.

O#	What are the CSFs for meaningful application of Scrum?
O#1	In our organisation, the emphasis has been mainly on an awareness training.
O#2	• Transparency and trust. • Open communication. • Do not promise more than you can make true. • Reliable in the sense of appointments. • The trade-off cannot be planned long in advance.
O#3	Time to market must be achieved as well as a cost reduction.
O#4	Agile Scrum starts with Agile Management, ensuring the right context.
O#5	• Every sprint delivers software. • Good customer participation for feedback on what has been developed. • Acceleration in development. • Being able to work in a multidisciplinary way (engineers and testers).
O#6	Timely delivery of customer requirements, within the costs.
O#7	• End with an application that matches the expectations of the internal and external customer. • Fast feedback when the built applications do not meet expectations.
O#8	• Customer satisfaction. • Visualizing work.
O#9	Customer satisfaction, employee satisfaction, craftsmanship, First Time Right (FTR) deployments, FTR bugs after DoD, Productivity (hours per operation), wastes and defects.
O#10	• Commitment of management. • An involved product owner. • Necessity in relation to purpose and timeline.

Table 4-5, Critical Success Factors for applying Scrum.

It is not easy to clearly define immediately the interface between Scrum and service management. There are also a number of failure factors that require careful attention. An important question is therefore what the critical success factors have been that have to be monitored.

Possibly, there is, for example, a duplication of activities such as recording changes / features or carrying out double tests. A potentially critical success factor is in that case to sharply define of the roles and the execution of activities, both inside and outside the Scrum team.

O#	What are the CSFs of applying Scrum in combination with service management?
O#1	• Generic & Specific Acceptance Criteria (GSA). • The management of incidents and changes in Scrum teams.
O#2	• The service management team works closely with the Scrum team, which is why they must also be located close to each other. • Fixed high release frequency and subsequent routines help. • In the event of a break down (high priority incident), the Scrum team is always ready for support. • The service management team also has a voice in the product backlog and prioritization.
O#3	• Requirement management. • Regression tests. • Distribution of features across teams.
O#4	Intensive service management involvement in Scrumming and vice versa.
O#5	Business case: • Better insight into what we can deliver. • Productivity improvement. • Less is more. • Focus on the things that matter. • At last something is delivered CSF: • Multidisciplinary teams, insight into the development process / maintenance. • An important CSF is to keep the maintenance within the Scrum teams in the first 6 months after the release. • There is a lot of profit there (knowledge, throughput time, no boundaries culture).
O#6	Faster delivery times and better connection customer wish realization.
O#7	• Definition uncertainty. • Short feedback lifecycle.
O#8	Time to market was the consideration not to let DevOps fall under control of the service management processes. The multidisciplinary team composition led to informal contacts with other teams faster than formal contact.
O#9	• Being able to respond flexible to the question, if the urgency is high it can be picked up right away. • Working more predictably. • Small teams with focus deliver higher performance. • We have set requirements for competences: Proactive, result-oriented, flexible.
O#10	The CSF for the ESB Scrum team is to get more control of the workflow. We can ask for a clearer priority. There is a more streamlined collaboration with operations. Currently, operations are a great deal of time busy to ensure the uptime of the systems. As a result, the time for innovation (T / A and A / P) has decreased. With the introduction of continuous integration / continuous delivery, cooperation with operations must also improve.

Table 4-6, CFSs for applying Scrum in combination with service management.

4.2.5 Scrum-patterns

The layout of the Scrum team is closely related to the architecture of the application that has to be realized. If the application depends to a large extent on other applications, such as in a chain, then this is called a tightly coupled architecture. Another complexity-raising characteristic of an application is whether one or more business models must be configured in the application. In that case, the user interface, the business rules and the data model must support this multiple use. This is also called a multi tenancy architecture. The case organisations were asked which application architecture they develop and / or maintain with the Scrum team and which scope the Scrum team has.

O#	Loosely coupled / tightly coupled	Single tenancy / multi tenancy	Scope of the team
O#1	Loosely coupled	Multi tenancy	The Scrum team is solely responsible for the Enterprise Service Bus (ESB). There are no heterogeneous features. The Scrum team is therefore not dependent on other teams for their performance.
O#2	Loosely coupled	Single tenancy	There are two isolated Scrum teams.
O#3	Tightly coupled	Multi tenancy	Scrum teams are organized on horizontal splitting of the features.
O#4	Tightly coupled	Single tenancy	The teams are closely linked due to the chain formation of applications.
O#5	Tightly coupled	Multi tenancy	Kanban team maintains the entire application.
O#6	Loosely coupled	Single tenancy	There is only one Scrum team.
O#7	Loosely coupled, there is little or no chain formation.	Single tenancy, one business model per application.	Loose Scrum teams. The teams work independently of each other.
O#8	Loosely coupled	Single tenancy	There is only one team.
O#9	Loosely coupled	Single tenancy	Independent teams. Every team currently has its 'own' label for which work is being done.
O#10	Tightly coupled	Multi tenancy	The Scrum team only has the responsibility for the enterprise service bus. There are no heterogeneous features. The Scrum team is therefore not dependent on other teams for their performance. Other teams are dependent on deliveries from this team for their performance.

Table 4-7, Critical Success Factors for applying Scrum.

4.2.6 Scrum-roadmap

A new Scrum development team needs time to evolve. This maturation goes through a number of stages, as shown in Appendix A on the basis of an assessment. Some organisations want to give direction to this maturation. This can be done by defining a migration path between the current situation and the desired situation (Target Operating Model). This migration path can be mapped out in a roadmap including milestones. In that case, we speak of a top-down approach.

Leon de Caluwé has defined various change strategies and labelled them with colours. This top-down change strategy is labelled with the colour blue (Table 4-8). Another approach is the bottom-up change strategy. The Scrum team itself gives substance to the maturation. This change strategy is indicated by the colour green.

O#	Target Operating model	Milestones	Dashboard	Caluwé colour
O#1	No	No	No	Blue with management and green on the work floor.
O#2	No	No	No	Blue frame, green content.
O#3	Yes	No	Yes	Was blue (top-down) but is now completely green.
O#4	No	Yes	No	Organisation is yellow with blue areas. The teams are shaped green in this organisation. For the application of Scrum, we started green with, among other things, team building, gaming and InterVision. It is only when scaling up to several teams that blue areas have been added to establish a minimum form of agreements for the teams, so that a link with the 'old world' is guaranteed for the moment. The target situation is green / white.
O#5	Yes	No	No	Blue (top-down prescribed) and green filled in (organize work).
O#6	Yes, the team was pre-assigned plus the corresponding division of tasks.	Yes, milestones have been recognized	No	The Scrum process is Caluwé green and the control in Caluwé blue.
O#7	No	No	No	The Scrum process is shaped Caluwé green.
O#8	No	No	No	The Scrum process is shaped Caluwé green.
O#9	Scrum / Agile is one of the primary pillars of the factory model that we have adopted. The factory model is described in a TOM.	Yes. The factory model has now been operational for about 3 years. At that time, it was implemented over the period of about 6 months. By the use of a plan.	Yes, based on the milestones.	Blue frame, green content.

O#	Target Operating model	Milestones	Dashboard	Caluwé colour
O#10	There are regular teams defined. Within frameworks they can decide themselves which method to use.	No	The teams are observed on the development of agile maturity.	The organisation has defined standards that must be followed within which teams determine their own process. So Caluwé blue top-down and Caluwé green bottom-up.

Table 4-8, Roadmap.

4.2.7 Scrum establishment bottlenecks

When setting up a new development process, there are always surprises revealed that were not anticipated. The case organisations were asked which bottlenecks they experienced and which solutions were used.

O#	Bottlenecks in setting up Scrum development process	Selected solutions
O#1	• Understanding Scrum. • Willingness to cooperate. • Documentation.	• Awareness training. • Fun.
O#2	• Still locally implemented. • For our own team there is an expansion of the work area and there are smaller assignments, creating a broad set of stakeholders. So, there is no real product owner to designate.	The Product owner role has been filled in for a long time from the own team, at the moment it is being filled in by the supervisor in close consultation with project managers and Scrum master.
O#3	• Scope determination of the teams. • Multidisciplinary teams. • Discussions about how to deal with requirements, changes, releases across more teams. • There are different images with different officials.	• In general, the shaping of the organisation is started Caluwé blue and finished Caluwé green. Which means that much has been worked out in advance in terms of team composition, division of tasks, use of tools and the like. • The reorganisation shows that this top-down approach has been embraced as the departure point of the management, but has not been taken over in the construction of the Scrum teams due to the lack of a governance structure. • The organisation of teams is now filled in bottom-up based on the needs of the business partners.
O#4	• The Agile development process is simple, but very difficult to implement.	• Combined and phased approach of Scrum, Kanban, Agile architecture and portfolio management. Starting with one team and then scaling up in a controlled manner.
O#5	• Learning to be multidisciplinary. • Estimating the user points. • Learning new methods (Scrum method).	• Hire external Scrum coach.

O#	Bottlenecks in setting up Scrum development process	Selected solutions
O#6	• Delivering at the end of a sprint. We could not remove features from the release that were not finished at the review. Therefore, it was not always possible to deliver. This made it difficult to weigh up when a sprint had to end.	• Developing at different branches, delivering more often, even during the sprint.
O#7	• It took a lot of effort to explain to management what Scrum exactly means. • This is still difficult, because it is regularly thought that extensive designs are needed before the Scrum team can get to work.	• The Scrum master always takes an extra layer of management along in the Scrum process to really get them to understand what it means.
O#8	• No.	• Does not apply.
O#9	• Other mindset. • Scrum mastering is a profession. • Not something that you will do just that. • Developers also had to get used to the short cyclic and continuous improvement aspect.	• Training. • Explanation. • Sense of urgency. • Power of repetition. • Especially celebrating successes.
O#10	• Getting along the business and service management departments. • Push from the business, No dedicated product owner. • Platforms that do not lend themselves to short-cycle work.	• Apply Business DevOps. • Scaling of working Agile.

Table 4-9, Establishment bottlenecks.

4.2.8 Other methods besides Scrum.

Many case organisations use other methods in addition to Scrum to implement changes. The case organisations were asked to indicate what the primary Agile method is for shaping changes (Scrum, Kanban, Scrumban) and what the secondary method is to shape changes (PRojects IN Controlled Environments (PRINCE2), International Project Management Association (IPMA) etcetera. In case more methods are used, it is also asked to indicate the criteria for applying the primary or secondary method.

O#	Primary Method	Secondary Method	Criteria to choose between the methods
O#1	Scrum	PRINCE2	If the requirements are fixed in advance, then PRINCE2 is chosen.
O#2	Scrum (10-20%)	PRINCE2	Software development projects are controlled with PRINCE2. But development is also being done with Scrum. Demarcation is a team assignment that is not a project. An assignment that falls within the existing service provisioning is assigned to a team. The team carries out the work using Scrum. So, there is no choice. Currently there are only Scrum teams for Business Intelligence (BI) and software development.

O#	Primary Method	Secondary Method	Criteria to choose between the methods
O#3	Scrum (95%) Kanban (5%)	No.	Does not apply.
O#4	Scrum (100%) as defined in the manual.	PRINCE2	Scrum is used for software development of internet applications. PRINCE2 is always applied to projects. PRINCE2 and Scrum can be used in a complementary manner, using PRINCE2 for project control and Scrum for software development.
O#5	Scrum (100%) Kanban (100%)	No.	Does not apply.
O#6	Scrum (100%) Scrumban	Yes, PRINCE2, waterfall.	Create design, realization, testing. Is also used within Scrum to work out the operation of the functionality. That which works is applied (small waterfall within Scrum). Indication is <300 hours is service team. But for other customers this can be different. There are no formal rules.
O#7	Scrum (100%)	Waterfall.	We use waterfall for regular product development (more maintenance). We use Scrum for the new product development.
O#8	Scrum (100%) Kanban (100%)	No.	There is only one team, but there are two processes within it. Scrum we use for large features that also affect the back office. The smaller features go through the Kanban process. We therefore have two boards on which we manage.
O#9	Scrum (100%)	No, not within our depart-ment. But elsewhere within the organisation.	Does not apply.
O#10	Scrum	Kanban, Scrumban, Waterfall, PRINCE2 / IPMA.	Kanban is often chosen by maintenance teams. Scrum more often by project teams. There are still a few teams that work incrementally waterfall.

Table 4-10, Critical Success Factors for applying Scrum.

4.2.9 Other teams

Scrum is a framework for shaping a development process. In addition to Scrum teams, other teams are often recognized, such as a service management team or a deployment team. All case organisations have indicated the involved teams.

O#	Service desk	Release team	Service Management team	Others
O#1	Yes.	-	Yes.	-
O#2	Yes.	-	Yes.	-

O#	Service desk	Release team	Service Management team	Others
O#3	Yes.	No. Assigned to DevOps teams.	No. Assigned to DevOps teams.	• Technical management team.
O#4	Yes.	Yes.	Yes.	• Support team (support functions for Scrum teams - team-transcending disciplines). • Kanban team (solve incidents and carry through minor changes).
O#5	Yes.	Yes.	Yes.	• Integration team.
O#6	Yes.	-	-	• Service team.
O#7	Yes.	Does not apply.	Does not apply.	• Generic development team. • Documentation and test team. • Service delivery team.
O#8	Yes	-	-	• Application management team. • Infrastructure team.
O#9	General service desk (non-Scrum).	Yes, IT exploitation Windows performs the releases on the A and P environ-ment (non Scrum).	MicroSoft Competence Center (MScc) RUN (non Scrum).	• Database services. • SAP services (backend) (non-Scrum).
O#10	Yes.	Yes.	No.	-

Table 4-11, Other teams.

4.3 Agile governance

In this research attention has been paid to the following governance subjects:
- governance roles;
- governance model;
- governance instruments;
- governance aspects;
- governance tollgates.

4.3.1 Governance roles

Scrum provides a clear definition of the roles that apply in the Scrum development process. This does however not mean that these are also applied in practice. The roles that the case organisations recognize are listed in Table 4-12. Per role the characteristics are indicated:
- is dedicated, the officer is only connected to this team for this role;
- is a line officer, the officer is also a manager;

- part-time, the job involved is not a full-time job / one FullTime-Equivalent (FTE);
- back-up present, there is someone who can take over this role in case of absence.

O#	Product owner	Scrum master	Developer	Others
O#1	Is dedicated. Is line officer. Is part-time, 25%. Backup available.	Is dedicated. Is part-time, 30%. Back-up by colleagues.	Is dedicated. Partly multifunctional.	Classic roles. Is dedicated.
O#2	Is dedicated. Is line officer.	Is dedicated. Backup available.	Is dedicated. Full time. Partly multifunctional.	Release manager (not in the Scrum teams).
O#3	Is dedicated. Are mostly line officers from information management. Backup No.	Is dedicated (some teams). Is Part time, 10%.	Is dedicated. Specialists.	Is dedicated. Release manager. Integrators. Architects. Change manager. Service manager.
O#4	Is dedicated. Is line officer. Is full-time. Backup available.	Is not dedicated. Is full-time. Backup available.	Is usually dedicated. Is multifunctional. Backup available.	-
O#5	Is dedicated. Is not a line officer. Is Fulltime.	Is dedicated. Is part-time 15-20%. Is also an engineer.	Is dedicated. Is multifunctional.	Product manager, software architect, business architect.
O#6	Is dedicated. Is line officer. Is part-time, 20% Restricted backup.	Is dedicated. Full-time at start, now 30%. Backup not available.	Not dedicated. Specialists.	Developer, tester and designer.
O#7	Is dedicated. Is line officer. Is Fulltime. Backup yes.	Is dedicated. Part-time 80%. Is also programmer. Backup is a team member.	Is dedicated. Is multifunctional, but also, specialists.	Front enders. Java specialists. Test engineers. Product manager.
O#8	Is dedicated. Is not a line officer. Part time, 50%. Is ICT information analyst.	Is dedicated. Part time 50%. Is ICT information analyst.	Is not dedicated. Is multifunctional, but also specialists.	-
O#9	Is not dedicated[1]. Part time 50%. Is team manager. Backup Yes.	Is not dedicated. Part time 50%. Backup is team lead.	Is in principle multifunctional, but also specialists.	-
O#10	Is line officer. Part time.	Is dedicated. Is also a team member Part time, 70%.	Is dedicated. Specialist team.	Mandator. Project Manager.

Table 4-12, Governance roles.

1) No, we use a delegated product owner within the Component Factory who is in contact with the product owner who communicates with the business. There is one product owner.

4.3.2   *Governance model*

Various governance models are used within Agile. A portfolio management process is often present at strategic level. A product roadmap is often defined for an individual application. A release plan is then available at the tactical level. The product roadmap and the release planning are reflected in the product backlog. Operational control usually takes place on the basis of the sprint backlog. The question is how the case organisations implement this control.

O#	Portfolio control	Themes, epics, features and stories control	Cross team features control
O#1	There is a strategic decision-making body.	Themes and epics are not recognized.	The control takes place at a feature level over more teams. The teams give substance to the assigned stories.
O#2	Assignments, small-scale changes and new development.	Release planning. We had a product roadmap, but we do not have it anymore. We also looked at themes. Now we are more in the maintenance phase. However, we are now working on building up for another product set.	Product backlog. Sprint backlog.
O#3	A target architecture has been drawn up. In this target architecture, portfolio adjustments have also been indicated.	The great innovation is still quite waterfall-like. Lumps of functionality are delivered. There are also projects that work more in a Scrum manner on the basis of themes (phases) and divide this into sprints with user stories.	Separate role for defined and operationalized. These people receive support from blueprint experts and integrators.
O#4	Via portfolio management (business).	Via prioritizing of the portfolio backlog respectively the product backlog.	This control is given by the architecture function in the phase prior to the Scrum phase and where necessary during the Scrum phase. This steering is team transcending.
O#5	Not.	From the product backlog.	By means of the roadmap, followed by the sprint backlog after which the stories are distributed over the teams by coordination between the product owners.

O#	Portfolio control	Themes, epics, features and stories control	Cross team features control
O#6	It is more a series of (functional) wishes that are submitted to the organisation. If there are enough wishes (as was the case in the past period), a project is set up here.	Through steering committee consultation. Further in the hands of Scrum master. The themes have been named by means of a "walking skeleton". Within the sprint, these themes have been further divided into epics, then into features and then into user stories.	Does not apply.
O#7	A product portfolio is drawn up from 'Policy & Architecture', (see Figure 7-7). A roadmap for each product is also drawn up.	The product owner fills the product backlog on the basis of the roadmap team 'Policy & Architecture'.	At this moment we do not do anything with this.
O#8	The application is designed bottom-up from marketing. There is no portfolio. There is architecture involvement.	Epics are recognized. The user stories are managed through Kanban (product backlog and sprint backlog).	Does not apply.
O#9	Change is a pillar under the factory model. By cutting disciplines apart, they can be managed better on craftsmanship. Architecture roadmaps ensure planning.	The Kanban board is used for this purpose (at initiative and feature level).	The Kanban board is used for this purpose (at initiative and feature level). Our teams consist of developers and one tester. The tester uses the same Kanban board (in addition to the development tasks of the developers, the tester creates test tasks under the same user story).
O#10	We try to implement portfolio management through the standard integrated tooling for backlog management.	For the change teams, we use / implement standard integrated tooling for backlog management.	Using standard integrated tooling for backlog management, the feature / story is put on the board of another team.

Table 4-13, Governance model.

4.3.3 *Governance instruments*

In Table 4-14 a number of specific governance instruments are included. Per case organisation is shown whether they are in use or not.

Governance instruments	O#1	O#2	O#3	O#4	O#5	O#6	O#7	O#8	O#9	O#10
Policies	No	Yes	No	Yes	No	Yes	Yes	Yes	Yes	No
Release sprint	Yes	No	Yes	Yes	Yes	Yes	Yes	No	No	No
Product portfolio	Yes	No	Yes	Yes	Yes	Yes	Yes	No	Yes	Yes
Vision	No	No	Yes	Yes	Yes	Yes	Yes	No	Yes	Yes

Governance instruments	O#1	O#2	O#3	O#4	O#5	O#6	O#7	O#8	O#9	O#10
Product roadmap	Yes	Yes	Yes	Yes	Yes	Yes	Yes	No	No	Yes
Release plan	Yes	Yes	Yes	Yes	Yes	Yes	Yes	No	Yes	Yes
Sprint plan	Yes	Yes	Yes	Yes	Yes	Yes	Yes	Yes	Yes	Yes
Sprint review	Yes	Yes	Yes	Yes	Yes	Yes	Yes	Yes	Yes	Yes
Sprint retrospective	Yes	Yes	Yes	Yes	Yes	Yes	Yes	Yes	Yes	Yes

Table 4-14, Governance instruments.

4.3.4 Governance aspects
There are a number of important aspects that strongly influence the management of the development team. Three aspects have been investigated:
- Which officer has been given the role of product owner, or to which domain has this role been assigned?
- Is scaling used such as Scrum of Scrums or a Scaled Agile Framework (SAFe) framework?
- Is there a steering based on the velocity?

O#	Who is the product owner?	Do you use scaling?	Velocity measurement
O#1	Information management.	No.	Yes / No.
O#2	Line manager Scrum team.	No.	Yes.
O#3	Domain information management.	There is a separate Agile Transformation workgroup that deals with scaling.	Is measured on the basis of the realized stories per sprint.
O#4	Product developer.	Is under construction towards SAFe.	Based on the realized story points.
O#5	Analyst.	No.	Through story points in ScrumWise.
O#6	Mandator from the customer.	No.	Normally on the basis of the number of story points that are realized within a sprint.
O#7	A business consultant in the service delivery team. Our service delivery team is responsible for providing service to our customers in the area of our product.	No.	During each sprint the number of story points spent in the previous sprint is checked. This way we look at how many story points are available for the next sprint.
O#8	ICT information analyst.	Does not apply.	Yes, based on the number of story points and the number of hours.
O#9	The solution delivery manager.	Scalability is one of the primary pillars under the factory.	By calculating the story points (number of operations) that are delivered per sprint.

O#	Who is the product owner?	Do you use scaling?	Velocity measurement
	He communicates with the stakeholders on behalf of the entire factory and determines the priority on the basis of this.	Teams have a strong individual responsibility (1. design team, 2. component factory (design middleware / backend you might say), 3. frontend development). Scalable per discipline. (Factory has started with three teams, currently scaled up to about twenty teams by near and off shoring.)	In addition, we use the focus factor (total hours spent / target hours related to the sprint).
O#10	Line manager from the business.	This is being looked at.	The effort based on breakpoints.

Table 4-15, Governance aspects.

4.3.5 Governance tollgates

Whether or not to promote a change into production can be decided at different levels. This is often referred to as a tollgate. The following tollgates can be recognized:
- DoD at release level, this includes the generic criteria for all releases;
- DoD per feature, this includes the generic criteria for all features on the product backlog;
- DoD per story, this includes the generic criteria for all stories;
- DoD per phase, this includes the generic criteria per Scrum or Kanban phase.

These tollgates are included Table 4-16.

Governance tollgates	O#1	O#2	O#3	O#4	O#5	O#6	O#7	O#8	O#9	O#10
DoD per release	Yes	Yes	Yes	Yes	No	Yes	No	No	Yes	No
DoD per feature	Yes	Yes	Yes	Yes	No	Yes	No	Yes	Yes	No
DoD per sprint	No	No	Yes	Yes	Yes	Yes	Yes	No	No	No
DoD per story	Yes	Yes	Yes	Yes	No	Yes	Yes	Yes	Yes	Yes
DoD per phase (todo, doing and done)	No	Yes	No	No	No	No	No	Yes	No	Yes[1]

Table 4-16, Governance tollgates (1).

[1] The DoD contains agreements for each phase of the change process.

The application of change management in relation to Scrum is dealt with differently. Some organisations use changes at a higher abstraction level (assignments), than the features and stories. Other organisations equate a change with a feature. The use of a lifecycle of a change at the level of an assignment gives an extra tollgate that has to be passed.

In addition to the lifecycle of features and stories, it is advisable to also identify a lifecycle of requirements. The feature / story then contains the governance data and the requirements the actual functional and non-functional demands. The reason for choosing this is to be able to reuse the requirement and thus also the underlying test cases that are linked to the requirement. In addition to these tollgates at change / requirement level, Table 4-17 also shows which aspects the case organisations have applied in their DoD at release level.

O#	Content DoD releases	Own lifecycle requirements?	Own lifecycle changes?
O#1	User story - specific acceptance criteria.	The start architecture contains requirements. These are converted into a user story, but the requirements continue to have their own cycle.	Everything expressed into a feature. Only RFCs with an agreement to be included in the next release are entered in the sprint planning.
O#2	Release notes, installation / configuration manual and a test report.	Requirements are integrated in the feature / story.	Changes for correction or improvement follow the Scrum development process. For this capacity is reserved in the Scrum team. Registration and management of changes takes place in the issue management tool (HP Quality Center). IT Service Management (Mexon) plays a role in the service management process for configuration management, change management and incident management.
O#3	Especially attention points for maintenance deliverables and risk controls.	No.	No, changes must come as a feature request on the product backlog.
O#4	All requirements in the DoD have a focus on the release. In addition to the requirements regarding a user story, we have a separate DoD at integration level. The DoD release includes: • Technical Architecture Document (TAD) updated. • Release Notes created / updated. • Master Test Plan final (1.0 available). • Integration tests performed. • Test report available. • Release documentation available. • System Integration Test report available. • Functional Acceptance Test Plan (including regression test and planning).	Integrated in user story / use case.	RFCs are also generated through incidents. In addition to Scrum, there is a separate process for realizing corrective maintenance. For this a team is available that works on the basis of the Kanban method and can quickly bring small changes to production.

O#	Content DoD releases	Own lifecycle requirements?	Own lifecycle changes?
	• Functional Acceptance Test Plan (including regression test and planning). • Chain test plan. • Test data acceptance test environment. • Data migration plan (if applicable).		
O#5	• Code. • Functional. • Delivery. • General.	Integrated.	Yes.
O#6	• Compilable code. • Test scripts present. • Test scripts performed. • If unit test then green. • Screens are displayed within 3 seconds. • User's manual updated. • Release notes. • Installation manual. • Web configuration documentation. • House style screens. • Review.	Depends on the sort of requirement. Some are part of the lifecycle (business / technical requirements), some part of feature (functional requirements). Functional requirements are part of the functional design. In Jira the description of the functional requirements is registered. Technical requirements are included in the vision document and have been added to Jira at the time of realization. Requirements do not have a unique number and the test case does not refer to which requirement has been tested. Sometimes, the test case refers to requirements by enumerating the requirements.	Generally, they have a separate process.
O#7	No. A release is coordinated by the product manager with the product owner, but also with the Sales and Delivery team.	A requirement is in the minds of others and is translated into a user story by the product owner.	Developers can submit their own changes to the product owner.
O#8	No.	No.	No, only improvement, issues and standard (regular feature).

O#	Content DoD releases	Own lifecycle requirements?	Own lifecycle changes?
O#9	Build quality reporting, TFS configuration, documentation, etcetera. This is a checklist in MS Excel.	Integrated to the feature / User Story (described in the DDD).	Yes, in addition to additive changes, we also recognize corrective changes, which are initiated by service management from problem management.
O#10	For this we use a CAB procedure with its own set of rules.	One half of the teams manages the requirements apart / separately, the other half manages the requirements via the registration of acceptance criteria in user stories.	Yes, changes are recognized for both the projects and for the maintenance process.

Table 4-17, Governance tollgates (2).

4.4 Agile tools

4.4.1 Tool support

In the research the organisations are also asked which tools they use for the development process.

Subject	Tools
Administration user stories.	<ul><li>Ice-Scrum.</li><li>Standard integrated tooling for backlog management is used for this purpose and in the past also other tooling.</li><li>HP Quality Center.</li><li>Jira (mentioned three times).</li><li>Sparx Systems Enterprise Architect (Enterprise Architect).</li><li>ScrumWise.</li><li>LeanKit.</li><li>Team Foundation Server.</li></ul>
Versioning and baselining.	<ul><li>IBM Rational ClearCase ClearQuest (CCCQ) (mentioned two times).</li><li>Own release tool, Excel, standard integrated tooling for backlog management.</li><li>Jira.</li><li>Serena Dimensions.</li><li>Subversion (mentioned twice).</li><li>Subversion with transition to Global Information Tracker (GIT).</li><li>GIT.</li></ul>
Continuous integration.	<ul><li>Mavim.</li><li>Standard integrated tooling for backlog management and continuous integration. Jenkins (mentioned twice).</li><li>Build servers with tools for CI are under development.</li><li>ClearCase and TestComplete.</li><li>Jenkins and Nexus.</li></ul>
Continuous delivery.	<ul><li>standard integrated tooling for backlog management and continuous delivery.</li><li>Jenkins.</li></ul>

Subject	Tools
	• Build servers with tools for continuous delivery are under development. • ClearCase and Installshield. • RepliWeb Operations Suite for SharePoint (ROSS). deployment tool & Automated PowerShell script (PowerShell).
Regression tests.	• HP Application Lifecycle Management (HP ALM). • Robot framework / Apache JMeterTM (JMeter). • Standard integrated tooling for backlog management and automatic testing / regression testing. • Selenium (mentioned twice). • Manual according to regression test script. • TestComplete. • Selenium. • SOAtest. • Own tooling. • A self-built test framework, Selenium and Twist.
Software configuration management.	• ClearCase (mentioned twice). • Own release tool, MS Excel, standard integrated tooling for backlog management. • Subversion. • Subversion, supplemented with Nexus. • Subversion / #define amongst other WinMerge / Jenkins. • GIT (mentioned twice). • Serena Dimensions. • PowerShell.

Table 4-18, Tool support.

4.4.2 Tool integration

In order to realize a traceable development process, it is necessary to make links between tools. This can be done on the basis of an identification and on the basis of an automatic linking of tools. The better the integration of tools, the sooner continuous integration and continuous delivery is possible.

Subjects	Tools
Linking user story and Software Configuration Items (S-CIs).	• Via standard integrated tooling for backlog management. • No direct links, but within HP Quality Center (HP QC) for test scripts there are direct links. • Link between Enterprise Architect and ScrumWise. • Jira link with Subversion. • Subversion link with Jenkins. • HP ALM. • Both are ensured in TFS.
Are you still using your service management tool, or has it now been changed / linked to the Scrum tools?	• Yes, standard integrated tooling for backlog management and standard integrated tooling for service management that however are not linked to each other. • Yes. • Yes, HPSC and HP ALM linked on a manual basis with Scrum tools.

Subjects	Tools
	• Clientele IT Service Management (Clientele) is linked to the Software Configuration Management (SCM) system for the tracking of the defects. • Yes, Open source Ticket Request System (OTRS), which is not linked to the Scrum tools. • Yes, Clientele, as source not as management for our team. There is a manual link between Clientele and the Leankit in case of adjustments to the CMS or the interface with the back-offices. • TOPdesk is used on the business side. • Omnitracker is used on the ICT side. • TFS, MicroSoft Competence Center (MSCC) RUN, HP Service Manager.
How do the Scrum teams deal with the infrastructural tools?	• We use standard tooling for starting processes and moving files. We do not implement it but do create the design. The infrastructure maintainers are responsible for the actual implementation. • The maintenance domain does this. • Not, there is a technical management team. • No. • We do it ourselves or we write work instructions for the customer. • On an ad hoc basis, we do it partly and partly the supplier. • Monitoring / scheduling, etcetera. Is not done by Scrum team but DoD entries are delivered such as installation manual. • Is requested. The developer provides the script.

Table 4-19, Tool integration.

5 Agile risk management

Message:
- Processes of which the risks are well controlled are financial management for ICT services, information security management, availability management, capacity management and change management.
- The processes whose risks are less well controlled are service level management, event management, incident management and problem management.

Reading guideline:

This chapter is divided in the phases of the service life cycle of ITIL v3. For each phase, the risks per related process are presented to the case organisation. For each risk, the management of the Agile development process was requested. The risks and possible countermeasures are published in the book 'Agile Service Management with Scrum' [Best 2018]. This chapter therefore only provides a summary of the countermeasure. The first section discusses the general questions about the service management processes. Section 5.2 describes the risk control in the first phase, the service strategy. The second phase include the risks of the service design phase (5.3). The third phase is the service transition phase. This phase is discussed in section 5.4. The fourth phase is service operations. This is described in section 5.5. The continuous service improvement phase is not included in the study.

5.1 General questions

5.1.1 Service management processes

There are organisations that have explicitly chosen not to recognize process owners and / or project managers anymore. There are also organisations where people no longer believe in the added value of service management processes. That is why the research also is focused on the question of whether there are indeed process owners and process managers.

ALG A01	Which service management process owners and process managers are still in position after the introduction of Scrum? Which have become superfluous (change management for example)?
O#	
O#1	The service management processes are as they were before the introduction of Scrum.
O#2	Incident management, change management, configuration management, release management (not process-based), service level management, capacity management and IT service continuity management.
O#3	All service management processes are still active and have an owner. Governance is agile implemented.
O#4	All service management processes are still in use.
O#5	All service management processes are as they were before the introduction of Scrum.
O#6	All service management processes are still in use.
O#7	The existing process implementation has remained unchanged.
O#8	The Kanban team has been working for a year to realize the portal function. The service management processes are not involved, neither operationally nor tactically. We do consult with the service management organisation to share information.
O#9	The development team performs the work under the control of the change management process. But most service management processes are performed within the run organisation.

ALG A01	Which service management process owners and process managers are still in position after the introduction of Scrum? Which have become superfluous (change management for example)?
O#10	All service management processes (ITIL processes) are applied.

Table 5-1, ALG-A01 – Service management processes.

ALG A02	Is there still a role for process owners?
O#	
O#1	Yes, incident management, change management etctera.
O#2	Process ownership for ITIL processes is assigned to (managers of) departments. Process managers are appointed from these departments. Responsibility for compliance is assigned to the main contractors for services (management maintenance teams).
O#3	Yes, process owners / managers are recognized.
O#4	Yes.
O#5	Yes, incident management, change management etcetera.
O#6	Yes.
O#7	The line manager development is the owner of all service management processes.
O#8	No.
O#9	Yes.
O#10	Yes, process owners are recognized.

Table 5-2, ALG-A02 – Process owners.

ALG A03	Is there still a role for process managers?
O#	
O#1	Yes, process managers are still being recognized for incident management, change management, etcetera.
O#2	Yes, incident management, change management and service level management.
O#3	Yes, process owners / managers are still being recognized.
O#4	Yes, process managers are still being recognized.
O#5	Yes, process managers are still being recognized for incident management, change management, etcetera.
O#6	Yes, process managers are still being recognized.
O#7	Yes, there is still a role for process managers. Change management is performed by the Scrum team. The product owner and the quality assurance team determine the acceptance.
O#8	No.
O#9	Yes, process managers are still being recognized.
O#10	Yes, process managers are recognized.

Table 5-3, ALG-A03 – Process managers.

Looijen recognizes five forms of application management [Looijen 2011]. Additive application management is adding functionality. Adaptive application management is the modification of an application due to a change in the environment of the application, such as a new operating system, database management system and so on. The corrective application management is adjusting an application based on an incident.

The perfective application management is the maintenance of the application to better adapt it to the needs of the user, such as reducing the number of screens and reducing the number of clicks to carry out a business transaction. Preventive application management includes the work required to prevent incidents such as the installation of security patches.

ALG A04	Which forms of application management are performed by the Scrum teams? A. Additive application management B. Adaptive application management C. Corrective application management D. Perfective application management E. Preventive application management
O#	
O#1	All five forms are performed by the Scrum team.
O#2	All five forms are performed by the Scrum team.
O#3	All five forms are performed by the Scrum team.
O#4	Additive, adaptive and perfective application management.
O#5	All five forms are performed by the Scrum team.
O#6	All five forms are performed by the Scrum team.
O#7	All five forms are performed by the Scrum team.
O#8	All five forms are performed by the Scrum team.
O#9	All five forms are performed by the Scrum team.
O#10	All five forms are performed by the Scrum team.

Table 5-4, ALG-A04 – Application management.

The role of product owner is similar to that of the service level manager. The question is therefore whether the product owner has received these roles.

ALG A05	Has a double function been recognized? Is the product owner also a service level manager?
O#	
O#1	No, the product owner is not the service level manager.
O#2	No, there is no product owner. The change calendar is of a higher level (assignments). The priorities of the product backlog are determined by the line manager.
O#3	No, Service management within application management is limited to process governance in 2015, from 2016 connection with information management is provided and Service Management could be introduced in practice.
O#4	No.
O#5	No.
O#6	No.
O#7	No.
O#8	No.
O#9	No.
O#10	No, the product owner is not the service level manager.

Table 5-5, ALG-A05 – Is the product owner also a service level manager?

The role of product owner is similar to that of the change manager. The question is therefore whether the product owner has received these roles.

ALG A06	Has a double function been recognized? Is the product owner also a change manager?
O#	
O#1	There are changes that go outside change management to the Scrum team, but that are not application changes where governance is applicable, because they are configuration changes.
O#2	The product owner is not also a change manager. There is a distinction between the responsible person / party for the change management on the application (product owner) and the ITIL change management process (change manager). In the current set-up of the Scrum development team, there is a contact point for each managed application from the application management (change manager). The line manager of the Scrum team ensures mutual prioritization between change requests (product owner - supplier perspective).
O#3	Yes, within the teams the product owner takes on the role of change and release coordinator for his team. The coordinators are managed by the change and release process manager.
O#4	No, but at release level there is a change manager.
O#5	No.
O#6	No.
O#7	Yes.
O#8	No.
O#9	No.
O#10	No, a double function is not recognized.

Table 5-6, ALG-A06 – Is the product owner also a change manager?

ALG A07	Which service management processes play a role in the Scrum development process?
O#	
O#1	Lifecycle product management, license management and change management on the development environment.
O#2	The Scrum team is dealing with service management processes of ASL / ITIL. This affects, among other things, the DoD. The development team is also involved in the service management processes.
O#3	Service management processes are included in the DevOps teams. The processes are primarily intended as an adhesive layer over DevOps teams for control and information transfer.
O#4	The service management processes are used for governance.
O#5	All ITIL v2 service management processes play a role in the Scrum development process.
O#6	The incident management, release & deployment management processes play a role in the Scrum development process.
O#7	The incident management process plays a role in the Scrum development process.
O#8	The incident management and request fulfilment processes play a role in the Scrum development process.
O#9	All ITIL v3 processes play a role in the Scrum development process.

ALG A07	Which service management processes play a role in the Scrum development process?
O#10	The incident management, problem management and change management processes play a role in the Scrum development process.

Table 5-7, ALG-A07 – Which service management processes play a role within Scrum?

5.1.2 Policies

Another word for a strategic choice is a policy. Various service management processes require the use of policies in order to achieve the process goals. An example is that certain changes must always be put into production via the DTAP street. But a policy can also relate to more service management processes. For example, the use of a service management tool for various processes can be made compulsory, as well as the correlation of the objects of those processes.

For example, in most organisations, incidents, problems and changes must be linked to configuration items. But a policy can also relate to a concept, such as applying a service orientation for incidents, problems and changes. The question is to what extent these policies are included in the DoD. Scrum does not mention the possibility to use policies from service management in the DoD. However, it is much easier to name the compliancy to the service orientation as DoD entry than to name all possible requirements individually as a result of the service orientation.

ALG A08	Which policies related to service management processes do you recognize?
O#	
O#1	We do not use policies from service management in the Scrum team.
O#2	We use the WIP limit, release frequency and incident handling times as policies.
O#3	Every process is provided with policies. These play a role in the DoD and the administration of information in the tooling.
O#4	There are no policies from management processes for the DoD, other than that changes must be adequately documented, and the correct release documents are delivered. Only from release management there is a policy that there is a release twice a year. With smaller releases, the policies become important.
O#5	Service management processes set requirements for the Kanban process.
O#6	The release policy and Installability policies are included in the DoD.
O#7	We use the incident handling time as a policy. We also apply the policy that only one story can be handled by a team at the same time and only one task per person.
O#8	There are no policies from management. We do, however, use a WIP limit and a lane policy that indicates for each phase when a ticket may stay in a phase.
O#9	The following policies apply from release & deployment management: system test, system integration test, functional agreement, etcetera.
O#10	We do not explicitly apply policies in the DoD from service management in the Scrum team.

Table 5-8, ALG-A08 – Policies from service management processes.

5.1.3 Service desk

The service desk is an important function of operational service management processes. The question is whether that function still applies with the use of Scrum.

ALG A09	Is there a service desk? Which service management processes play a role in this?
O#	
O#1	Yes, there is a service desk. The service desk executes the incident management process and the request fulfilment process. Change management is not assigned to the service desk.
O#2	Yes, there is a service desk. The incident management process has been assigned to the service desk. The following processes are not assigned to the service desk: change management, problem management and configuration management.
O#3	Yes, there is an end user support desk. This is the entry point for incidents and feature requests.
O#4	Yes, there is a service desk. The incident management and problem management process are assigned to the service desk. Changes are registered at the service desk, but these are the more technical changes. There is a counter function on the business side for the functional changes. An RFC starts its lifecycle there.
O#5	Yes, there is a service desk. The incident management, problem management, configuration management and deployment (publication portal) process are assigned to the service desk.
O#6	Yes, there is a service desk. The incident management, change management and service level management are assigned to the service desk.
O#7	Yes, there is a contact person for customer questions. The following processes play a role here: incident management, request fulfilment and change management.
O#8	Yes, there is a service desk. The following processes play a role in this: incident management and request fulfilment.
O#9	Yes, there is a service desk. The following processes play a role here: incident management, request fulfilment, problem management, service asset & configuration management and access management.
O#10	Yes, there is a service desk. The following processes are involved: incident management, problem management, change management and configuration management.

Table 5-9, ALG-A09 – Policies from service management processes.

5.2 Service strategy

5.2.1 Service Portfolio Management

Scrum is primarily a bottom-up shaping of the change. This implies the risk that there is no connection to the mission, vision, business objective and strategy of the organisation. ITIL does address this risk by defining at a strategic level a service portfolio management process that gives direction to the innovation and ensures that these connect with the business processes in cooperation with, for example, demand management. In practice, in addition to the ITIL approach, an alignment is also necessary at the architectural level. This means that attention has to be paid to architecture frameworks such as TOGAF / IAF.

SPM RO1	How do the Scrum teams ensure that the service continues to be aligned with your business processes?
O#	A solution is to connect the Scrum development process to architecture. For example, by applying the Integrated Architecture Framework (IAF) that has been defined within TOGAF.
O#1	Changes are designed under architecture. The decision-making process lies with the decision-making body.
O#2	This responsibility is assigned to architecture.

SPM RO1	How do the Scrum teams ensure that the service continues to be aligned with your business processes?
O#3	The service is service-oriented. A relationship has been established between business services - business information services - information system services and infrastructure services.
O#4	Control from portfolio management takes place at business level. At the architectural level via DYA / IAF.
O#5	The Kanban team does not see this. There is no service orientation yet. Information & Automation (I & A) has started.
O#6	Vision document in combination with functional wishes and changes from legislation are translated to the product backlog and the planning.
O#7	Consultancy does the business analysis.
O#8	This is not ensured.
O#9	Multidisciplinary design teams work in the form of co-creation with IT Demand.
O#10	We are mainly product-oriented. The frameworks from architecture are given to the teams.

Table 5-10, SPM-R01 – Business alignment.

Based on a starting point from architecture, it is possible to prevent Scrum teams from inventing redundant solutions. The question is therefore how this is prevented from the Scrum approach.

SPM RO2	How do the Scrum teams prevent patchwork in your service, product and tool portfolios?
O#	A solution direction is defining the current situation (IST), the desired situation (SOLL) and the migration path to achieve this. On this basis, a product roadmap can be composed. This architectural approach makes it possible to prevent the patchwork.
O#1	We use a start architecture, which means that patchwork is prevented.
O#2	This responsibility is assigned to architecture.
O#3	This is prevented by architecture.
O#4	Architecture is involved and responsible in the preliminary phase with regard to the solution architecture, coherence and dependencies. Intensive collaboration in the entire process between the various architectural functions (business, IT, software and infra- / integration architect).
O#5	This is not applicable.
O#6	This is prevented by using a vision document.
O#7	Product management is responsible for the patchwork control. The Scrum team builds on open standards.
O#8	This is not prevented.
O#9	The design team checks the applications for reuse.
O#10	The blueprint of architecture should prevent patchwork.

Table 5-11, SPM-R02 – Patchwork.

5.2.2 Demand Management

ITIL provides insight into customer's demand by identifying user profiles and usage characteristics (patterns of business activities). The future demand can also be looked at. This makes it possible to establish high level non-functional requirements in the sense of performance indicators and service norms.

DEM R01	How do the Scrum teams ensure that the future use of the information system align with the information to be delivered?
O#	A solution direction is the recognition of user profiles and patterns of business activities.
O#1	This is not implemented. We do not recognize user profiles. We do have a forecast based on a trend analysis.
O#2	Architecture establishes user profiles and patterns of business activities.
O#3	From the service architecture it is clear what the services are. The non-functional requirements are defined from Operations (Ops) / service management role. Patterns in business requirements have been recognized.
O#4	We use user profiles and patterns of business activity.
O#5	This is not applicable.
O#6	User profiles are recognized. The product owner sometimes indicates what happens. Sometimes this is reported from the use of the application It is not an issue at the moment.
O#7	Product management recognizes user profiles and patterns of business activities, but these are not recognized for all applications.
O#8	This is not ensured.
O#9	This must be part of the performance stress test. The tests are carried out on the basis of non-functional specifications that are based on the business forecasting.
O#10	This is not recognized other than from architecture. We do not recognize user profiles or patterns of business activities.

Table 5-12, DEM-R01 – Future use.

By applying demand management, it is possible to establish service packages that uniformize the service provision and on the other hand give a limited degree of freedom.

DEM R02	How do the Scrum teams prevent sprawl in service levels and service norms?
O#	Service packages, core services, enhancing services and enabling services.
O#1	We use a generic SLA.
O#2	Management carries out the service level management process. Service management is responsible for preventing the sprawl of service level and service standards.
O#3	The services are clustered into service packages. There are as few different norms as possible.
O#4	There is only an image on information system service. Architecture has to bridle the sprawl. Non-Functional Requirement (NFR) programs are constantly baselined on application level.
O#5	Integration team performs the integration test (only a performance test) and makes a generic deployment available to operations (service desk). The basic service levels and norms are laid down in the basic service provision document. This applies to every customer, regardless the size. In addition, a customer can receive a supplement to the base by agreeing an SLA in which the service levels and norms are of a higher level.
O#6	Scrum teams carry out stand-alone projects that are embedded in existing service levels.
O#7	This is not applicable.
O#8	This is not prevented.
O#9	Service level management is highly standardized.

DEM R02	How do the Scrum teams prevent sprawl in service levels and service norms?
	The factory model hosts a standard platform. Only this standard deviates from a strong business case. The factory-based sites (fast-lane) are provided with a standard SLA. The fast lanes are simple websites that consist of standard building blocks and can therefore quickly pass through the process (directly to acceptance and production, development and testing do not have to be carried out in this situation).
O#10	This is not done structurally.

Table 5-13, DEM-R02 – Sprawl in service levels and service norms.

5.2.3 Financial Management for ICT services

Most organisations spend 80% of the ICT budget on maintenance. That is why it is important to reduce these costs. This requires the Scrum team to take measures in the sprints.

FIN R01	How do you prevent the costs for information provision from boiling over?
O#	A solution direction is using refactoring and / or renovation.
O#1	There is no control on this.
O#2	The maintenance department is responsible for this. We do the refactoring of the source code. See also CAP-R03.
O#3	Standard packages have been purchased and are being configured. Renovation or refactoring is not the case.
O#4	Refactoring is applied. In addition, software quality measurements take place and steering at the reduction of technical debt takes place.
O#5	Refactoring is applied.
O#6	Removal of obsolete software, refactoring of existing parts, execution of annual software control that provides an overview of the status of the application and gives recommendations.
O#7	Refactoring is applied.
O#8	Both refactoring and renovation are applied.
O#9	Both refactoring and renovation are applied.
O#10	Architecture uses the strategy to look at the future system landscape. The portfolio is used to managed this. The team uses both refactoring and renovation.

Table 5-14, FIN-R01 – Maintenance costs.

Information systems have a certain lifespan. It is important to take this into account. The maintenance of the application can become more expensive because the technological knowledge is no longer available and as a result the hourly rates become more expensive. It is also possible that the application needs to be replaced because it is no longer compatible with the current state of technology.

FIN R02	How do you monitor the economic value of the information system?
O#	A solution direction is lifecycle management and monitoring the Return on Investment (ROI). The removal of of not used and irrelevant code during maintenance is also an important factor to keep the economic value high.
O#1	We do not use Total Cost of Ownership (TCO). We do recognize lifecycle management.

FIN R02	How do you monitor the economic value of the information system?
O#2	Service management monitors the economic value of the information system together with the owner.
O#3	At strategic level. There is still no dead wood.
O#4	There is a steering on the reduction of technical debt, including the removal of not used and irrelevant and complex code.
O#5	Recognizing dead wood is done. The dead wood is removed.
O#6	Scrum team eliminates dead wood and performs refactoring where necessary.
O#7	We also understand under refactoring the elimination of code that is no longer used.
O#8	We remove dead wood.
O#9	The reuse matrix provides insight into what is used and what is not. If it is not used, we can remove it. That is then a point of improvement that does not have a high priority.
O#10	This aspect is also shaped by architecture and not by the Scrum team. However, the Scrum team is looking at cleaning up. Turning functionality off is a continuous challenge.

Table 5-15, FIN-R02 – Economic value.

5.3 Service design

5.3.1 Service level management

A Scrum team can be regarded as an internal or external provider of services. The primary service here is the provision of software (production orientation) or a supporting functionality (service orientation). The secondary service is the handling of escaped defects, urgent changes, etcetera. A service Scrum team could prepare a service catalogue for this primary and secondary service. A service level manager could also agree on an Operational Level Agreement (OLA) with the Scrum team.

SLM A01	Do the Scrum teams use a service catalogue and an SLA for the services they provide?
O#	
O#1	No, we only use a generic SLA.
O#2	No.
O#3	Yes, now mainly at team level but is always agreed between teams.
O#4	No.
O#5	No. Incidents have to be solved, that is a remit for the service desk. The Kanban maintenance team only receives problem tickets. There is no OLA between the Kanban maintenance team and the service desk. There is a common interest. The Kanban maintenance team also has KPIs that are in line with the SLAs. The management steers on these KPIs.
O#6	No.
O#7	No.
O#8	No.
O#9	No.
O#10	Not specific for the Scrum team. When the SLA norms are exceeded, the cause is looked at.

Table 5-16, SLM-A01 – Service catalogue and an SLA.

The question is who fulfils the role of service level manager. If the product owner is a co-worker of information management, he would have to fulfil the demand side (external specsheet). In that case he may not fulfil the supply side (internal specsheet). If the product owner was appointed from the ICT organisation, he would be able to fulfil the full role of service level manager. He is then in any case responsible for the demand side. In fact, the product owner must always fulfill in the demand side. The question is therefore what in practice is the collaboration between the product owner and the service level manager.

SLM A02	Who fulfils the role of service level manager and how is the governance on the Scrum team organized?
O#	
O#1	The responsibility to agree on the SLA with the customer is placed outside the application development and the application maintenance organisation.
O#2	There is a service level manager, the application maintenance team is responsible for achieving the agreed service level. The Scrum team acts as supplier of the software and provides support. No explicit agreements have yet been made about the manner in which the service level manager is steering the Scrum team in the sense of governance.
O#3	The role of service level management is carried out centrally. This has not yet been formalized.
O#4	The service level manager fulfils the role from a distance.
O#5	No one fulfils the role of service level manager. There is no governance on the Scrum team from service level management.
O#6	Service level management fulfils this role. The governance has been organized by participating in a development team as a functional designer / tester.
O#7	The architect carries out an initial analysis. The product owner only determines the functional requirements. The service level manager has the final responsibility.
O#8	No one.
O#9	The product owner fulfils the service level manager role. The governance is determined from the design authority.
O#10	The role is assigned to maintenance. There is no governance on the Scrum team from service level management.

Table 5-17, SLM-A02 – Service level manager role.

The Scrum teams can be held responsible for the delivery of a service as this can be the case with a business DevOps team. In that case they will have a need to make agreements with parties they depend on.

SLM A03	Which OLAs do the Scrum teams have with internal service management parties (infrastructure, service desk)?
O#	
O#1	No OLA has been agreed with the Scrum team. There are informal agreements. These are partly based on the generic SLA.
O#2	None.
O#3	None. There is an agreement with infrastructure.
O#4	None.
O#5	None.
O#6	This is not formalized.
O#7	None.

SLM A03	Which OLAs do the Scrum teams have with internal service management parties (infrastructure, service desk)?
O#8	None.
O#9	None.
O#10	The maintenance department draws up OLAs. No OLA has been agreed for the Scrum team.

Table 5-18, SLM-A03 – Internal agreements.

SLM A04	Who communicates about what regarding the service norms?
O#	
O#1	This is not applicable. This falls outside the scope of application development and application maintenance.
O#2	The service level manager.
O#3	Has not been implemented yet. This is mainly done by the Ops side of the DevOps teams based on information from HP Service Center (HP SC), HP ALM, and the monitoring facility and batch processing.
O#4	This is outside scope.
O#5	Via the service desk.
O#6	The service level manager.
O#7	The service level manager.
O#8	We apply underpinning contracts to suppliers. There is no communication about SLAs to the customer.
O#9	The Business Solution Manager (BSM) communicates this from his role as service level manager in collaboration / coordination with the service management organisation. This BSM also has the role of product owner.
O#10	The service norms are communicated by the service level manager and the maintenance department. The product owner is not primarily involved in the formulating of the NFRs.

Table 5-19, SLM-A04 – Communication about service norms.

In most, if not all organisations, the product owner is not also the service level manager. The question is therefore whether there is close collaboration between these officers. The question can also be asked more broadly: 'how is the demand / supply relationship fulfilled'.

SLM R01	How do you ensure the connection of the supply and demand side in terms of quality KPIs?
O#	A solution is to have external specsheets prepared by the product owner and internal specsheets by the service level manager.
O#1	This is not applicable.
O#2	There is an SLA and a service reference manual. The SLA specifies the norms of the service. The service reference manual describes how it is delivered. Service level management is responsible for monitoring the connection between demand and supply. For this purpose, the service reference manual is drawn up in advance. This is accepted in a chain meeting. There is a meeting and a formal acceptance for the acceptance of the SLA.
O#3	Supply and demand come together at various levels: portfolio, advisory boards, release boards and DevOps teams.
O#4	Service level manager uses the non-functional requirements.

SLM R01	How do you ensure the connection of the supply and demand side in terms of quality KPIs?
	NFRs are part of the RFC and the impact is based on the established baseline.
O#5	This is not ensured.
O#6	Weekly meeting with product owner and the sprint reviews.
O#7	Architecture determines the requirements. The service level manager has the final responsibility.
O#8	Nobody ensures this.
O#9	Quality control has been standardized through quality gates.
O#10	There are no concrete NFRs from the business. The SLA is initially drawn up and negotiated. But this has little effect on the system. This means the quality control is often at operations. There are audits of information security. But the Confidentiality, Integrity and Availability (CIA) codes have not been made concrete for the business.

Table 5-20, SLM-R01 – External and internal specsheets.

As soon as the first increment of the application (or service) has been taken into production, it may be that additional or other quality needs arise from the user due to future increments. A set of best practices is available for this purpose from service level management, but what does this mean for the Scrum team?

SLM R02	How do you ensure that mutual expectations are not out of step?
O#	A solution direction is the application of an SLA and a DAP. However, this cannot be set up by the product owner if he is a representative of the business.
O#1	This is not applicable.
O#2	There is regular consultation.
O#3	The service manager sets up the NFRs in collaboration with the Ops people of the DevOps teams. This is not yet implemented.
O#4	The service level manager uses the non-functional requirements. NFRs are part of the RFC, these are introduced via the product owner and are impacted against the established baseline (in this case SLA).
O#5	This is not ensured.
O#6	Weekly meetings with product owner and the sprint reviews. NFRs are recorded in DoR and DoD.
O#7	Based on an SLA.
O#8	This is not ensured.
O#9	Through forecasting over the entire factory model that is being matched with the business forecasting.
O#10	There are no concrete NFRs from the business. The SLA is initially drafted and negotiated. But this has little effect on the system. This means the quality control is often at operations. There are audits by information security. But the CIA codes have not been made concrete for the business.

Table 5-21, SLM-R02 – Expectation management.

Ensuring an SLA with OLAs, and Underpinning Contract (UC) is a best practice from service level management, but does this also apply to a Scrum team?

SLM R03	How do you ensure that the expectations created in the SLA are fulfilled?
O#	A solution direction is the handling of an OLA and a UC. The OLA can be concluded with the Scrum team.
O#1	This is not applicable.
O#2	These expectations are ensured by carrying out acceptance tests and monitoring during the production phase. However, there is no OLA with the Scrum development team. This is formally ensured within the maintenance.
O#3	There is no formalization between the service desk and the DevOps teams in the form of OLAs.
O#4	The Scrum team does not have an OLA.
O#5	Kanban is applied by software development for maintenance. Operations (service desk) fulfils the role of product owner. They determine which problems / changes must first be handled by the maintenance team. All software that is older than 2 releases, with an average of 6 months, is carried out by a separate maintenance team. The maintenance team assigns problems / changes from recent software to the relevant Scrum team. The agreement with the Scrum teams is that they comply to the service levels and norms.
O#6	Not explicitly, only by means of an assignment.
O#7	The internal organisation ensures this. No OLAs and UCs are required.
O#8	This is not ensured.
O#9	This is centrally arranged.
O#10	There are no OLAs for the Scrum team. There are OLAs and UCs. These are set up and managed by the maintenance team, but do not apply to the Scrum team.

Table 5-22, SLM-R03 – OLA and UC.

The product owner must include both functional requirements and non-functional requirements in the product backlog. In practice, the non-functional requirements sometimes remain underexposed. The question is how the case organisations deal with this. An example is the handling of the GSA.

Architects make landscape pictures that indicate the scope of the change in terms of business processes / services, application modules and infrastructural facilities. Subsequently, architects define building blocks for a change. These determine the scope in more detail and make it possible to organize a targeted risk session, in which especially the quality aspects come forward. This is a solid basis for obtaining non-functional requirements. This approach is described in detail in the book 'Acceptance criteria' [BEST 2014].

SLM R04	How do you ensure the non-functional requirements in the Scrum teams?
O#	GSA on the basis of a risk and impact analysis from architecture.
O#1	This is not applicable.
O#2	Where formalized, these are ensured in the acceptance criteria. This is also taken into account in the design and testing.
O#3	This is ensured by GSA based on building blocks. Criteria are part of the generic controls that must be implemented at the various moments in the change and release cycle.
O#4	We use the non-functional requirements as acceptance criteria. There is a template non-functional requirements and a checklist of NFRs. The user story handling must comply with DoD. NFRs are tested at the earliest possible stage.
O#5	This is not ensured.

SLM R04	How do you ensure the non-functional requirements in the Scrum teams?
O#6	This is ensured as part of the technical design / vision document and in DoR, DoD.
O#7	Acceptance criteria per story. Given the context, there are not many non-functional requirements.
O#8	The performance is measured by means of a performance stress test. The availability and performance are measured by the supplier on the basis of an under-pinning contract with the supplier. For security purposes, we agree that the deliverables are tested annually with PENetration (PEN) tests by an external party.
O#9	This comes from design. This is ensured through quality gates and reference architecture.
O#10	This is not done. Initially with new applications. Then there are guidelines from architecture.

Table 5-23, SLM-R04 – GSA.

The delivery of software is only part of what a user requires. A workable application that performs as expected requires a lot more. The question is therefore to what extent the Scrum team now provides a monitorable service. Often the plugs and sockets with the infrastructure are forgotten and the application is a black box that can only be measured on whether or not it is available.

SLM R05	How do you ensure that the customer can steer on the actually delivered services? How is this monitoring implemented?
O#	A solution is that the Scrum team provides a monitorable service and draws up a Service Improvement Plan (SIP) for the deviations.
O#1	This is not applicable.
O#2	The customer can steer the result in the demo that we give at the end of the sprint. Furthermore, monitorability is made possible by logging, among other things in consultation with maintenance.
O#3	Monitoring is only implemented at component level. Furthermore, there is control and monitoring on the batch processing.
O#4	This is integrated in the development cycle.
O#5	The customer cannot steer, there is no direct contact.
O#6	There is monitoring on infrastructure: disk space, memory usage, status database backup, availability application. The application log file is not monitored.
O#7	There is a Simple Network Management Protocol (SNMP) monitoring and a self-built dashboard.
O#8	Internal monitoring with logging and alerting. It is also ascertained whether processes are running or not and whether action must be taken. There is no integral overview. The customer does not steer this.
O#9	This is included in the acceptance criteria. These are included the DoD and are incorporated in the build. Monitoring takes place via the Scrum master (point of contact) and / or TFS. The client can monitor the progress at component level through the Kanbans and / or through the implemented release management page for components releases.
O#10	We use standard internal monitoring and end user monitoring.

Table 5-24, SLM-R05 – GSA.

Many organisations argue that the non-functional requirements are not feature specific, but are related to the entire product backlog. However, this is not always a valid statement. Non-functional requirements can also apply at increment level or even at feature level.

SLM R06	How do you ensure the risk and impact analysis of the non-functional requirements?
O#	A solution direction is not only to handle non-functional requirements for the entire application, but also for a specific feature.
O#1	This is not applicable.
O#2	These are included if this plays a role for the relevant feature.
O#3	NFRs are linked to features. Generic controls are part of the DoD of the DevOps teams.
O#4	Risk and impact analysis takes place at the earliest possible stage with the cooperation of all relevant parties, including maintenance. We use the non-functional requirements as acceptance criteria for the intake of an RFC for the realization by a Scrum team. The user story handling must comply with DoD.
O#5	This is not applicable.
O#6	Through user stories.
O#7	The only non-functional requirement is sizing.
O#8	This is not done.
O#9	By including NFRs in the DoD.
O#10	NFRs are also recognized at feature level by operations. Operations is also a stakeholder of the product owner. There are also NFRs at release level. These are also recognized by operations.

Table 5-25, SLM-R06 – NFR for specific features.

Delivering an increment at a fixed time is a requirement for Scrum. But Kanban also has agreements about productivity. The question to the case organisations is which control they use.

SLM R07	How do you control the time to market?
O#	A solution is to make SLA agreements about quality aspects such as the maximum Work In Progress (WIP) and the sprint length.
O#1	This is not applicable.
O#2	The time-to-market is ensured by the sprint and the release. These are fixed. The content of the release is not fixed.
O#3	By applying agreements about the sprint length. There are no formal agreements about the WIP limit, apart from the DevOps team.
O#4	By using the WIP limit and the sprint length.
O#5	By using a three-weekly cycle (patch).
O#6	Because of the sprint length and the agreements about the promotion of the releases to production.
O#7	By using the WIP limit and the sprint length.
O#8	Applying a WIP limit and the sprint length. We use Kanban for the small adjustments. In addition, we use Scrum for the major changes that also require the integration with the back-office.
O#9	By using a sprint of 2 weeks.
O#10	By using a sprint length of three weeks. A release is delivered every month.

SLM R07	How do you control the time to market?
	The approval is on the first Friday of the month.

Table 5-26, SLM-R07 – Time-to-market.

5.3.2 Supplier management

Many organisations argue that a Scrum team can only organize and manage itself if they can also choose the means themselves. In that case, the danger of fragmentation of purchasing arises. Whether this is freeware packages or not, there is a great risk in this approach. Not only the possible cooperation of teams is hindered, but also the interchangeability of people or knowledge and skills is a lot lower.

SUP R01	How do the Scrum masters prevent fragmentation of purchasing?
O#	A solution direction is to apply a supplier policy at strategic level.
O#1	In our organisation, vendor management and the application manager must prevent this fragmentation.
O#2	We do not do the purchasing ourselves.
O#3	There is a target architecture for tooling. This is under development.
O#4	Neither Scrum masters nor Scrum teams buy in themselves. If necessary, a support team arranges this team transcending.
O#5	The Kanban management team has a Scrum master (one of the seniors working on the team). There is no fragmentation of purchasing because it is centrally assigned.
O#6	This is not applicable.
O#7	There are a number of standard tools. That must be complied with.
O#8	This is not prevented.
O#9	There is a central policy of tools that prevents this.
O#10	This is prevented by having the purchase take place via a central purchasing department.

Table 5-27, SUP-R01 – Supplier policy.

There are several reasons why Scrum teams are forced to frequently exchange information. This may be due to the fact that they simultaneously make changes in the same chain. But it is also possible that scaling has been applied in which Scrum teams produce a solution together. In those cases, it is important that the Scrum teams work closely together. The same tooling helps with this. The question is how to design this alignment of tool use.

SUP R02	How do the Scrum masters ensure the connection of tools between different teams?
O#	A solution direction is to recognize a tool portfolio in which three levels are recognized. At the highest level, tools have been defined that are mandatory to use. At the middle level a set of tools to choose from and at the lowest level the Scrum team can submit their own tools.
O#1	This is not applicable.
O#2	There are no connections.
O#3	There is a target architecture for tooling. However, the connections between the tools have not yet been fully dealt with.
O#4	This is done by architecture and the support team.
O#5	Company-wide agreement for the choice and implementation of the tooling.

SUP R02	How do the Scrum masters ensure the connection of tools between different teams?
O#6	This is not applicable.
O#7	This is not applicable.
O#8	At the highest level, Leankit was chosen to work with digital Scrum boards.
O#9	There is a central policy of tools.
O#10	There is an architectural policy for tooling.

Table 5-28, SUP-R02 – Tool integration.

5.3.3 Information Security management

An important aspect of information security is preventing information from being lost. To this end, measures can be taken in both the software and the infrastructure. In some cases, the software must take account of infrastructural measures such as cluster awareness.

ISM R01	How do the Scrum teams prevent loss of information? Who is responsible for this?
O#	A solution direction is to use Return Point Objective (RPO) - / Return Time Objective (RTO) agreements and determine the necessary measures in the software to give substance to this. A possible measure is a standard transaction mechanism or a reconciliation control in information processing.
O#1	The Scrum team limits the data loss by adding extra controls in the software where necessary. The application manager must monitor the programming aspects (but not at code level). Infrastructure management must also signal the loss of messages.
O#2	Integration architecture takes this into account. There is also someone responsible for the security aspects. We also look at the implementation of products and services that transcend over the teams. We also use standards and guidelines.
O#3	There are agreements with infrastructure for the maximum RPO / RTO. And there are controls in the software such as different types of reconciliation to determine if data loss has occurred.
O#4	Use is made of Secure Software Development (SSD) policy, control transactions and monitoring & logging.
O#5	However, rules and guidelines are available in the field of information security management. These are also used in code reviews. The application is a straight through application that writes every change real time in its database. The software of the application is not multi-tier. If the application is placed in a multi-tier environment, then it must be configured so that the application sees it as one environment.
O#6	All information from the entire team is on the portal. The software contains means to prevent information loss such as transactions, approval of critical processes by someone with a different profile, and so on.
O#7	This is not applicable.
O#8	We prevent this by taking various measures: • the use of a message queue for front-end side (website / BizTalk); • in the DoD as requirements; • an RPO / RTO appointment in the UC with the supplier; • performing a PENetration (PEN) test.
O#9	Via database services. This is centrally arranged through the database management department that manages all MS Structured Query Language (SQL) databases.
O#10	Rules and guidelines from Information Security Policy (ISP).

ISM R01	How do the Scrum teams prevent loss of information? Who is responsible for this?
	The RPO / RTO are determined by the CIA service norm. In the meantime, the CIA service norm has been laid down in the ESB. With new developments with protocols and protections, the CIA service norm is included, or if applications are given a different use.

Table 5-29, ISM-R01 – Loss of information.

The information processed by the software can be changed unintentionally in the process, either deliberately, by accident or by a bug. This unintentional change must be prevented or observed so that timely measures can be taken.

ISM R02	How do the Scrum teams prevent loss of integrity of information? Who is responsible for this?
O#	A solution direction is to analyse corruption of information and take countermeasures such as a Cyclic Redundancy Check (CRC) check.
O#1	The messages are not changeable. These can only be presented again by the application maintainer).
O#2	See ISM-R01, a policy has been drawn up for this.
O#3	There are reconciliations at the application level. The file deliveries are also provided with checks.
O#4	An SSD set of 31 requirements is included in the DoD. The SSD policy is actively applied by the Scrum teams and included in the various tests.
O#5	The team is responsible for this. There are no Standards, Rules & Guidelines (SRG) 's present.
O#6	Integrity of data is ensured by designing changes and taking into account the integrity. Corrupt information is analysed and removed ad-hoc.
O#7	This plays a role in one application. An external database is used. The risk at this moment is that data that our customers have worked on is being lost. We will record in a procedural way that this data will be backed up. The Lead Architect (not part of the Scrum team) ensures matters such as (data) security, integrity, etcetera during the development of the various applications.
O#8	A lot of attention has been paid to this, especially on the web side. Self-signed certificate, Internet Protocol (IP) filter, Secure web services, etcetera.
O#9	By implementing Secure Development Lifecycle (SDL) and quality gates. Responsibility for the design lies with the design authority.
O#10	This has been done once for the ESB.

Table 5-30, ISM-R02 – Corruption of information.

The confidentiality of information has to do with access to the information processed by the application. It is important to know who has access to which information.

ISM R03	How do the Scrum teams prevent the confidential information from falling into the wrong hands? Who is responsible for this?
O#	A solution direction is the use of a CIA-coding per information system / feature. The CIA-coding then also provides the countermeasures of the risks to be managed.
O#1	Messages cannot be viewed.
O#2	See ISM-R01.
O#3	There is a role model and a strict control on access rights.

ISM R03	How do the Scrum teams prevent the confidential information from falling into the wrong hands? Who is responsible for this?
	A CIA code is used in information areas.
O#4	An SSD set of 31 requirements is included in the DoD. In addition, the target binding principle is applied from design. In the production phase, policies apply, for example, the anonymization of test data, access to the DTA environments.
O#5	This is not used.
O#6	The portal is shielded. Users must be authorized to access. The application contains roles and authorization mechanics. Penetration tests are regularly performed by external parties to test the security.
O#7	This needs to be further developed.
O#8	Everything is Secure Socket Layer (SSL) encrypted, certain data requires to login. The CIA code has not yet been fully implemented.
O#9	This is included in the design. This is generic for all components.
O#10	There is no list of approved messages. We do check the confidentiality. More and more work is being done with standard solutions in combination with services.

Table 5-31, ISM-R03 – Confidentiality of information.

5.3.4 Availability management

Availability management is responsible for drawing up an availability plan that includes measures to prevent unavailability. This in alignment with the wishes of the customer. The result is an SLA agreement about availability.

Any change in the sense of an increment of a Scrum team is a potential threat to this availability. The availability manager must therefore ensure that design criteria are drawn up that are passed on to a Scrum team. An alternative is that the Scrum team is responsible for the implementation of this process. However, the same requirements apply.

AVI R01	How do the Scrum teams prevent unscheduled unavailability? Who is responsible for this (AVI-R01)?
O#	One solution is to analyse Single Point Of Failure (SPOF), to test for cluster awareness, to design an adequate monitoring facility and the like.
O#1	No, this is not the responsibility of the Scrum team but of the maintenance team.
O#2	This involves working with the maintenance and taking it into account in the design.
O#3	The infrastructure is simple and robust. The applications have been purchased.
O#4	Architecture is responsible for preventing unplanned unavailability by bringing together all relevant disciplines, including maintenance, as early as possible and testing the solution on the aspects of availability, performance and stability.
O#5	Availability of the application for the business is under the attention of the management, but no availability management process has been set up.
O#6	By making an availability schedule. Unplanned unavailability is unavoidable. Business Unit Managers (BUM) are responsible in combination with the Scrum master as an escalation level.
O#7	The unavailability is in the development and test platform that is used for the application. Availability is ensured by following the architecture and by setting up monitoring for those platforms. The availability of the application is therefore determined by the platform.
O#8	The Kanban team is responsible for the application. The supplier is responsible for the platform. Unavailability is prevented by incorporating robustness into our architecture.

AVI R01	How do the Scrum teams prevent unscheduled unavailability? Who is responsible for this (AVI-R01)?
	The monitor facility is also being expanded to monitor the health of systems.
O#9	This is part of the architectural design.
O#10	This is not a responsibility of the Scrum teams.

Table 5-32, AVI-R01 – Unplanned unavailability.

In analogy with availability, reliability is also an aspect that an availability manager must pay attention to, outside the Scrum team or within the Scrum team. The reliability here is the degree to which disruptions occur. Disruptions can be prevented by checking the quality of the source code, for example a scan of the source code by a tool such as Tiobe. Another possibility is to verify the behaviour of the application with each increment in an acceptance environment.

AVI R02	How do the Scrum teams prevent unreliability of the delivered products?
O#	A solution direction is to use source code scanners.
O#1	We perform regression tests for this purpose.
O#2	By carrying out acceptance tests, regression tests and performance stress tests, unit tests. Various code quality tools are also used.
O#3	Code scanning is performed from a security aspect. There are Standards, Rules and Guidelines (SRG) for programming.
O#4	We use Jenkins with a SonarQube plugin to check the quality of the source code. In addition, independent measurement of software quality is used.
O#5	Code standards are checked. Also, for ISO standards. That is where numbers come from and that is steered on.
O#6	By carrying out a good inventory in advance. In addition, by testing afterwards, also with the end user.
O#7	By applying static code analysis. There are a number of scanners.
O#8	By doing automated petests using McAfee. By regression tests and intake tests after delivery of software. Quality Assurance (QA) actions after delivery of software by developers.
O#9	By using source code scans from Microsoft.
O#10	The tooling enforces standards. We do not use tools that scan source code.

Table 5-33, AVI-R02 – Unplanned unavailability.

The maintainability is also an aspect of availability. As with availability and reliability, the question here is which controls apply and who is responsible for this. Important aspects are modularity, reusability, traceability to architectural building blocks, and so on.

AVI R03	How do the Scrum teams ensure the maintainability of the delivered products?
O#	A solution direction is the structuring of documentation based on architecture building blocks.
O#1	We apply refactoring. The software is modular in terms of structure. We also apply decoupling. The quality of the software is monitored through Software Improvement Group (SIG) measurements.
O#2	The maintainability is ensured by the modularity of the software. In addition, standards and guidelines ensure the maintainability. We also use peer review and refactoring of source code. Finally, we also use Subversion for the management of the source code.

AVI R03	How do the Scrum teams ensure the maintainability of the delivered products?
O#3	The documentation is Agile, but not standardized. There is a lot of diversity.
O#4	By re-using code / services such as building blocks and where possible documentation.
O#5	By documentation of an RFC. Design documents of the object are being updated. By drafting release notes and a description of the functionality. Also executing reviews on delivered software.
O#6	By drafting release notes and a description of the functionality. Also executing reviews on delivered software.
O#7	By using coding guidelines and refactoring. By the documentation about the project design, but not about the code. Documentation can be generated from the code. Annotation is used for the generation of documentation.
O#8	Functional designs, technical designs, mock ups, wire frames (design drawing of the GUI) and process flows are drawn up on the basis of utility and necessity. There is no reference to architecture here.
O#9	This is guaranteed in the DoD. TFS information is stored as part of the change set. TFS does the documentation integrated.
O#10	We have a global technical design with components within the bus. The overall technical design is modular in design. The bus is standardized, which is also reflected in the technical design. And there is a service overview. Management of the documentation is a point of attention.

Table 5-34, AVI-R03 – Maintainability.

There are organisations that have outsourced development through Scrum. In that case the contractibility is at risk. This can be compensated through Escrow contracts. But the Scrum team can also be responsible for the configuration of a purchased product, for example SAP or Siebel. In that case the contractibility also plays a role.

AVI R04	How do the Scrum teams ensure the contractibility?
O#	A solution direction is to make agreements about who is responsible for the Serviceability.
O#1	The application manager is responsible for this.
O#2	This is a responsibility of the maintenance team.
O#3	This does not play a role.
O#4	This is not the responsibility of Scrum teams.
O#5	This is not applicable.
O#6	By making arrangements with service level management.
O#7	This is not applicable.
O#8	The supplier is responsible for lifecycle management alerts and the roadmaps of new releases. Internally, this is also done for the backside (back office).
O#9	Customization, therefore contractibility is not at stake.
O#10	Scrum team is not responsible for the product choices. That is architecture.

Table 5-35, AVI-R04 – Contractibility.

The application must be resilient. For example, it may not be possible that the application will fail due to a wrong key combination. This also applies to the connection with other applications.

An input check must therefore take place. The same applies to changes such as peak loads. In that case, the application must display normal behaviour again after the peak load. In doing so it is sometimes important that changes in the infrastructure are taken into account when programming. An example is to prevent a session from being lost as a result of routing traffic through a load balancer.

AVI R05	How do Scrum teams ensure the resilience of the delivered products?
O#	A solution direction is to include a load test in the release schedule. But PEN tests are also a possible test of resilience.
O#1	All messages that deviate from the agreed format are removed from the message traffic. These are stored in a separate database. There is a failure process that inspects and handles these messages.
O#2	The resilience is guaranteed by acceptance tests and design criteria. If applicable, a load test is also used here.
O#3	PEN tests are performed regularly, just like secure code reviews. Regular disaster recovery tests are also carried out.
O#4	This is further in the chain, in the acceptance performance, load / stress and PEN tests are performed. This is also ensured in the SSD guidelines.
O#5	This is ensured in the code guidelines and the regression tests.
O#6	This does not take place.
O#7	This is ensured by performance testing, input validation testing and the like.
O#8	This is ensured in the filtering of the input. We use message queuing so that message traffic is robust.
O#9	We do not use destructive tests.
O#10	Everything is implemented twice. There is a message validation that prevents this.

Table 5-36, AVI-R05 – Resilience.

5.3.5 Capacity management

In analogy with availability management, a planning must also be made for the capacity and design criteria must be provided to Scrum teams. Here too, the alternative is that the Scrum teams are responsible for carrying out this process. The danger of lack of capacity planning is that ad hoc infrastructure extensions are needed. These are also called panic purchases that are often many times more expensive than the measures that can be taken proactively.

CAP R01	How do the Scrum teams prevent panic purchases for infrastructural capacity that must be purchased on an ad hoc basis?
O#	A solution direction is to translate the non-functional requirements into infrastructural facilities. Use can be made here of User Profiles (UP) and Patterns of Business Activities (PBA). This is especially true for the initiation of a new service.
O#1	Architecture collects the information. Application maintainers gets the measurements from the architect and gives a forecast.
O#2	We make forecasts. We also carry out business analyses.
O#3	Capacity management is under development.
O#4	An impact analysis on technology is carried out in the preliminary phase. Based on the information about non-functional requirements and solution architecture, an estimate of the impact on the infrastructure is also made. This is validated during the acceptance tests. This prevents panic buying or shortages in production.
O#5	The Kanban management team does not do anything with this.

CAP R01	How do the Scrum teams prevent panic purchases for infrastructural capacity that must be purchased on an ad hoc basis?
O#6	This is not applicable.
O#7	The monitor function of the application itself shows the analysis.
O#8	There are no characteristics. We do look at the performance stress tests.
O#9	This does not apply because everything is done virtually, and the scalability is adequate for the business forecast.
O#10	This risk does not play a role in our organisation. The capacity is a flat line.

Table 5-37, CAP-R01 Panic buying.

The capacity management process is not only responsible for capacity but also for performance. In the case of a lack of capacity, the performance often decreases.

CAP R02	How do Scrum teams ensure that performance standards are met?
O#	A solution direction is to define the performance in advance in terms of User Profiles and Patterns or Business Activities.
O#1	The application maintainer receives reports of operations.
O#2	We monitor the performance on the basis of performance stress tests.
O#3	No PBAs / UPs have been drawn up. Occasionally we look at it for reports.
O#4	We include the performance norms in the NFRs of the user story. Testing is carried out as early as possible. Performance tests based on PRA are carried out in the acceptance phase.
O#5	Is not ensured from Kanban team, but in a regression test of a release.
O#6	This is ensured by testing this.
O#7	The Scrum team ensures the performance norm by drawing up a performance baseline and performing regression tests against this baseline with each successive release. No PBAs / UPs are drawn up from the context of our product organisation. For one application it was done for a specific customer.
O#8	This is not ensured. We monitor and act accordingly. Furthermore, we look at the performance stress tests.
O#9	This is guaranteed by the performance test in the acceptance environment. The types of users and behaviour are taken into account by the designers.
O#10	We keep an eye on how many messages per week go over the bus. There is also a Quality of Service (QoS) implemented. It is about the message type and not the user groups. Certain documents must be available immediately.

Table 5-38, CAP-R02 Performance.

A part of capacity is the innovation of technology to prevent that the capacity and / or performance of the information system is no longer sufficient. Innovation can be postponed by refactoring where the code is rewritten. Renovation is a coarser approach in which an application can be rewritten in its entirety to meet a new context of hardware and software. But finally, a standard package can also be chosen that, in terms of functionality, largely corresponds to the customized software.

CAP R03	How do the Scrum teams ensure the innovation of the technology used?
O#	A solution direction is to set criteria for the choice of refactoring, renovation or innovation by means of a standard package.
O#1	A specific department ensures this.
O#2	The Scrum team is responsible for the health of the software and makes choices for refactoring, replacement and upgrades of libraries in consultation with application management. However, there are no hard criteria for this. However, application management is responsible for the service and therefore ensures that agreements are made with surrounding parties, including the Scrum development team. This also includes the choices for refactoring, renovation or innovation through a standard package.
O#3	This is not the case now.
O#4	This is ensured by structural space (20%) for refactoring and renovation.
O#5	This is ensured by refactoring, renovation and innovation.
O#6	By drawing up a vision document in advance.
O#7	There is no active renovation, but there is actively looking for new technologies that are discussed in the Scrum team. The new technology can be chosen for new applications.
O#8	This is guaranteed by both refactoring and renovation. This is included in the regular development process. We also receive an alert from the supplier at the moment that changes to ICT resources arrive where we depend on. Technical infrastructure plus the CMS and your own code that require refactoring or renovation.
O#9	Both renovation and refactoring are applied.
O#10	Both renovation and refactoring are applied.

Table 5-39, CAP-R03 Innovation.

5.3.6 IT Service Continuity Management

The contingency provision is in many organisations centrally implemented and not for one application per se. Yet it is interesting to do a check on this. That is why this question was also submitted to the case organisations.

ITSCM A01	How do you deal with contingency provision?
O#	
O#1	There is a generic contingency provision.
O#2	There is a generic contingency provision. Support for contingency provision is a requirement for a product that is supplied by, for example, a Scrum team.
O#3	This is organisation-wide organized from infrastructure.
O#4	There is a generic contingency provision.
O#5	This is not applicable.
O#6	This is not implemented.
O#7	We use Disaster Recovery Plans (DRP), but these are not completely up-to-date.
O#8	This is arranged integral, so everything or nothing.
O#9	This is centrally arranged.
O#10	There is a contingency test twice a year. This does not affect the Scrum team.

ITSCM A01	How do you deal with contingency provision?
	It does affect the operations side. This is because session loss can occur. But that has already been negotiated at system level.

Table 5-40, ITSCM-A01 – Contingency provision.

5.4 Service transition

5.4.1 Change management

Some organisations make a difference between changes that add new functionality and changes that are needed to resolve incidents. The question is therefore how this is handled in practice.

CHM A01	Do you make a difference between additive (Scrum?) and corrective (ITIL?) changes?
O#	
O#1	Additive changes take place via the policy body. The rest is done through corrective application management. Both forms of application management are performed by the same Scrum team.
O#2	Yes, capacity is reserved for maintenance changes, such as corrective, preventive, adaptive and perfective maintenance and capacity for renewal and expansion. These changes occur on the backlog and are prioritized in the sprints with monitoring of both maintenance and renewal interests.
O#3	No, we do not make a difference between additive and corrective changes.
O#4	Yes, we make a distinction between additive and corrective changes. The corrective management follows the Kanban process with a reduced throughput to production, the additive, adaptive and perfective management follows the Scrum process.
O#5	The product backlog for the Kanban team is Clientele. The Scrum teams have their own product backlog. Additive changes are excluded from the Kanban management team. There is no CAB (nor was there). There is no change process for Scrum. For the Kanban team the change process is embedded in Clientele.
O#6	Yes, a difference is made, and the type is registered.
O#7	Both are handled in the Scrum team.
O#8	The team performs both additive and corrective changes.
O#9	Yes, we make a difference between the two.
O#10	The teams carry out both additive and corrective changes. A difference is made in booking the hours and reporting on this.

Table 5-41, CHM-A01 - Additive and corrective changes.

The Agile terminology recognizes various classes of changes ranging from Themes to Stories. As a format for the stories, the user story format is often used. That is why the term story is often replaced by user stories. The question is which classes are recognized in relation to the change management process.

CHM A02	Which classes of RFCs do you recognize (e.g. Themes, Features, Epic Stories / User stories)?
O#	
O#1	We use features and user stories.
O#2	We do not use this format. A feature is split into stories.

CHM A02	Which classes of RFCs do you recognize (e.g. Themes, Features, Epic Stories / User stories)?
O#3	We use all classes.
O#4	We use themes, features, epics and user stories.
O#5	The Kanban maintenance team only recognizes changes.
O#6	All classes are used.
O#7	We use stories, not the rest.
O#8	We use epics, stories, issues, improvements, expedites (killing issues that are solved via the fast lane) and finally there are fixed date requests (request that must be resolved / completed on a certain date).
O#9	We use initiatives, features, user stories and tasks. We possibly handle bugs. These can be created by the maintenance organisation and put on the backlog (though via the product owner, think of critical production incidents and the like in relation to a component).
O#10	We use themes, feature and user stories. These are administered in standard integrated tooling for backlog management. The user stories give substance to the RFC.

Table 5-42, CHM-A02 – Classes of RFCs.

With the arrival of the Scrum team, the product owner is responsible for the priority of the entries on the product backlog. The development team is responsible for the commitment of the contents of the sprint backlog for the next sprint. The question is therefore what the role of the CAB still is.

CHM A03	Is there still a CAB? And if so, who participates in this? What is the role of the product owners?
O#	
O#1	A decision body has been set up in which an architect, project manager, feature manager, application maintainer and senior developer participate. The decision-making body meets every two weeks and can be regarded as a CAB. The Scrum teams carry out the approved feature requests and the maintenance team takes care of the acceptance.
O#2	There is a functional CAB (within ICT) for assessment and routing of questions and a Technical CAB for monitoring risks and impact implementation of changes. The functional CAB is separate from the Scrum device. New questions go through order intake and come to teams after assessment via CAB. Assignments are on the backlog. The manager of the Scrum team participates in the functional CAB.
O#3	There are different CABs. The role of the product owner is to represent the business user in the CAB and from that mandate prioritize for his / her DevOps team. The CABs include product owners, line managers, IT representatives, blueprint experts, change and release managers.
O#4	There is still a CAB. This ensures overall prioritization of changes at the level of releases (what is pre-sorted for which release). Participants of the CAB are: business managers, information managers, team managers of agile development and waterfall development. The product owner is not involved directly, other than to indicate the business value adequately for an RFC.
O#5	There is no CAB. But before it was not there either.
O#6	There is a steering committee. The product owner has an active role in this.

CHM A03	Is there still a CAB? And if so, who participates in this? What is the role of the product owners?
O#7	The CAB is formed by the product owner, the product manager, the Chief Information Officer (CIO), the Vice President of Sales (VP-sales), and the line manager development. Product owner is in the CAB for the GO. The product owner does not determine the roadmap.
O#8	No, there is no CAB.
O#9	There is a CAB, the product owner does not participate in the CAB.
O#10	The CAB is only a deployment CAB. This deployment CAB is a part of operations. There is no role for the product owner in the CAB. The product owner does say which changes he wants in his sprint. The Scrum team agrees with the deployment CAB. In addition, there is a sign-off of the FAT and UAT test results by the business.

Table 5-43, CHM-A03 – CAB.

Within Scrum, risk management is not an explicit focus area. The question is therefore how to deal with the risk and impact analysis. The impact involves two types of impact namely the scope (what is affected by the change) and the implications (what are the consequences when things go wrong).

CHM A04	Do the Scrum teams use risk and impact analysis on the basis of a change process? And if so, who perform these?
O#	
O#1	This is included in the start architecture. We also look at the non-functional requirements.
O#2	The Scrum team and the maintenance team carry out the risk and impact analysis. Impact and risks of changes are monitored within the change process.
O#3	This is done layered: architects, blueprint managers and Scrum teams.
O#4	The Scrum team and the change management process together carry out a risk and impact analysis before the definition step is initiated.
O#5	Yes, both use a risk and impact analysis, but not basis on a structured method.
O#6	Yes, the risk and impact analysis are carried out by a member of the team.
O#7	The functionality and risks are determined during the planning session. There are two risk sessions: per product and per sprint.
O#8	No, this is not used.
O#9	There are no risk analyses performed in the Scrum team. The design team does this. They look at the impact, what is affected. The workload and the like also come from the design.
O#10	There is a risk and impact analysis. This is carried out by the team members. Teams with representatives of the line & maintenance organisation determine the risks and the impact. This is a kind of PRA. This is usually done for projects and for change requests. Most change requests fall into the small risk category.

Table 5-44, CHM-A04 – Risk and impact analysis.

Many people wonder how they should call an RFC when they switch to Scrum. Hence the question of how this is handled in practice. It is also important to know how to deal with acceptance criteria. Normally they are linked to an RFC. With Scrum, this will be linked to the feature or, if it is a generic acceptance criterion that applies to all features, to the DoD.

CHM A05	How do you call the RFCs (for example, feature request)? Which aspects of service management processes are included in your DoD?
O#	
O#1	A change is registered as RFC, later in the process the RFC becomes a feature.
O#2	We call the RFCs change requests and projects. In DoD various aspects important for maintenance are included such as release notes, installation / configuration manual and a test report.
O#3	We call the RFCs a feature request. The DoD contains the maintenance deliverables such as for service level management and IT information security management.
O#4	We call the RFCs change signal or change order. With the introduction of an Agile process, no change has been made at business level. The acceptance criteria are tested via the DoD.
O#5	The Kanban team calls the changes based on the problem ticket an RFC.
O#6	The RFCs are called epics, features and user stories.
O#7	We call the RFCs stories.
O#8	The RFCs are called epics, stories, issues, improvements, expedites and fixed date requests.
O#9	We get changes in the format of a user story or bugs.
O#10	Our organisation uses the terms themes, feature and user stories for an RFC. The DoD includes the functional intake criteria. There is a release moment, but not a separate sprint for a release. The management aspects are included in the implementation plan. There is a disconnect from the development cadence and release cadence.

Table 5-45, CHM-A05 – Aspects of service management processes in the DoD.

In practice, more than 60% of the incidents are the result of changes. Within Scrum these are called escaped defects. From the Scrum team, measures are possible to get this percentage to a lower level.

CHM R01	How do the Scrum teams prevent the incident that occur as a result of the change (consequence incidents)
O#	A solution direction is building knowledge through standardization of tooling and the use of SRGs.
O#1	We apply regression testing, peer review, unit testing and refactoring. We do not do pair programming. We also do standardization.
O#2	We perform tests and regression tests. The users and maintainers also carry out acceptance tests. There is also an DTAP street. A configuration of the DTAP environment is managed, so that of each environment it is known which versions are installed. The deployment of an application is modular and layered.
O#3	We test based on the user stories. There is a Global Tooling Architecture (GTA) for tooling emerging. This is not being complied yet.
O#4	Tooling is standardized, for example the use of #define.
O#5	The Scrum team and Kanban maintenance team work on the same development street. They use the same tools.
O#6	This is prevented by using a functional design and testing in the DTAP street.
O#7	This is prevented by using SRGs for programming, peer-to-peer and refactoring.

CHM R01	How do the Scrum teams prevent the incident that occur as a result of the change (consequence incidents)
O#8	This is prevented by using peer reviews, unit tests, quality checks, Definition of Ready (DoR) and Definition of Quality (DoQ).
O#9	In addition to a number of test types, a component must comply with the new reference architecture. It must be considered how this can best be implemented. SRGs are also used.
O#10	We use retrospectives. Also, more and more is being done with Peer-2-Peer programming. We do not use SRGs.

Table 5-46, CHM-R01 – Prevent consequence incidents.

Following a change is an important part of the management that change management exercises on the changes. The question is how this is done within Scrum teams. You often see Kanban boards with post-its and the like.

CHM R02	How do the Scrum teams do the tracking of changes (registration and status)?
O#	A solution direction is the administration of metadata for features, such as the status, the relations with other features, CI's, etcetera.
O#1	This is not done by them. The application maintainer is responsible for this.
O#2	We bundle changes in a release. In the past, a release was rolled out in two versions. But now this is more flexible. The tracking of changes is carried out by change management based on the tool: IT Service Management (Mexon). The Scrum team uses HP Quality Center (HPQC) for this.
O#3	Yes, through HP ALM. Metadata is not tracked.
O#4	TOPdesk is used for process control. Omnitracker is used on the technical side. The portfolio portal is also used for the administration of change orders (meta information). This portal is overlapping and complementary to TOPdesk. The portal also includes the release information. The portal and TOPdesk are connected. TOPdesk has a link with #define in which the user stories are included.
O#5	Yes, through Clientele.
O#6	Yes, we do the tracking of changes with Jira. In the phases a peer review is used to see whether there are deviations.
O#7	For the tracking of user stories Jira and for test cases we use Twist (with reference to the user stories).
O#8	We do the tracking with Leankit (this is an electronic Kanban board).
O#9	We do the tracking with Kanban boards at different levels, these are in registered in TFS.
O#10	Yes, this is done through standard tooling. Objects can be linked, but a good CI tree has not yet been prepared for the standard integrated tooling for backlog management. The control of the RFCs is now based on status data. We are working to add requirements as a separate object. Requirements can then be related to features. But we are not yet that far.

Table 5-47, CHM-R02 – Tracking of changes.

Different change authorities are identified through change management. The impact of the change then determines who is allowed to decide on the change. Preferably, decision-making is placed as low as possible in the organisation (for example, an employee or the change manager). Higher decision-making bodies (e.g. the CAB or the MT) often have a lower frequency of decision-making.

CHM R03	How do the Scrum teams prevent the delay over the decision-making of changes as a result of vertical escalation?
O#	A solution direction is to recognize a layered change authority structure, for example: • defining a queue for changes that the team may implement themselves; • defining a set of features that can only be handled through cross product owner consultation; • defining a set of regular features.
O#1	We do not use a mandate.
O#2	The decision making of changes concerns functional change management. A layered structure is used for this. In this, the responsible application maintenance team plays an important role (also towards the Scrum / development team).
O#3	There is a list of applications and components and it has been determined how to deal with this. In this way, the change authority of almost all changes is known in advance. There is no layered change authority structure yet.
O#4	Everything follows the same flow except the fast-lane for incidents and minor changes. For small changes to be realized in the feature, the product owner has a mandate to implement these.
O#5	The Kanban team only does application management. There is no delay in decision-making. In addition, problem management and change management have been merged. The Kanban management team also has a weekly stand-up with service desk to determine the priority of outstanding problems (changes). The Kanban management team handover the problems (changes) on to the Scrum teams if these incidents are the result of a release that was published less than six months ago. These problems (changes) are handed over in the daily stand-up of the Scrum teams. Where we want to go is that this is considered as overtime. This is a pressure tool to prevent escaped defects. This creates a self-correcting ability.
O#6	The product owner is responsible for the planning of sprints. If something is not clear enough, it will not be included in the sprint. The functional requests are done by the product owner. Own findings are added.
O#7	The product owner is the only client. There is a fast-lane for incidents for one application. There is also an own responsibility for refactoring.
O#8	In BizTalk there is a separate connection so that changes can be implemented quickly. With our CRM everything is included in a release. So, no scope determination is known based on the product backlog items.
O#9	Everything goes through the product owner, except the 10% incidents.
O#10	Each change is discussed separately by the team. The product owner participates. Based on the priority, it is included in the sprint. It is true that improvements that we see ourselves are sometimes pushed aside.

Table 5-48, CHM-R03 – Avoid delay of decision making.

Recognizing risks depends on the professional knowledge of the involved employees. In addition, this is also determined by the way in which this analysis takes place. A brainstorming session does deliver a lot. But a brainstorming session based on an adequate impact analysis is not only more effective but also more efficient, see also SLM-R04.

CHM R04	Which risk analysis method do the Scrum teams use for changes?
O#	A solution direction is to use the GSA approach whereby an impact and risk analysis take place from architectural landscape images and architectural building blocks. A PRA can also be used.
O#1	There is only a risk analysis from architecture. The test strategy of the master test plan is based on a PRA. Architecture is involved in the PRA and organizes it.
O#2	No specific method is used for the risk analysis.
O#3	We use Generic and Specific Acceptance criteria based on architectural building blocks. But this is not applied by all teams.
O#4	Yes, it is done by architecture. Architecture building blocks are used, and PRAs are used.
O#5	There is no specific risk analysis approach.
O#6	No risk analysis method is used.
O#7	The acceptance of products takes place on the basis of an initial impact and risk analysis. Use is made here of the architectural landscape images and architecture building blocks of both the business processes, application and infrastructure. In addition, a risk and impact analysis take place with every sprint. This is mainly done afterwards at the end of the sprint.
O#8	No risk analysis method is used.
O#9	There are generic acceptance criteria. There are no specific acceptance criteria. A risk analysis is done in the design phase. This analysis is part of the design that goes to the (construction) Scrum teams.
O#10	We perform a PRA.

Table 5-49, CHM-R04 – Risk and impact analysis.

Often an auditor will want to know who has adjusted something and who has released something for production. In order to be able to prove this, it is necessary that an administration has been kept showing this evidence.

CHM R05	What evidence do the Scrum teams provide to the auditors for this process?
O#	A solution direction is to handle a requirement registration for those aspects that must be verifiable afterwards.
O#1	There is no auditing.
O#2	There is a formal procedure for this. A limited number of people may carry out changes. For changes on production, this is part of the change management process and the administration around it. For software changes, this is completely logged in the version control system.

The combination of a controlled version management and DTAP procedure provides the evidence. HP QC provides information on the release for individual issues and changes. Test scripts and test cases are also used, that can be used as evidence. |
| O#3 | The workflow in HP ALM contains tollgates. In order to be able to pass it, evidence must be provided for the controls that belong to the tollgate. |
| O#4 | The (non) functional requirements are baseline and set against the changes. Commitment takes place via the user stories in combination with use cases and version management. |

CHM R05	What evidence do the Scrum teams provide to the auditors for this process?
O#5	The teams provide evidence via Clientele. Also, the evidence via traceability: • Enterprise Architect (requirements); • ScrumWise (user story); • IBM Rational ClearCase ClearQuest (CCCQ); • TestComplete (automated testing). The integration of TestComplete with CCCQ has not yet been realized. In case of an incident / change, the Kanban management team looks at Enterprise Architect and with the linked user story in Scrum-wise.
O#6	All documentation (functional design, test, reports and schedules) is available on the customer portal.
O#7	There are no auditors.
O#8	The Scrum teams do not provide evidence.
O#9	There is no relationship between the auditors and the Scrum teams, information can be found in TFS.
O#10	Via standard tooling.

Table 5-50, CHM-R05 – Evidence for auditors.

It is important to determine in advance who is responsible for taking decisions in case changes have conflicting interests in terms of priority. A possible solution is to identify the components of each application. For example, an application often consists of a user interface, a database part, a processing unit (engine) and reports. An exhaustive list of types of changes is possible per component. For example, for a database can be established that new tables or attributes are needed. It can be determined once for each component and type of change which change authority is responsible. This information can be included in a governance spreadsheet.

Usually the change authority within Scrum is the product owner. But as soon as there is a change that requires the decision-making of different change authorities, there must be an escalation path. This can be a product manager, but often a type of CAB is established in this case in which the product owners are represented.

CHM R06	Who determines the priority in the event of conflicting interests?
O#	A solution direction is the usage of an application governance spreadsheet.
O#1	The product owner determines the priority in case of conflicting interests.
O#2	The CAB determines the priority in case of conflicting interests.
O#3	The CAB determines the priority in case of conflicting interests.
O#4	The CAB determines the priority in case of conflicting interests.
O#5	Within the Scrum team, the product owner is the first designated person to take a decision on conflicts priorities here. The Product Managers take the decision in transcending Scrum-team conflicts. The last escalation path is the manager Innovation & Architecture, Software Development and the Strategy Director.
O#6	The product owner determines the priority in case of conflicting interests.
O#7	The line manager development determines the resources.
O#8	A representative of our internal business customers in cooperation with the product owners.
O#9	The design team assesses every change. There is no governance selection based on an application / component change type analysis.

CHM R06	Who determines the priority in the event of conflicting interests?
O#10	The product owner determines the priority in case of conflicting interests.

Table 5-51, CHM-R06 – Conflicting interests.

5.4.2 *Service Asset & Configuration management*

With the introduction of Scrum, it is the question who is now responsible for maintaining the CMDB and if the CMDB also contains the administration of the application components (that the Scrum team produces. In this study, a difference was also made between a CMDB and a Software CMDB (S-CMDB). The CMDB is used by operations, for example for the registration of incidents. The S-CMDB is used by development, for example for version numbering of components. In this study, this is equated with the version management system, for example GIT or Subversion. An S-CMDB does not contain any CIs but software CIs (S-CIs).

SACM A01	Do Scrum teams use the CMDB? What level of detail do they use here?
O#	
O#1	The Scrum team uses a software CMDB. At a higher level, a CMDB is also maintained for the entire product. This CMDB is used by application management for lifecycle management changes.
O#2	There is a difference between an application version as a CI and versions of modules that the application is composed of. The CMDB is maintained by the maintenance teams at the level of applications, application versions, the connections of applications and the relationships with other CIs. The Scrum team maintains a registration with modules and interdependencies per delivery (and per environment).
O#3	Yes, but the CMDB is coarse. However, there is a configuration model per service.
O#4	Kanban is used. The following tools are used: • TOPdesk is used for the application CIs. • #define (issue tracker) is used for a definition of user stories. • Subversion, used for version management, does not recognize S-CI, but baselines are created based upon tagging of objects. • Jenkins contains the software baselines of Subversion on the basis of which builds are created.
O#5	Yes, CIs and version of CIs.
O#6	No.
O#7	No.
O#8	No.
O#9	No, the run organisation manages the CMDB.
O#10	The CMDB is mainly used to record) version control of the pieces of software that are in progress.

Table 5-52, SACM-A01 – level of detail CMDB.

The question is whether software CIs are also recognized.

SACM A02	Do the Scrum teams also use software configuration items (S-CIs)?
O#	
O#1	Yes, S-CIs are recognized.
O#2	Software CIs are maintained in the version management system Subversion.

SACM A02	Do the Scrum teams also use software configuration items (S-CIs)?
	There is no explicit relationship between the software CIs in Subversion and the CIs in IT Service Management (Mexon).
O#3	Yes, for this we use Serena Dimensions.
O#4	No.
O#5	We work with CCCQ, there is a test for GIT and Jira.
O#6	No, however GIT does contain ten containers with a version number. All containers are packaged. First, a three weekly sprint was used, after which it became a two-weekly sprint.
O#7	We use Subversion for S-CI.
O#8	No.
O#9	No, we do have identifiable source code.
O#10	Standard integrated tooling for backlog management and configuration items is used for version control. A tailor-made package for the DTAP control is also used. In this package it is described in which environment which version is. The build number is located in the MicroSoft Installer (MSI) package. The customized application fires all MSI packages. The MSI packages are used to configure the ESB in the acceptance and production environment.

Table 5-53, SACM-A02 – Software configuration items.

Often an S-CMDB is used in the form of a version management system. The question is how the Scrum teams ensure that this information is correct, complete, timely and accurate.

SACM R01	How do the Scrum teams ensure that the CMDB is correct, complete, timely and accurate?
O#	A solution direction is the direct or indirect connecting of the S-CMDB to the CMDB.
O#1	We use ClearCase with baselining. Everything that is delivered has a CI number.
O#2	The quality (correct, complete, timely and accurate) of the CMDB is monitored by the change management process. The administrator registers the software packages in the CMDB. In Subversion there is meta information about the structure of a product. We define releases based on predefined versions of packages. There is a tool that ensures that a package is correctly installed in the target environment (specifically for one application). The correct version is checked on the basis of a hash code from the production environment and the administration in Subversion. The correct versions of software in the production environment can therefore be verified with the versions as administered in Subversion. There is a division of responsibilities between keeping the CMDB up to date by the maintenance team and maintaining the registration of the modules and their mutual dependencies per delivery (and per environment) by the Scrum team, see SACM-R01.
O#3	There is a manual relationship between Serena Dimensions baseline (S-CI) and HP ALM (releases / features / stories). There is also a manual connection between HP SC (CIs) and HP ALM (releases). Compliance with release management.
O#4	For code modification, there must be a relationship between TOPdesk, #define, Subversion and Jenkins.

SACM R01	How do the Scrum teams ensure that the CMDB is correct, complete, timely and accurate?
	The relationship is as follows: • #define: issue-tracker has a TOPdesk ID. • Subversion contains the change-set, which receives an ID from #define. • Jenkins build the software that gets a buildID. If the build needs to be promoted Jenkins gives a release tag and puts it in Subversion.
O#5	There is a connection between Clientele and CCCQ, but there is still no continuous integration / continuous delivery connection.
O#6	No. Checking source code indicates which Jira code has been resolved. Test cases refer to Jira. So, from GIT it is possible to view what has been checked in without a test case. There is a direct connection between Jira issues and GIT.
O#7	No. The test cases are also in Subversion. So, the delivered software is therefore checked for completeness.
O#8	Not.
O#9	There is a checklist in the DoD. Windows SharePoint (WSP) is a total package. We deploy via the DTAP principle. The whole environment is promoted.
O#10	-

Table 5-54, SACM-R01 - right, full, timely and accurate.

With service asset & configuration management, verification is used to monitor the quality of the CMDB. This means that during the use of the CMDB the correctness and completeness is checked, for example by incident management. The question is how the Scrum team performs the verification for the S-CMDB.

SACM R02	How does the verification of the S-CMDB take place?
O#	A solution direction is to provide all objects (S-CIs) that are taken into production with a tag.
O#1	This is built in, we can see this for ourselves. Packages are sometimes installed incorrectly.
O#2	Software supplied by the Scrum team uses hash totals, among other things, to ensure that the target environment has the correct version of the software. However, the link with the central CMDB and quality monitoring of the CMDB is not automated for this component, but has different granularity (application version versus module version).
O#3	Objects that were rolled out are not identified on the basis of a tag. Therefore, no relationship can be established between the Definitive Media Library (DML) and production. Versions of S-CIs are brought to production on the basis of a unique baseline that is linked to a story.
O#4	There is a verification option to determine whether a particular version in the DML is also in production on the basis of the BuildID.
O#5	Every object that is modified has a timestamp and version. Each object has a build and version number that is identifiable in production.
O#6	The verification does not take place.
O#7	In production can be monitored which version of the components are in production.
O#8	The verification does not take place.
O#9	All components have a tag (solution ID).

SACM R02	How does the verification of the S-CMDB take place?
O#10	With .net tagging can be used but not with MSI.

Table 5-55, SACM-R02 – Verification CMDB.

5.4.3 Service Validation & Testing

The efficiency of the service validation and testing process is closely related to the correct focus of the test effort. In general, this is done by using a (PRA). However, more structured methods are also possible. The question is what is used within Scrum. See also SLM-R04 and CHM-R04.

SVT R01	How do the Scrum teams determine the test strategy (SVT-R01)?
O#	A solution direction is to determine the scope and risks from architectural building blocks, including the infra and business risks.
O#1	We use a PRA in the form of a brainstorming session. A classification of components is applied. The master test plan also includes the FAT and the UAT. A master test plan is drawn up per release.
O#2	The test strategy is based, among other things, on a risk analysis.
O#3	We use generic and specific acceptance criteria based on architectural building blocks. In the tooling (HP ALM) building blocks must be linked to stories, making impact analysis possible.
O#4	Non - PRA should be performed.
O#5	The service desk is the product owner for the Kanban team. The priority of a change is determined by the Service Desk. Partly on the basis of this priority, the Kanban maintenance team determines the test strategy: Priority low / medium: • The Kanban management team carries out the unit testing and UAT testing. • The customer receives the patch. Priority high: • The Kanban maintenance team carries out the unit tests and the UAT. • The service desk reports and installs the fix at the customer. • The fix is included in the patch. All changes (including patches) are included in the release and enter the regression test.
O#6	Best practice, in particular functional testing of the adjustments, both happy and "unhappy" flow. No structured risk analysis has been performed. The unhappy flow is of course based on thinking about exceptions.
O#7	The risk session CHM-R04 determines the focus of the test approach.
O#8	The Scrum team do not determine a test strategy.
O#9	We do not have a test manager who draws up a test plan. We have a fixed approach (generic test approach) for standard components. For this we do make a logical test case document. Components that are not standard (not testable with our self-built test tooling) we analyse, and we explain our test approach in the logical test case document.
O#10	This is done at project level in consultation. We focus on the technical operation. All paths of the ESB bus are tested.

Table 5-56, SVT-R01 – Test strategy.

The question is to what extent the acceptance tests actually show that the counter-measures of the identified risks have the desired effect. To this end, it is important to know what the coverage ratio of the acceptance tests is. See also SLM-R04 and CHM-R04.

SVT R02	How do the Scrum teams determine the coverage level of the acceptance tests?
O#	A solution direction is to define the relationships between services, building blocks, components, S-CIs and test cases. This provides a good coverage ratio analysis option.
O#1	The master test plan has a cover ratio analysis.
O#2	Methods are used to determine the degree of coverage.
O#3	Services, building blocks, components, S-CIs and test cases are recorded in a structured manner in HP ALM. All teams have access to it.
O#4	Based on the user stories and the PRAs. We use a happy flow and an alternate flow.
O#5	There is yet no real mechanism for this. It can be indicated which functionalities are affected in a test.
O#6	No degree of coverage is determined, but a test plan is drawn up per change that tests the happy flow and a few exceptions. The FAT and UAT largely takes place by the customer out of sight of the Scrum team.
O#7	The user stories contain acceptance criteria based on the risk analysis. The test cases are related to the acceptance criteria. No test coverage on functionality, but we have coverage on technology.
O#8	The degree of coverage of acceptance tests is not determined by the Scrum teams.
O#9	Scenarios are known for components, which can be performed. The question is which scenarios have or have not been included.
O#10	The coverage ratio is determined by the paths that we go through.

Table 5-57, SVT-R02 – Cover ratio.

Testing is an extremely important aspect of the application's life cycle. Particularly due to the high rate of change, the quality has to be determined even better than before. Techniques such as Test-Driven Development (TDD) help with this. But reusing test cases based on metadata is also an important success factor.

SVT R03	How do the Scrum teams ensure the efficiency of your test activities?
O#	A solution direction is the integration of the administration into tools. For example, the service can be related to a test case as well as the architecture building blocks, requirements and S-CIs. This allows the promotion of reuse of test cases.
O#1	Everything is automated. In the end there are manual tests, because not everything is automated yet - the testware is lagging behind.
O#2	This is not done.
O#3	Test management is in transition to agile way of working. Test cases are reused based on requirements and building blocks. Regression testing has not yet been taken up. Test automation has started.
O#4	No integration of information for testing. Regression tests are set up where integration has been done, but this is at user story level.
O#5	A subset of existing test cases is used (Enterprise architect, CCCQ / TestComplete).
O#6	Making test scripts, this increases repeatability, for the different flows (both happy and "unhappy").

SVT R03	How do the Scrum teams ensure the efficiency of your test activities?
O#7	Build server (Jenkins) interacts with Jira. Functional tests are not integrated. The regression test is the reuse of test cases that have been used until then.
O#8	This is not done.
O#9	Reuse matrix of test cases. Relationship between components and test cases. Test cases are not in TFS.
O#10	We use the test suite with SOAtest. We build test cases in this. These can be used as a regression test.

Table 5-58, SVT-R03 – Efficiency of test activities.

The prevention of incidents in production is related to the extent to which the development process is traceable. This traceability is needed throughout the chain from idea to deployment. In this way it can quickly be determined whether things have not been tested or forgotten to be taken into production, etcetera. The minimum traceability is that of the story with the baseline in which the modified software CI is included.

SVT R04	How do the Scrum teams steer to prevent recurring defects?
O#	A solution direction is the use of version control, linking user stories, S-CI and baselines.
O#1	This is not done.
O#2	Recurring defects are prevented by using regression tests. The version management system Subversion also prevents recurring defects. Furthermore, we also use a peer review and a controlled deployment process.
O#3	Version management for S-CIs has been adjusted and is being applied. Test cases are related to features and stories. Through a unique baseline reference at story level, versions of S-CIs are related to the story. Stories are released to production. Traceability is therefore possible.
O#4	Recurring defects are prevented by means of version control. See SACM, SACM-A01 and SACM-R01.
O#5	Recurring defects are prevented by: • a double check before the implementation of a change; • a cause analysis; • a review by a second person after performing checks; • developing on the same street; • a continuous build (every day); • traceability through tools (each object is recognizable in the production environment).
O#6	Recurring defects have occurred sporadically. Can be prevented by having the delivery done by another team. Programmatic unit and integration tests have been drawn up for complex components.
O#7	The commits are recorded in Subversion. This indicates which user story belongs to this (Jira). Jenkins looks at changes in Subversion to create a build. We use continuous integration. Each commit provides a new build.
O#8	Recurring defects are prevented by unit testing, code peer review and QA. QA includes checking the quality of the deliverables that a software builder has delivered before being tested by the customer. The QA takes place after the test of the builder himself.

SVT R04	How do the Scrum teams steer to prevent recurring defects?
O#9	Recurring defects are prevented by versioning. Change sets can be defined in TFS. A change set consists of deliverables: features + code + assurance quality through quality gates.
O#10	This is not yet integrated. We do this separately, such as the use of standard integrated tooling for version and backlog management.

Table 5-59, SVT-R04 – Prevent recurring defects.

A regression test is a test that shows that the unchanged functionality still works. Selecting the test cases to demonstrate this requires stringent administration of the static requirements and related test cases.

SVT R05	Do the Scrum teams perform regression tests?
O#	A solution direction is to make the development process traceable, the automation of the development and deployment processes, the recording of metadata such as S-CI and requirement as an independent object.
O#1	Yes, the Scrum team performs regression tests.
O#2	Yes, the Scrum team performs regression tests.
O#3	Not yet, is part of the test management transition to agile.
O#4	No integration of information for testing. Regression tests are set up where integration has been done, but this is at user story level. The follow-up steps with regard to test automation and automation of the deployment processes are now being set up.
O#5	In the release focus period. For each RFC, the related) unit test cases are examined.
O#6	Partly (became more during the sprints).
O#7	Yes.
O#8	Yes, manually.
O#9	System tests are done. Regression tests are done on the basis of improvements made on the basis of the findings of the system tests.
O#10	Regression tests are performed.

Table 5-60, SVT-R05 – Regression tests.

5.4.4   Release & deployment management

From time to time, provide, management and guarding must be kept separate. In maintenance this applies mainly to the segregation of D-T and A-P environments. A developer should never change anything in the A or P environment. With the introduction of DevOps and continuous integration / continuous delivery, there is a danger that the borders will fade. The question is therefore to what extent this is still being controlled.

RDM A01	Is each Scrum team allowed to independently perform a software rollout? Or is this a collaboration? Or is this left to a separate team?
O#	
O#1	No, the rollout is done by a separate team. But there are other Scrum teams where that is allowed.
O#2	The software rollout is performed by maintenance in collaboration with the Scrum team.
O#3	DevOps teams do that themselves. Collaboration is necessary for dependencies. Governance is centrally regulated.

RDM A01	Is each Scrum team allowed to independently perform a software rollout? Or is this a collaboration? Or is this left to a separate team?
O#4	Not for the acceptance and production environment.
O#5	The integration team delivers a fix, patch or deploy set to Operations. Operations does the physical rollout.
O#6	No, the software is delivered to the maintenance organisation that then puts it into production. Completion must comply with fixed standards in the field of documentation and Installability.
O#7	Does not apply. The Scrum team is allowed to do the promotion to the development and test environment.
O#8	Yes, the team can do this themselves.
O#9	No.
O#10	No, maintenance does the software rollout.

Table 5-61, RDM-A01 – Independently perform a software rollout.

In order to be able to restore the production environment at all times, the ICT organisation sometimes makes use of a repository in which both the source code and the object code that has been promoted to production are maintained. This makes it at all times possible to return in time and to use an older version of an information system. In many cases, only the object code is placed in the DML and the source code in the version control system. This is not entirely justified because the DML is meant to include all products approved for deployment, including the source code. If this final source is not stored in the DML, but in the version management system, then it must be required that the downloaded source code versions can never, ever be modified. Also, the associated sourced version must at all times be identifiable from each deployment to production.

RDM A02	Do the Scrum teams use a central Definite Media Library (DML)? Or is every team responsible for keeping this up?
O#	
O#1	We use ClearCase for the version management system. In it, the source code is saved. The infrastructure management team keeps a DML of the object code that has been rolled out.
O#2	As a DML, Apache Maven Project (Maven) / Nexus is used complemented with own tooling.
O#3	Yes, through set baselines in Serena Dimensions.
O#4	Yes, Subversion in combination with Jenkins.
O#5	Yes, GIT and that is now CCCQ.
O#6	Yes, the Scrum team uses a DML.
O#7	Yes, Nexus contains the builds.
O#8	No.
O#9	Yes, TFS.
O#10	Yes, Central is this standard integrated tooling and our customized application for the DTAP control.

Table 5-62, RDM-A02 – DML.

Standardization appears to be a must in larger organisations. This makes cooperation with other teams much easier and knowledge and expertise can be exchanged.

RDM A03	Do the Scrum teams use a prescription for the use of test tools? Or can each team decide this themselves?
O#	
O#1	Yes, this is prescribed (HP ALM).
O#2	Yes, this is prescribed. For issue management use is made of HP Quality Center (HP QC) and there is a policy for testing.
O#3	Yes, this is prescribed. HP ALM is used and FitNesse as test automation.
O#4	Yes, this is prescribed.
O#5	Yes, this is prescribed. The Kanban management team uses the same tools as the Scrum teams.
O#6	Not applicable (one team).
O#7	No, the team itself is responsible for this.
O#8	No, the team is free to choose.
O#9	Yes, this is prescribed. The teams use the same tools.
O#10	Yes, certain tools have been designated.

Table 5-63, RDM-A03 – Choice of test tools.

In RDM-A02 there was a question about the use of a DML. The question, however, is whether each Scrum team has its own DML, with its own rules or that this takes place centrally for the entire organisation.

RDM A04	Is there a central repository of rolled-out applications / configurations? Or can each team implement this?
O#	
O#1	The Scrum team has its own ClearCase environment for the source code. The object code is maintained in several DMLs throughout the organisation.
O#2	There is not one central repository. The Scrum team that manages the care application does use one repository.
O#3	There is one central CMDB repository for the entire organisation. We use Serena Dimensions with logical S-CI for lifecycle management.
O#4	Yes, there is one central repository, for this we use Jenkins in combination with Subversion.
O#5	Yes, we use a publication portal / CCCQ
O#6	Yes, there is one central repository. The package is created from GIT. The package is stored on a website. Per release, the installers and release notes are registered.
O#7	Yes, there is one central repository, for this we use Nexus.
O#8	Yes, there is one central repository, for this we use GIT.
O#9	Yes, there is one central repository, for this we use TFS.
O#10	Yes, there is one central repository, for this we use standard integrated tooling for source control.

Table 5-64, RDM-A04 – Centrale repository.

The time-to-market is promoted through the use of Scrum because of the incremental approach. However, some organisations use a separate release sprint to deploy the software. The time-to-market could be accelerated many times by making continuous integration and continuous delivery possible.

RDM R01	How do the Scrum teams prevent the continuous integration and continuous delivery process from taking too much time?
O#	A solution direction is the automation of the build, package and deployment of software. There are also possibilities to integrate the version management tool, test tool, repository tool and deployment tool.
O#1	Continuous integration is automated. Continuous delivery is not the responsibility of the Scrum team.
O#2	We do not have continuous delivery. The deployment is automated and formalized.
O#3	Continuous integration and deployment are still in the initial phase.
O#4	Continuous integration has just started, continuous delivery is not yet.
O#5	Daily build. Partial integration, only TestComplete is not linked.
O#6	Deliver often, scenario together with operations department. Automation of the deployment process. Using Azure connected to GIT as a test environment.
O#7	No deployment, the rest is.
O#8	There is an automatic build, package and deployment (this is not done continuously). We are actually close to continuous delivery.
O#9	TFS (daily build) + TFS makes WSP + auto deploy.
O#10	We are trying to get more maintenance in the team. Operations has little time for release & deployment management. Releases are automated with MSI including the parameters.

Table 5-65, RDM-R01 – Continuous integration and continuous delivery cost too much time.

A risk in the production of software is that it is unintentionally changed in the going through of the D-T, T-A and A-P steps. The question is which risk management applies to this.

RDM R02	How do Scrum teams prevent the object from not being identical during the O-T-A-P steps?
O#	A solution direction is the use of hashes, signature etcetera.
O#1	There is no protection. There is also no testing. However, a baseline is used.
O#2	The identically is guaranteed through the use of versioning with hash totals. There are tools for maintenance and controlling the configuration of the DTAP environments.
O#3	There is no protection of the objects by the DTAP.
O#4	Not researched.
O#5	The object is delivered by one central integration team. We have a D-T-A. Version management system ensures this. A build is made that goes from D to T.
O#6	By always going through the DTAP. Make agreements with product owner about the differentiating of versions and the duration of Acceptance tests.
O#7	This is secured by Nexus, which uses hashes.
O#8	This is not ensured.
O#9	WSP is inviolable.
O#10	You can only deliver one MSI package and then you cannot change it.

Table 5-66, RDM-R02 – Loss of integrity of the software that has to be promoted.

Organisations often use purchased software that is then configured. This could include ERP packages, reporting facilities and the like. The question that arises is how the Scrum team deals with changes to the standard packages by these external suppliers. An adaptation of these packages often takes a lot of time, varying from days to weeks.

After all, a new release or version has to be installed in the entire D-T-A-P and patches may also be available. The own adjustments that have been made in the past must also be re-applied and tested. Where necessary, adaptive changes must be made to their own modifications, and that while the sprints that realize the additive changes just have to continue.

RDM R03	How do the Scrum teams deal with the interconnectedness between LifeCycle Management (LCM) changes and Scrum changes? LCM changes sometimes still take a long time!
O#	A solution direction is to recognize lifecycle management and Scrum changes and to coordinate them. Use can also be made of separate D-T-A streets.
O#1	In our case the LCM changes concern those of the message broker or the application server. These changes to system software are solved by the Scrum team itself.
O#2	The LCM changes and Scrum changes are realized together in one team, in coordination with various teams and / or projects with which there is a dependency.
O#3	LCM change and Scrum changes follow the same process and governance.
O#4	Life cycle management changes and configuration changes are handled by the same Scrum team.
O#5	The lifecycle changes and own changes use the same release stream.
O#6	Separate routes.
O#7	Does not apply. At most from our central engine that needs to be upgraded to a higher version. This is solved with branching.
O#8	We first test the lifecycle change in a separate test environment. Then we test the custom software for that new version of the standard software.
O#9	Platform lifecycle management gives few conflicts.
O#10	That is difficult. It often happens in consultation with operations. For example, it still happens that operations have already upgraded everything. But the source tooling has also been upgraded. If you do not change anything about the MSI package, everything works. But when the new version of the ESB and MSI packages are modified, the deployment no longer works exactly the same. That is because stricter rules are build-in in the upgrade of the standard software that we configure. You often ONLY notice this only when you roll out.

Table 5-67, RDM-R03 – LCM- and Scrum-changes.

Going through the D-T-A-P steps can be delayed because defects are found so that features cannot be brought to the production environment or not completely. An example of a cause of defects is the use of a complex version management strategy, such as the frequent branching off of the software (branching). Defects delay the time-to-market. The question here is whether this delay can be prevented.

RDM R04	How do the Scrum teams prevent delays in the D-T-A-P street?
O#	A solution direction is to take components of objects into production without using them. Also, a pre-acceptance can be done in a test environment such as pre-FAT and pre-UAT.
O#1	Branching is only used occasionally.
O#2	Different strategies help here. That is among other things: • reducing the risk of acceptance by early demos during development and testing; • maintain of some flexibility in the content release through proper isolation of changes;

RDM R04	How do the Scrum teams prevent delays in the D-T-A-P street?
	• in certain cases, not activating functionalities in production. These are all applied. For version management, a single stream is used as much as possible (no branching unless).
O#3	Partial Working solutions are allowed in production that are not yet being used by the business. The acceptance tests may be carried out in the test environment.
O#4	Applying a Feature toggle: taking (tested) into production without activating.
O#5	This is not applicable.
O#6	This is prevented by working with separate branches and testing them.
O#7	Parts of objects are already being taken into production without using them.
O#8	We use feature toggles.
O#9	This is not very common, but it can happen.
O#10	In consultation with maintenance, parts of objects are taken into production without using them. This is indeed being done.

Table 5-68, RDM-R04 – Delays in the D-T-A-P street.

The degree of continuous integration and continuous delivery largely determines the time-to-market for a Scrum team. That is why automation is an important aspect in delivering a new increment. It is therefore necessary to consciously look at the extent to which manual tasks can be eliminated.

RDM R05	What degree of automation do the Scrum teams use to minimize manual tasks?
O#	A solution direction is to recognize the manual tasks and, based on a business case, eliminate them by automating them. Which tasks do you carry out manually and why?
O#1	We use continuous integration. Creating a BAR file is still manual.
O#2	The tasks to be performed are 80% automated.
O#3	Continuous delivery is still in its infancy. However, DevOps teams use their own created tools for carrying out standard activities and test cases.
O#4	Continuous integration and continuous delivery are still being developed. Some of the test tasks have already been automated.
O#5	We look at tools and connections between tools. Kanban maintenance team has automated all the tasks they perform.
O#6	Tooling but still quite a lot manually.
O#7	Deployment is manual.
O#8	There is an automatic build, package and deployment. We still perform regression tests manually.
O#9	XMLs (input messages) are still done manually.
O#10	We do have an automatic release. There is no automatic build (for .net) and no automatic regression test.

Table 5-69, RDM-R05 – Manual matters.

Overwrite objects in production with an older version or with a version that was not yet allowed to be taken into production must be prevented. The question is how this is handled in practice.

RDM R06	How do the Scrum teams prevent overwriting in the production environment?
O#	A solution direction is the standardization and the use of tools.
O#1	Our baseline is waterproof. Configuration conflicts may still occur, but we can test that in the acceptance environment.
O#2	There is version management and packages and scripts for deployment are sometimes supported with tooling. The DTAP procedure has been formalized with a release process across the DTAP street. Downtime and risks for critical applications are limited, among other things, by rolling out on the inactive production environment and activation after release.
O#3	We prevent overwriting by standardization of tooling.
O#4	We prevent overwriting by standardization and good version and configuration management.
O#5	Does not apply. A newer version is always placed in the portal. The version numbering is automatic.
O#6	The Scrum teams have no access to the production environment.
O#7	Deployment infrastructure prevents data / configuration from being overwritten.
O#8	We first deploy the changes to the staging environment. Only after approval, the change is taken into production.
O#9	We work 100% component oriented, so there is no overwriting.
O#10	Production release is done by maintenance and not by Scrum teams. We only have one source and one production branch. There are therefore few integration problems.

Table 5-70, RDM-R06 – overwriting in the production environment.

5.5 Service operations

5.5.1 Event Management

One of the most important performance indicators of an SLA is availability. To limit unavailability, it is important to trace the cause as quickly as possible. During the design of an application, this can already be taken into account by analysing the possible error causes and the information on the basis of which this error can be noticed. In addition to this proactive measure, unfortunately, often only reactive measures are taken in practice, such as monitoring availability. For example, on the basis of a robot that periodically uses the application. As a result, much less information is available to facilitate a quick and adequate incident analysis.

EVT R01	What support do the Scrum teams build in during the realization for the signalling of events?
O#	A solution direction is the application of a health model and a footprint analysis when drafting / further developing the design.
O#1	We use a definition of events.
O#2	We provide the service desk with instructions for the handling of exceptions. There are also work instructions based on exceptions programmed by the Scrum team.
O#3	We monitor (DevOps). From time to time we compose a health model. There is no footprint analysis.
O#4	The event catalogue is not yet a requirement of the DoD. It is also not an acceptance criterion of a user story.

EVT R01	What support do the Scrum teams build in during the realization for the signalling of events?
O#5	In the case of exceptions, there are routines in the application that help the customer to resolve the error. Before the software is built, we look for possible exceptions. There is no health model and there is no footprint analysis.
O#6	This is not done.
O#7	We do not use a health model and also no footprint analysis. There is, however, a central error handler and a generic log.
O#8	There is a list of risks that you can always encounter (generic). They have been described and we have looked at possible mitigation and technical solutions. There is also a specific list of issues. There is a list of events. Sometimes it is prescribed what you have to do. There is also a preventive effect in the operation by passing on down times to Kanban team.
O#9	The realization of a component takes place in two teams: the design team and the development team. The question is to what extent the design team take these aspects (A, B and C) into account. Event logging is implemented as standard via reference architecture. Logging to tooling which correlates on the basis of metadata.
O#10	Exception management is arranged from ESB. 1. Standard tooling measures whether the service is available from outside of the application. 2. Internal error handling is passed on to standard tooling and is published on a separate portal for application maintainers. On the bus there are standard components for the validation of the input. In case of an error, an exception is made. Features are standardized in terms of processing. There is no upfront analysis of exceptions.

Table 5-71, EVT-R01 – Signalling of events.

Not all events must lead to incidents. Often many events occur in succession to exactly the same incident. By programming tags in the event during programming, it is possible to filter events.

EVT R02	What support do the Scrum teams build in during the realization for filtering events?
O#	A solution direction is the formatting of events, the inclusion of tags in the event, the maintenance of an event catalogue and the use of a white-list / black-list.
O#1	We build tags in the application. We also keep counters in order to monitor the frequency of an event.
O#2	There are levels of exceptions possible (information, warning and exception).
O#3	This is not yet done, but in the long term this will be done centrally.
O#4	Not researched.
O#5	Events do not have a fixed format. Though how it should be reported and what should be in there is defined. Where it goes wrong is not traceable, but with debugging it is. There is no white-list / black-list of events.
O#6	There is a log function at certain events. There are also successful events of status changes. Unexpected events come in an event log. There is no list of events or an event white-list or an event black-list.
O#7	We use an event format. Furthermore, one application has a classification of events. These can be included in a white-list or black-list.
O#8	No event format has been agreed. Also, there is no white-list / black-list composed.
O#9	Our chain logging is guaranteed by a tool that we have developed ourselves.

EVT R02	What support do the Scrum teams build in during the realization for filtering events?
	Through this tooling, logging (through correlation IDs) is implemented over the entire stack. Tooling is part of our reference architecture. Implementation is checked / verified by Run and the controlling architect.
O#10	An event format has been defined. There is no white-list / black-list. Some applications send incorrect messages that cause maintenance to ignore certain issues. So, it can be better. There is no event catalogue.

Table 5-72, EVT-R02 – Filtering of events.

In addition to the filtering of events, it is also possible that completely different events from different CIs indicate the same incident. For example, an application that can no longer function due to the overloading of a database. An event can then be written to a log file from both the database management system and from the application. These two events could be correlated if the correct metadata is provided in the event.

EVT R03	What support do the Scrum teams build in during the realization in order to simplify the correlation of events?
O#	A solution direction is the handling of event correlation rules.
O#1	This is not done.
O#2	The event indicates which PC or user it concerns. There was no conscious thought about exception management and a design for this.
O#3	This is not yet done, but in the long term will become central.
O#4	Not researched.
O#5	There are no correlation rules of events.
O#6	This is not done.
O#7	This is not done.
O#8	The application architecture makes it possible to monitor message traffic (BizTalk). The external errors (functional) are matched with the internal error (technical). So, there is a matching of events.
O#9	See EVT-R02. This is supported. Our self-developed tool provides a correlation ID. Through this ID a functional flow can be traced through the technical chain.
O#10	The maintainer does the correlation. There is no metadata in the events to automate this.

Table 5-73, EVT-R03 – Event correlation rules.

5.5.2 Incident Management

A service desk offers many advantages for a Scrum team, such as the function as Single Point Of Contact, the registration function, etcetera. The question is to what extent this central function is still being used in practice.

ICM A01	Is there a central registration of incidents in a service management tool for more Scrum teams?
O#	
O#1	Yes, there is a central registration.
O#2	Yes, there is a central registration.
O#3	Yes, there is a central registration, we use HP SC for that.
O#4	Yes, all incidents are registered centrally. Omnitracker is used on the technical side.

ICM A01	Is there a central registration of incidents in a service management tool for more Scrum teams?
O#5	Yes, there is a central registration.
O#6	Yes, there is a central registration in Cherwell Software (Cherwell), registration at a central Service Desk.
O#7	Yes, there is a central registration.
O#8	The customer reports to the branch that it is not working. The branch reports it to the service desk. The service desk cannot provide support. The service desk passes it on to the Scrum team but there is no control.
O#9	Yes, there is a central registration. For this we use HP service manager.
O#10	Yes, there is a central registration. We use standard tooling for this.

Table 5-74, ICM-A01 – Central registration.

Some organisations use a separate service team to deal with incidents. Other organisations designate the Scrum development teams as solution groups. The question is what works well in practice.

ICM A02	Are the Scrum teams solution groups?
O#	
O#1	Yes, the Scrum team is a resolution group. But the work is functionally controlled by the maintenance team. In fact, matching is therefore the responsibility of maintenance. A timebox of 30% is used for this.
O#2	Yes and no. Maintenance teams are a resolution group in the IT Service Management tool (Mexon). The Scrum teams are the third line. The database developers are also in IT Service Management (Mexon) and have maintenance tasks.
O#3	Yes, Scrum teams are resolution groups.
O#4	Scrum teams solve their own test findings (no incident) up to and including the phase acceptance. A separate team focused on the Kanban method does the production incidents. So, the Scrum teams are not resolution groups.
O#5	Kanban maintenance team (Scrum teams are the resolution team for the first 6 months).
O#6	The Scrum teams are partially resolution groups. They handle escaped defects. Incidents of previous versions, however, not, these are picked up by the maintenance team which is not part of the Scrum team.
O#7	Yes, Scrum teams are resolution groups.
O#8	Yes, Scrum teams are resolution groups.
O#9	A bug or user story can be created within TFS.
O#10	Yes, Scrum teams are resolution groups.

Table 5-75, ICM-A02 – Resolution groups.

If an incident needs to be resolved by more teams, collaboration is needed. This requires sharing the same tooling, or double tracking of an incident on the product backlog or sprint backlog. The question is how the case organisation deals with this in practice.

ICM A03	How do you deal with (heterogeneous) incidents?
O#	
O#1	Does not occur because we only have one team.
O#2	A single incident management tool is used, in which the handling is assigned to solution groups. Where necessary, the Scrum (development) team supports the maintenance team in analysis and solution. If necessary, a team from more disciplines is formed.
O#3	The service desk coordinates the collaboration of teams.
O#4	The incidents are analysed and solved by one team.
O#5	This is not applicable.
O#6	Incidents relating to the Scrum team are monitored by Scrum and informally resolved by the service coordinator.
O#7	An incident is examined on a case-by-case basis whether it needs to be picked up by one or more teams. Jira internal, OTRS with the customer.
O#8	Heterogeneous are resolved and administered both within the team and outside the team.
O#9	This is not applicable.
O#10	Management routes these incidents. One team is the main contractor.

Table 5-76, ICM-A03 – Heterogeneous incidents.

It is possible that different Scrum teams will solve an incident when this is actually the same incident. The question therefore is to what extent a Scrum team gives metadata during an exception to make this matching possible. The question is also who does the matching, is that the service desk or is this done by the Scrum teams themselves.

ICM R01	In what way do the Scrum teams simplify the matching of incidents across Scrum teams during the development phase?
O#	A solution direction is to add error search criteria in exceptions.
O#1	No, this is not done.
O#2	There is a very limited number of Scrum teams that do not have an overlap. That is why this issue is not applicable for us.
O#3	Will not be done yet. If it is done, then this is done by the service desk. Is not yet supported from the programming method.
O#4	Error IDs are not all transferred from the application log to the service desk (if they are already logged).
O#5	This does not apply to the Kanban team.
O#6	This is not applicable.
O#7	The context of an incident is logged. Features are: name, error code and error message.
O#8	No, this is not applicable, there is only one Scrum team.
O#9	We use separate codes in the design and which handlings have to be programmed. Component names are included in the event. Service (ID) is included in event logging.
O#10	No metadata for matching is provided. Often the incident that the user sees is not what is registered in the incident. The applications do log, but the log information is not sent to the service desk.

Table 5-77, ICM-R01 – Matching incidents.

It is often difficult to determine to which team an incident should be routed. By including characteristics in the exception, it is possible to facilitate this.

ICM R02	How do the Scrum teams simplify the routing of incidents during the development of the software?
O#	A solution direction is to provide metadata in the exceptions that are monitored and registered as incidents. This simplifies routing or even better, makes it possible to automate routing.
O#1	The service desk routes the incidents. Maintenance steers the Scrum team functionally to solve this. For this they get a timebox of 30%. The routing does not have to be simplified by the Scrum teams, this is covered by functional management.
O#2	The maintenance teams route the incidents to the Scrum teams.
O#3	The routing takes place via the service desk or with each other. No metadata is included in the exceptions to automate routing.
O#4	This is not done.
O#5	There is never a routing problem and the routing is only based on a problem (reproduction is possible).
O#6	This is not applicable.
O#7	The component of the event is included in the event notification.
O#8	No, this is not applicable, there is only one Scrum team.
O#9	System test must record an incident in TFS and correlate it to a User story. Everything registered in TFS.
O#10	Incidents are set ad-hoc on the sprint backlog, depending on priority. There are no measures to support the routing of incidents at source code level.

Table 5-78, ICM-R02 - Routing incidents.

When writing an exception during programming, it is possible to include the severity of the event as metadata. On this basis, an initial priority can be given.

ICM R03	How do the Scrum teams support the determination of the priority of the incidents during development?
O#	A solution direction is to include a severity code in the exception.
O#1	There is a generic SLA indicating the initial priority. The priority is not determined by the product owner but by the application manager. No severity code is incorporated in the source code.
O#2	The maintenance team determines the priority.
O#3	Severity code is included in the exception. On that basis the priority is determined by the DevOps teams.
O#4	This is not done.
O#5	The exception codes are unique. Based on these codes, the service desk knows what the severity is.
O#6	The priority is determined in consultation with the product owner. No severity code is incorporated in the source code.
O#7	There is a severity code that is given in the incident.
O#8	This is inherent to the Scrum process. No severity code is provided in the event definition.
O#9	The solution architect aligns with the business. Bug triage by system integration tester.

ICM R03	How do the Scrum teams support the determination of the priority of the incidents during development?
O#10	All events are exceptions. There are no informational or warning events.

Table 5-79, ICM-R03 – Determine the priority.

Resolving incidents is sometimes very simple and sometimes very complex. Especially if more teams are involved in an incident, then the lead time increases. This could be prevented if during the occurrence of an event in application processing the application itself checks what the possible cause is. An example is the absence of another connected application or an infrastructure service. A return code from a database call can also be read and provided with a meaningful event error message.

ICM R04	How do the Scrum teams support the cross-Scrum team incidents during development?
O#	A solution direction is to look during the exception, from the application itself, which interfaces do not work properly. This requires extra programming work. But that way an incident can be solved much faster.
O#1	This is not applicable.
O#2	Meaningful error signalling is taken into account, so that analysis and solution can be as good as possible. Learning points from incidents are processed in improved logging and monitoring and / or measures in the software that reduce sensitivity to error situations (see PPE-R02).
O#3	Incidents are coordinated via the service desk.
O#4	There is only one solving team. The service desk is responsible throughout the chain.
O#5	This is not applicable.
O#6	This is not applicable.
O#7	Each engine component can at any time give a log of what is going on. A snapshot dump can also be made. For one application a health check has been made to check the interfaces.
O#8	This is not applicable.
O#9	There are not many ping-pong incidents. Component / back-end discussion. Mitigated by "factory model".
O#10	We do not provide any extra event information about this.

Table 5-80, ICM-R04 – Cross Scrum team incidents.

In case a user has a standard change, request, information request, etcetera, this can be handled through the request fulfilment process. Often these requests are provided with an automated handling where the service desk can facilitate. Information should then be available on how to handle these requests. The knowledge for this is available within the Scrum team But then this must be a deliverable that is recognized.

RFQ R01	How do your Scrum teams support the implementation of request fulfilment?
O#	A solution direction is a DoD entry for service desk handling.
O#1	This is not applicable.
O#2	This is primarily a maintenance team matter.
O#3	Are part of the DoD.
O#4	This is not applicable.
O#5	This is not implemented.

RFQ R01	How do your Scrum teams support the implementation of request fulfilment?
O#6	This is not an item on the DoD, it is done informally.
O#7	We do not use DoD entry for the service desk handling. If a service request is received for which a Scrum team member is required, the service request is assigned to this employee, after which he handles the request.
O#8	This is not done.
O#9	There is no separate item on the DoD for a service desk to identify / define service requests.
O#10	This does not apply to the team in this study. From the service desk, the service request handling is assigned to teams.

Table 5-81, RFQ-R01 – Support service desk handling.

5.5.3 Problem Management

The question is whether problems are also identified and solved within the Scrum development team.

PBM A01	Are there problems identified by the Scrum teams?
O#	
O#1	Application management identifies the problems and the Scrum team solves them.
O#2	The Scrum team participates in the analysis and resolution of problems and works closely together with the responsible maintenance team.
O#3	Problem management will be reorganized in 2015 and will be linked to the Product Backlog of DevOps teams.
O#4	Problems in the sense of production incidents that are recognized by problem management are not identified by the Scrum teams, however problems in the sense of repetitive coding incidents, are identified by the Scrum teams. These are handled as refactoring within the time allocated for this.
O#5	The service desk creates a problem ticket. The Kanban maintenance team itself also identifies problems.
O#6	Yes. Incidents are placed on the product backlog and grouped. Based on this, problems are recognized. The Scrum team uses Jira and the service team uses Cherwell for this.
O#7	No, problems are not recognized.
O#8	No, problems are not recognized.
O#9	No, problems are not recognized.
O#10	Problems are assigned to the Scrum teams.

Table 5-82, PBM-A01 – Problems.

Some problems require the collaboration of more teams. The question is how this is dealt with. This concerns both the cooperation and the administration by means of a tool.

PBM A02	How are heterogeneous problems dealt with (if more Scrum teams are involved in a problem)?
O#	
O#1	Does not apply.
O#2	There are heterogeneous problems that involve more teams. However, these are not Scrum teams. If necessary, a problem team is put together for a problem.

PBM A02	How are heterogeneous problems dealt with (if more Scrum teams are involved in a problem)?
	The coordination lies with the main contractor of the service and thus lies with the responsible maintenance team.
O#3	Not yet.
O#4	Problems are tackled in the first instance by the Kanban team. If a change is required, it can come to a Scrum team for the realization.
O#5	Does not apply.
O#6	Does not apply.
O#7	No, this is not done.
O#8	No, this is not done.
O#9	No, this is not done.
O#10	There is one team in the lead. A project manager is often also assigned to a problem. This project manager then functions as a problem coordinator. Problem management is a process. The problem manager works for the entire organisation.

Table 5-83, PBM-A02 – Problems.

If a Scrum team is responsible for problem management, then the question is whether the best practices of ITIL are indeed used.

PBM R01	How do Scrum teams prevent recurring incidents?
O#	A solution direction is to have the Scrum teams carry out a Pareto analysis.
O#1	This is the responsibility of the application maintainer.
O#2	No, the management team determines recurring incidents. The Scrum team analyses these incidents.
O#3	Process only becomes now relevant, because there have not yet been recurring incidents.
O#4	This is done by the Kanban team.
O#5	Collaboration with the service desk. They look at code that generates many incidents. The Kanban management team also carries out a Pareto analysis itself.
O#6	The Scrum team performs a problem analysis based on recurring incidents. Automated unit and integration tests are performed for complex parts.
O#7	No, this is not done.
O#8	No, this is not done.
O#9	No, Pareto analyses are performed within the RUN.
O#10	The most common exceptions are discussed in the Scrum team.

Table 5-84, PBM-R01 – Recurring incidents.

Proactive problem management is a way to obtain even higher availability. To this end, it is important to have analysis information. Often this information is only available to a limited extent. However, this can be taken into account during the development of the application.

PBM R02	What measures do the Scrum teams take in the source code to enable proactive problem management?
O#	A solution direction is to incorporate in the application measurements that continuously measure the behaviour of the application and pass the measurement data on to a monitoring facility.
O#1	The Scrum team builds in exceptions. These exceptions are monitored to check whether a certain threshold value is reached or to determine that something specific is happening. The events are handled by event management, which can lead to an incident. The ESB is monitored in this way. An end user experience monitoring has also been added.
O#2	This is taken into account and during the lifecycle learning points from the practice (incidents) are incorporated in improved logging and internal monitor functionality of the application and / or measures in the software that reduce the sensitivity to error situations in cooperation with management.
O#3	Functional and technical reports are written by applications to log files. These log files are actively monitored.
O#4	Standard measurements have been incorporated for the most important functionalities / transactions. These are constantly monitored. With new or modified functionality, these measurements are also adjusted.
O#5	No measurements are made on behaviour, but after each release by an external party a source code check takes place indicating whether we have deviated from the coding standards / guidelines or not. If deviated, this must be solved by the engineer who introduced it in the next release.
O#6	By having exceptions to be written to an event log.
O#7	No, this is not done.
O#8	No, this is not done.
O#9	The Scrum team only does the root-cause analysis at the request of the run organisation. The code base in TFS is also indirectly proactively scanned for possible vulnera-bilities. Indirectly because scans typically only take place when a build of the software is triggered. Proactive because the maintenance and security rules are actively updated.
O#10	This is not done.

Table 5-85, PBM-R02 – Proactive problem management.

6 Agile service management

Message:
- Many organisations still carry out waterfall projects.
- The interface between waterfall projects and service management processes has not changed due to the introduction of Scrum.
- The interface between waterfall projects and Scrum is implemented by a part of the organisations. This overlap then encompasses the control of the Scrum team, status information exchange and the phase transitions in which projects and Scrum come together.
- The interface between Scrum and service management mainly includes incident management and change management.
- The management processes of BiSL, ASL and ITIL are still being implemented by many organisations.
- Architecture plays a role in a part of the organisations in the intersection area of the waterfall projects, the Agile projects and the service management processes.

Reading guideline:
This chapter describes the impact of applying the Agile development process to the service organisation. Section 6.1 shows how the ten case organisations see the division of work between project management, service management and Agile development. Section 6.2 briefly shows how an Agile service management organisation can be implemented on the basis of requirement-based process design. Finally, paragraph 6.3 shows what conclusions can be drawn from the information provided by the case organisations regarding the changes to the service management organisation. The indicated redistribution of the work implicitly reflects how service management can be made Agile and how service management can be properly connected to the Agile development process.

6.1 Cooperation disciplines
An important question when introducing an Agile approach in an ICT organisation is the relationship between project management (PRINCE2), system development (Scrum) and management (BiSL, ASL and ITIL). In Figure 6-1, these disciplines are shown as a diagram.

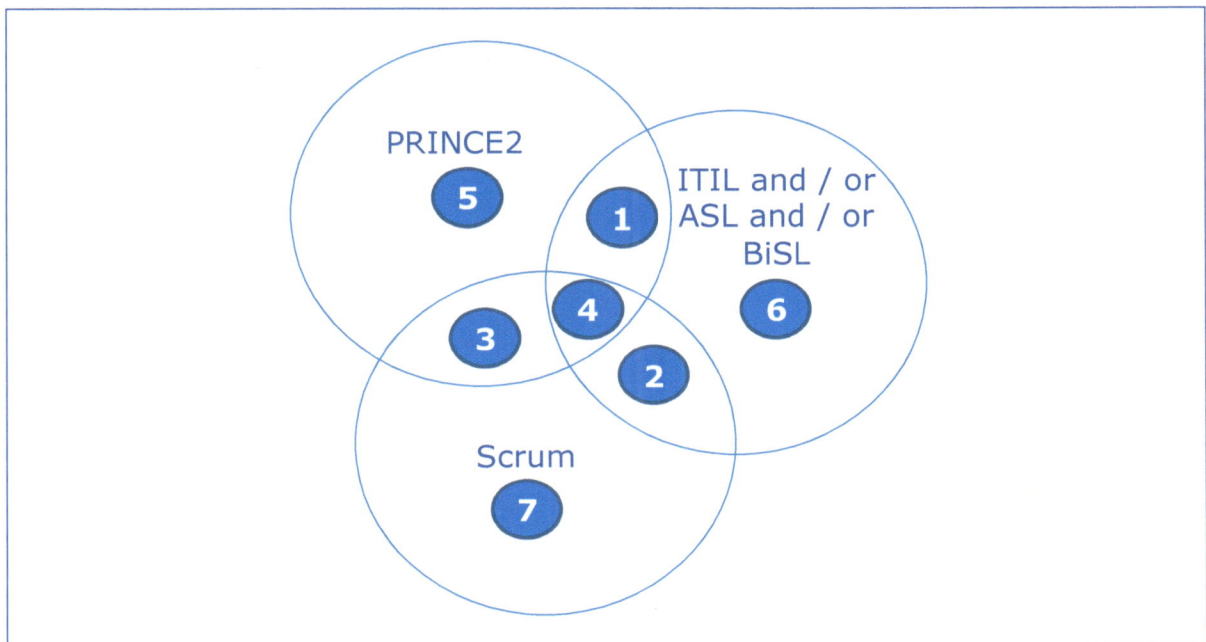

Figure 6-1, Cooperation disciplines.

In the research, each organisation was asked to indicate which work is done for these disciplines and how to deal with the intersection areas. This creates a good overview in the scoping of the Agile development process. The numbers in Figure 6-1 have the following meaning:

1. With projects there is always an interface with the service management organisations. Usually this is done by the change management process for the coordination between the project planning and the change calendar. There is also a relationship with release & deployment management for the rollout of the project deliverables. But there are more interfaces to recognize, such as those of service level management, etcetera. The implementation is different for each organisation.
2. The intersection of Scrum and service management is often located in the handling of incidents, problems and changes. As indicated in chapter 5, this interface is also different for each organisation.
3. The intersection between Scrum and PRINCE2 (waterfall) is more difficult. A possible interpretation of the combination of both is to complete a project in accordance with the waterfall with PRINCE2, but to give the phases details based on Scrum.
4. The central coordination of the changes is crucial when applying different development processes. This can be done, for example, from a strategic consultation, supplemented with the framework from architecture.
5. There will always be projects that are carried out by the waterfall approach. A list of criteria has been included for this purpose in [Best 2018].
6. As shown in this research, the exclusion of service management processes by the introduction of Scrum is absurd. The scope of Scrum is therefore far too limited. With a business DevOps approach, however, it is possible to implement the operational service management processes much more in an Agile way of working. But as a result, they will not be redundant.
7. The scope of Scrum is determined by the extent to which changes are realized through a waterfall approach and the extent to which the maintenance of the delivered software is or is not assigned to the maintenance teams that do not work in accordance with Scrum. Incidentally, more and more organisations use Kanban to manage the service management processes.

For all case organisations, the division of work over these 7 points is not stable over time. There are shifts to be observed. A tendency can be observed here to continuously bring areas 5 and 6 under control of an Agile way of working or, in any case, to apply Agile techniques in these areas. For each of these 7 points, the case organisations were asked how they implemented this. The answers are included in the tables below.

1	What overlap do you recognize between the waterfall approach and the service management processes of BiSL, ASL and ITIL?
O#	There are various overlaps that can be considered such as change management, release management (DTAP) and service level management (SLAs). But also planning & control (resource allocation of employees) and financial management for IT services (budgeting).
O#1	This collaboration has not changed with the introduction of Scrum. This is business as usual.
O#2	Change management and service level management (SLA and service reference manual (describes how the service is delivered)).
O#3	This overlap does not apply.
O#4	This overlap has been filled in at a traditional way.
O#5	This overlap does not apply.
O#6	This overlap includes change management. With major changes, the changes are picked up on a project basis.
O#7	Service desk is the interface for incidents.

1	What overlap do you recognize between the waterfall approach and the service management processes of BiSL, ASL and ITIL?
O#8	There are still regular projects. These projects have an interface with change management. BiSL is not applied.
O#9	This overlap includes change management and release & deployment management.
O#10	Change management is the interface between the project organisation and the service management organisation.

Table 6-1, Overlap of waterfall and service management processes.

2	What overlap do you recognize between the Scrum and the service management processes of BiSL, ASL and ITIL?
O#	Many organisations limit Scrum's role to delivering software. In that case, this intersection is for change management (governance), release management (deployment) and service validation and testing (acceptance).
O#1	Incidents are delivered by maintenance to the Scrum team (30% maintenance timebox). Incidents are sometimes scheduled through a user story but also ad hoc (IBM Tivoli Service Management Suite).
O#2	This overlap includes the service management processes release & deployment management and change management.
O#3	ASL is not applied. BiSL is not used within Scrum. However, features are provided with a form of requirements. ITIL is used within the front office at strategic and tactical level. At the operational level (run and changes) there is an overlap between Scrum and ITIL. This concerns incidents and changes that come as PBI on the product backlog. In addition, release management mainly has a relationship with the Scrum teams for continuous integration, continuous delivery and regression testing. However, this has not yet fully crystallized.
O#4	This overlap includes the RFC that is picked up as a user story (epic). Furthermore, this overlap also includes the risk and impact analysis and the planning.
O#5	Every 6 months, the software is transferred to the Kanban management team. The overlap lies in the use of the same development street and the same tooling. With a modification in the software, the Kanban team also ensures the updating of the documentation and the administration in the tools that are also used by the Scrum teams. The release focus period is used to fully integrate the quality (Scrum + Kanban).
O#6	The product owner is change manager because it is a small application. He has at least the last vote.
O#7	Service desk interface for incidents.
O#8	There is only interface regarding incident management. Change management has no interface, only informal meetings.
O#9	From D-T to A-P is release & deployment, also change management.
O#10	The Scrum team is solely responsible for development. The service management organisation does the governance.

Table 6-2, Overlap of Scrum and the service management processes.

3	What overlap do you recognize between the waterfall approach and Scrum?
O#	The interface between waterfall projects and Scrum concerns, for example, the release planning (roadmap), the sprint planning (phase plan) and the DoD (phase control).
O#1	The overlap is formed by the phase transitions in which projects and Scrum come together. The deliveries of the Scrum team must then wait for those of the project.

3	What overlap do you recognize between the waterfall approach and Scrum?
	This means continuous delivery is not possible.
O#2	Release / sprint planning: • A project letter and Project Initiation Document (PID) is also drawn up for Scrum activities. • There are three possible projects: New construction with PRINCE2, Scrum and a mix.
O#3	This is not applicable.
O#4	This overlap is zero and functions as serves as an interface and the issuing of the status.
O#5	This overlap does not apply.
O#6	Project steering committee manages the Scrum team. The steps of the waterfall are also used in the development process.
O#7	This overlap does not apply.
O#8	There is no steering from a project management board.
O#9	Sometimes a component is part of a project.
O#10	Previously, until 2010 these were the standard project management methodologies. In this segment, the steering is mainly on time and money monitoring.

Table 6-3, Overlap of waterfall and Scrum.

4	What overlap do you recognize between the waterfall approach, Scrum and the service management processes?
O#	The intersection of all circles lies in the planning and steering of the change at strategic level (policy & architecture). Quality control is also important (organisational objectives).
O#1	All changes pass the central decision-making body.
O#2	These work areas of project management, Scrum and service management come together in the order intake process. An order can result into a project or an RFC. The architects guide this.
O#3	This overlap does not apply.
O#4	In chain releases, there is a waterfall for the back-office systems and Scrum for the front-end systems. Upon realization, this provides specific coordination problems, particularly in the release process and integration / acceptance.
O#5	This overlap does not apply.
O#6	The application architect participates in the Scrum team. The application architect is also involved in projects and management.
O#7	This overlap does not apply.
O#8	Interfaces with the back office are a common interest but this is not formally managed.
O#9	This overlap is filled in by the solution architect.
O#10	In this intersection area, architecture and QA play an important role in our organisation.

Table 6-4, Overlap of waterfall, Scrum and service management processes.

5	Which projects are still being carried out in accordance with the waterfall?
O#	There will always be waterfall projects. These projects have a low degree of definition uncertainty ergo a high degree of up-front definition of functionality and quality. The business case can be set up well in advance and risk management can be assessed also well in advance.
O#1	The project organisation is still present. All types of projects are still being carried out. Also, projects that are not yet fully mapped out. In total 70% is still waterfall.

5	Which projects are still being carried out in accordance with the waterfall?
O#2	Most projects follow a traditional approach based on PRINCE2. Software development projects carried out by the development team follow as much as possible an Agile approach.
O#3	During the transition to agile, there will be a hybrid model of waterfall projects with agile DevOps teams. After the transition, features are realized and no waterfall projects anymore.
O#4	At present, policy is that all e-service applications are realized and maintained using agile development methods. In particular, projects around legacy systems are (still) being carried out. In addition, a set of criteria has been drawn up for when agile and when waterfall.
O#5	No waterfall projects are being carried out.
O#6	The project approach 'waterfall'.
O#7	A project also executes all service management processes.
O#8	Regular project management.
O#9	There are still waterfall projects.
O#10	This usually depends on the teams themselves.

Table 6-5, Work area waterfall projects.

6	Which service management processes are still being carried out?
O#	With the arrival of Scrum, a lot of work from the change organisation is shifting to Scrum and mainly the run-organisation remains. This therefore concerns the processes of service operations. In order to safeguard the knowledge, DevOps teams are therefore often formed.
O#1	The service management organisation is still responsible for the licenses, the roll-out, the vendor management, the capacity agreements, the execution of acceptance tests (UAT, FAT) and the design and maintenance of the DTAP environment.
O#2	The Scrum team (development team) works in close cooperation with the maintenance teams. The maintenance teams use their own process.
O#3	Especially strategic and tactical management processes.
O#4	Most service management processes are still being carried out. Until the transformation to DevOps is realized, this will remain the same on a sliding scale.
O#5	Kanban management team performs service management based on Clientele. External and internal notifications are put in the service desk tool. A flag marks the source (external or internal). The service management team plus the Kanban team and the Scrum teams have the same Problem Backlog. We only know one backlog that lists all our problems, both internally and externally reported problems. The problems have an earmark so that it can be recognized if reported internally or by a customer.
O#6	The service management organisation includes the plan and run processes of ITIL and ASL.
O#7	Interface to the customer for incidents, service requests and changes.
O#8	Regular service management.
O#9	The processes of drive, plan and run.
O#10	In this area, the operation is mainly performed on the basis of ITIL processes.

Table 6-6, Work area service management processes.

7	What is the work area of Scrum?
O#	This work area is reserved for Agile projects where development and testing techniques are focused on the incremental and iterative development of new functionality. The high degree of automation enables continuous integration and continuous delivery, enabling a short time-to-market.
O#1	We do not only work with Scrum. Scrum works better for isolated applications than for the complex applications.
O#2	Scrum is applied by the software development team in maintenance and new build projects.
O#3	The work area is DevOps.
O#4	Scrum is complementary. The Scrum work area includes the development of a phase of a project or an RFC.
O#5	Scrum develops the new functionality and maintains it for six months after being put into production.
O#6	This work area includes the development process.
O#7	The Scrum team also carries out all service management processes.
O#8	This work area includes a fully autonomous Scrum team.
O#9	Scrum's field of work is the change management process.
O#10	Scrum is mainly used to realize the desired software (development).

Table 6-7, Work area Scrum.

6.2 Requirement based process design

One way to implement the service management processes absolutely Agile is to identify a list of requirements per service management process that includes the complete functionality of the process as well as the quality assurance. Then, per requirement, it can be decided whether this has to be implemented. If it needs to be designed, the question is in which segment of the diagram of in Figure 6-1 this must take place. A planning must also be drawn up for those process requirements that are not yet in place. This principle is extremely powerful. The model that can be used for this is described in detail in the book 'Quality Control & Assurance' [BEST 2012].

Only one of the ten case organisations had a requirements-based process design approach. And that approach has indeed led to a high curve of maturity and a high degree of management attention.

6.3 Right of existence of ITIL after introduction of Scrum

A question that many process managers worry about is whether it is still possible to make a living by implementing service management in accordance with ITIL best practices. Or is that becoming an obsolete service management model. The same question applies to the BiSL and ASL models. The answer is simple: 'No', these models will not disappear and always offer added value. However, they must be made Agile. This Agile aspect must be based on two axes.

The first axis is to redistribute the task based on the Ven-diagram of Figure 6-1. This division is not static but will change over time. Ultimately, the division of the work stabilizes. But that's certainly going to take a few years. The second axis is the distribution of risk management per component of the Ven- diagram as shown in Figure 6-1. In Chapter 5 often the question of risk management is answered by mentioning that the control lies outside the Scrum team. That is not a problem at all. But then it must be ensured that the corresponding control function is also implemented in terms of design, existence and operation. On the basis of this risk distribution, the associated requirements per management process can then be examined.

An example is the release & deployment process. A risk that should be part of the Scrum team is the prevention of version conflicts through a version control system.

The ultimate control of the risk leads to a flawless continuous integration solution. Of the same process, the risk management of the rollout is often assigned to a separate deployment team. This means that an ITIL process is actually divided over a piece of development within Scrum and a piece of deployment outside Scrum. However, the entire process is still fully applicable, including the associated best practices.

Based on the research as reported in this book, an indication can be given of possible divisions as described above. For each service phase and per process, this section indicates the possible consequences of an Agile method on the service management processes. This also implicitly answers the question of how to make Agile processes.

7 Case organisations

Message:
- Every organisation gives its own interpretation to the Agile development process and the way in which they work together with the service management processes.

Reading guideline:
This chapter briefly describes each case organisation. For each paragraph, one organisation that has taken part in the study is described. The same template was used as much as possible. The same terminology has also been used as possible. On the one hand, this offers a better possibility of comparing the chosen organisational structure and on the other hand safeguards anonymity for the case organisation.

7.1 Casus #1
This case organisation is part of one of the ministries of the Dutch government. The organisation described in this case is responsible for the entire lifecycle of the applications.

7.1.1 Introduction
Traditionally, we work with a development organisation that uses PRINCE2 and a management organisation that applies ITIL processes. In recent years, the need for faster change grew. There was also a great need to make it more visible what exactly happens in a project.

7.1.2 Organisation
The organisation has made a split between Application Lifecycle Management (ALM) and Infrastructure Lifecycle Management (ILM). ALM is assigned to an ALM organisation and ILM is assigned to the ILM organisation. ALM includes both the development and the maintenance of applications that are then deployed and maintained by the ILM organisation.

7.1.3 Background
The ALM organisation traditionally worked with market standards such as PRINCE2 and ITIL. From the workplace came the notion that giving substance to the realization of applications could better take place on the basis of Scrum. This bottom-up choice of applying Scrum has expanded over the past years and several departments are currently working with a combination of PRINCE2, ITIL and Scrum. The best practices of all methods are applied together and brought into harmony with each other. The layout of Scrum is therefore evolutionary and can be characterized as Caluwé green on the workplace and Caluwé blue on management level.

7.1.4 Organisational model
In Figure 7-1 an overview is given of the ALM organisation. Due to the size, a split has been made within the ALM organisation between the front office and the back office. The front office consists of a service desk at operational level and an overarching decision-making body at a strategic level. The back office consists of different domains that are each responsible for a part of the product portfolio. A domain consists of one maintenance team and one or more Scrum teams.

Front office ALM
The service desk is the Single Point Of Contact (SPOC) for the end users. The service desk receives the incidents and the feature requests. The overarching decision-making body is responsible for the product portfolio and the controlling of the domains in the back-office. Representatives of the domains participate in this decision-making body. In a regular meeting it is decided in which domain feature requests belong and which budget must be allocated for the realization.

Back office ALM
The front office steers the back office of ALM. The back office consists of various domains. Each domain consists of a maintenance team and one or more Scrum teams.

Domains

A domain includes one maintenance team and one or more Scrum teams. A decision body has been set up per domain in which an architect, project manager, feature manager, application manager, senior developer and representative of the maintenance team participate. The decision-making body meets every two weeks and can be regarded as a CAB. The Scrum teams carry out the approved feature requests and the maintenance team takes care of the acceptance.

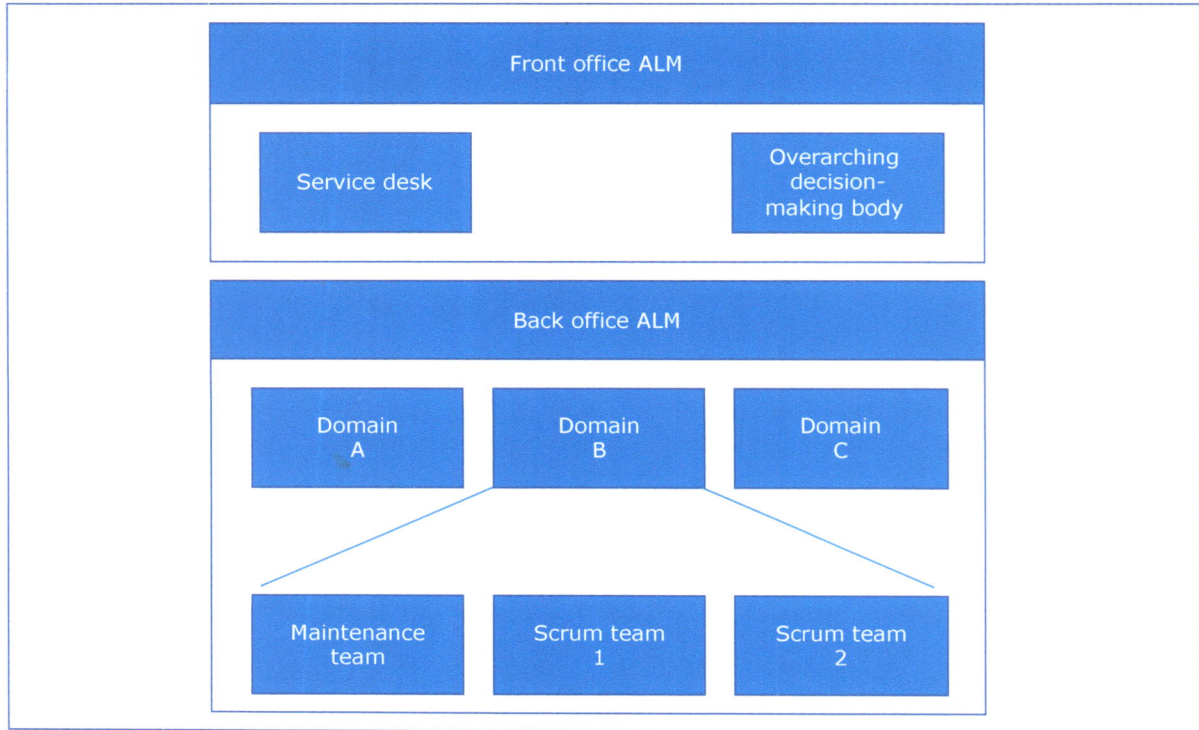

Figure 7-1, The ALM-organisation.

Scrum team

A Scrum team consists of ten dedicated employees. A dedicated product owner has been appointed who spends half an FTE of time on the team. There is a back-up for the product owner in case he is not available. The Scrum master role has also been assigned and also involves a half FTE. There is also a project architect assigned to team for half an FTE. The Scrum team is responsible for the design, construction, testing and delivery of software. However, the distribution and implementation of the software is not done by the Scrum team. The team members are not fully multifunctional. So, specialists have been assigned to specific tasks.

Maintenance team

The maintenance team consists of a service manager who is responsible for supervising the handling of incidents, problems and service requests. The service manager is also responsible for the acceptance of software from the maintenance team. The service manager also provides the interface with the outside world, such as deployments of completed software and the provision of tools to the Scrum team. The service manager is also responsible for the coordination with ILM.

Scope development process

Table 7-1 shows the scope of the development process. A red cross means that there is no relation at this level with the development process. A green tick means that the development process does give substance to this.

Control level	Information Management	Application Management	Technical Management
Strategic	X	X	X
Tactical	V (1)	X	X
Operational	X	V (3)	X
Innovation	V (2)	V (4)	V (5)

Table 7-1, Scope development process.

The first and the second tick indicate the relationship with the product owner. This determines the planning of the functionality at the tactical level. At the operational level, he gives direction to the development process. The third tick indicates that the development process is also part of the run processes. This is indicated because incidents are also solved by the development team. The fourth tick is the core of the development team's work, which is the development of new functionality. Finally, a fifth tick has been drawn because Scrum teams are also recognized on the side of the infrastructure.

7.1.5 Service management processes

SLA's
There are no specific agreements for the applications. Only generic service norms are used.

Service Management processes
All service management processes of ITIL are still used by the maintenance team. In this respect, the introduction of Scrum has not brought about any changes.

Incident management
The incidents are reported at the service desk. This routes the incidents to the management teams involved. The incidents are picked up by developers working in the Scrum teams. They are set hierarchically, for a part of their time, under the maintenance team, but are further functionally controlled by the product owner. The incidents are solved on the basis of a timebox window of 30% of the sprint time.

Problem management
The problems are also handled up by the developers who work in the Scrum teams.

Change management
Adjustments in the application portfolio are decided at an overarching level. For each application, the product roadmap is maintained at the domain level by the product owner. He drafts a project letter and Project Initiation Document (PID) for the changes. The architect advises the product owner by drawing up a start architecture that also includes the high-level requirements. Based on the PID and the start architecture, the release schedule is drawn up in which the sprints are defined. This release planning is the basis for the filling of the product backlog. The software is designed, built and tested in sprints. The high-level requirements are converted into user stories. The management team is one of the acceptors of the deliverables. They monitor the manageability of the delivered software. The maintenance team also ensures that the deliverables are transferred to the ILM organisation.

7.1.6 Challenges and solutions
In the beginning there was quite some resistance because the employees had no understanding of what Scrum really meant. As a result, there was not much willingness to change. There was an impression of: "You can only Scrum when you know the newly developed system" and "Once you know a system and the requirements, why would you Scrum, then you can also develop incrementally with PRINCE2". That is why Scrum awareness sessions have been organized. In this the fun factor played an important role. The second resistance was the fear that the documentation would contain too little information. The documentation is still getting the right attention. However, the scope of the project letter and the PID has been greatly reduced.

An important challenge in this organisation is the anchoring of the Scrum approach higher in the organisation. After all, the introduction of Scrum has arisen from the work floor. A second outstanding challenge lies in the fact that delivered products cannot always actually be taken into production because they are dependent on other developments that are not implemented in a Scrum manner.

7.2 Casus #2

This case organisation is part of a healthcare institution in the Netherlands and is responsible for the entire lifecycle of a medical application for logistics around patients, appointments, schedules, non-national Electronic Patient Document (EPD) and the like. This application is called in this case the care application.

Every resemblance to an existing product in the market is purely coincidental. In addition, the integration with other applications, that the healthcare organisation has purchased, has been implemented. In addition to the care application, this case organisation also develops, integrates and manages other applications based on Scrum.

7.2.1 Introduction

This organisation has traditionally been working with a development organisation that works according to PRINCE2 and a service management organisation that applies service management processes in accordance with ITIL. For the realization of the care application it was decided to use a Scrum approach.

7.2.2 Organisation

In this case organisation, application management and infrastructure management are combined together into one ICT organisation. Various teams have been set up with dedicated task areas.

7.2.3 Background

The reason to use Scrum for the development process arose around the renewal cycle of an existing application. Various projects were initiated for the expansion of functionality, integrations with other applications and maintenance changes. The problems with the regular project approach arose in a period in which the organisation had major ambitions for expansion. As a result, the development team was faced with various project managers, insufficient mutual prioritization and rapid expansion of the development team with external staff. This led to quality problems and an unreliable delivery. Scrum was introduced in the improvement track that started in response to this.

Line management has set the framework for the introduction of the Scrum teams to a reasonable level of detail (Caluwé blue). The Scrum team members have only taken care of the refinement of the implementation (Caluwé green). Senior management has given its commitment to this change of working method.

This case concerns the construction and management of the care application as well as the configuration of the applications with which communication is required. This means that the deliverables are both application components of the healthcare application and configuration files for the integration with other applications. In this case, therefore, it concerns a single application in a chain of other applications that together form the information provision of the care-providing institution.

7.2.4 Organisation model

In Figure 7-2 an overview is given of the ICT organisation. Due to its size, a split has been made within the ICT organisation between ICT support, the Front office and the Back office. The Business office and Policy & Architecture provide support within the ICT service. Policy and Architecture operate on a strategic and tactical level. The architects give guidance the changes regardless of whether they are designed on a project basis or by means of Scrum. The Front office consists of the Service desk and Service teams. The Service Teams perform work at both operational level and tactical level and are therefore involved in service design. Standard questions are dealt via the service desk and the service teams.

Customer questions that fall outside normal service provision and changes to the service provision are dealt on a project basis, where necessary as a project. This is the difference between the questions that are handled according to service management (ITIL) or according to project management (PRINCE2). The Back office consists of different teams for both the construction and the maintenance of applications and the infrastructure.

Front office ICT
At a strategic level, Policy & Architecture gives direction to the product portfolio from an architectural perspective. Here the architecture scenarios are detailed to changes at project level.

Then, at a tactical level, projects are started that are or are not realized through Scrum. The use or non-use of Scrum in projects is determined by the involvement of the teams in a project. A team does or does not work with Scrum. There are therefore no decision criteria which project can or cannot be realized through Scrum.

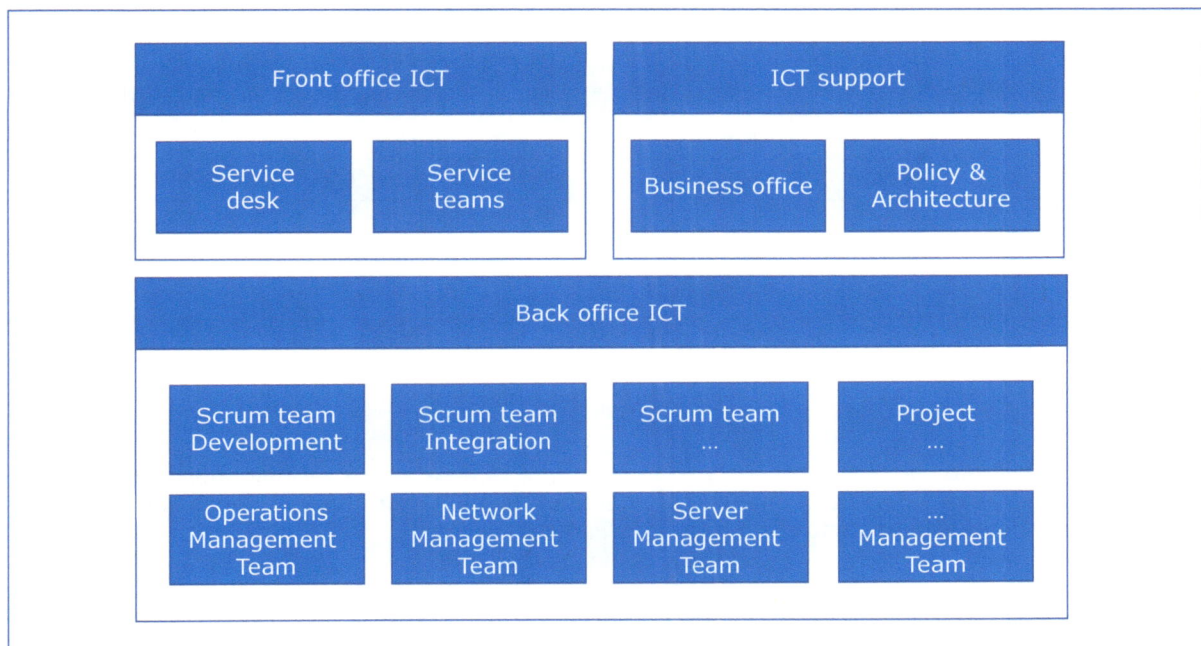

Figure 7-2, The ICT-organisation.

At the operational level, the change manager collects the change requests from the user organisation and the service management organisation. These assignments are managed in a dedicated service management tool in accordance with a standard change management process. If an assignment is approved by the CAB, it is assigned to the management teams involved.

Back office ICT
The front office manages the back office of the ICT organisation. The back office consists of various development and management teams. Two Scrum teams have been set up for the healthcare application. One team does the development and the other team the integration of the care application. The management teams and the Scrum development team work together for the deployment. The Scrum Integration Team, however, has the responsibility for the integration environment and does the deployment of software itself. The new building of the care application is governed in accordance with PRINCE2 and developed in accordance with Scrum. In practice, this means that the frameworks have been issued by the line / project organisation and that the development is in accordance with Scrum and these frameworks. All standard roles of Scrum are represented, namely the product owner, the Scrum master and the development team. The framework from the project organisation provides enough space to work with a product roadmap, release plan and sprint plan based on themes, features and stories. The Scrum development team therefore uses a product backlog and a sprint backlog.

Adjustments to the care application that are already put in production are received as approved assignments that are translated into features. These features are put on the product backlog. The Scrum teams also participate in resolving incidents.

Scrum team
A Scrum team consists of seven to ten dedicated employees. Each Scrum team has a Scrum master. The Scrum team is responsible for designing, building and testing. There are specialist roles in the Scrum team. The distribution and implementation are not done by the Scrum teams themselves. The management teams are responsible for the changes to the acceptance environment and the production environment in collaboration with the Scrum development team. This also applies to the deployment.

Scope development process
Table 7-2 shows the scope of the development process. A red cross means that at this level there is no relation to the development process. A green tick means that the development process does give substance to this. The first tick shows the planning of the product backlog. The second tick the realization of in the development process.

Control level	Information Management	Application Management	Technical Management
Strategic	X	X	X
Tactical	X	V (1)	X
Operational	X	X	X
Innovation	X	V (2)	X

Table 7-2, Scope development process.

7.2.5 Service management processes

SLAs
SLAs are used. From the Front office organisation there is a service level manager who draws up these SLAs and passes non-functional requirements on to the Scrum teams. These NFRs are used in the sprint when designing and testing the application.

Service management processes
All service management processes of ITIL are still being used. This involves both Front office and Back office staff.

Event management
The Scrum teams provide the service desk with instructions to handle exceptions. During the construction of the care application, no explicit consideration was given to the design of exception management in combination with monitoring provision and incident management. However, the exception message includes metadata such as localization information (who / where). However, no use has been made of the possibility to provide tags for filtering and correlation of events.

Incident management
The incidents are reported at at the service desk. This routes the incidents to the management teams involved. The RFCs arising from the incidents are placed on the backlogs of the relevant Scrum teams. In case an incident cannot tolerate postponement and the management team cannot solve it, the Scrum team will be involved. The coordination and progress monitoring of the incidents is assigned to the service desk.

Problem management
The management teams identify recurring incidents that are then analysed by the Scrums teams.

Change management
The Scrum team participates in the functional CAB for the planning and approval of assignments.

If the assignments for business applications fall within the agreed frameworks, no involvement of the functional CAB within ICT is required here. The risk and impact analysis are made by the Scrum teams. The changes are administered by the management team in a service management tool. The Scrum teams use a different tool for the lifecycle of features. There is a 1: N relationship between an assignment and the related features. The Scrum teams are loosely coupled, and the applications are single tenancy applications. As a result, no or hardly heterogeneous changes occur.

Configuration management
In the service management tool, CIs are used for applications such as the care application. Software CIs are recognized in the version management system used by the Scrum teams. However, no relationship has been established between these two tools. The version management system is used for the version management of the source code and the modules for the building process. Also, a tool is used in which the configuration of each deployment environment is managed. This tool ensures that the correct version of the software is installed in every environment.

Release and deployment management
The roll-out of the care application takes place by the management teams in collaboration with the Scrum development team.
A deployment of a release of the care application takes place at the end of two sprints. There is no question of a release sprint. Releases are compiled on the basis of predefined versions of packages. For the healthcare application such a package is defined in the version management system in the form of a data set. In addition to various tools that have been purchased to give shape to the deployment process, there is also a separate management shell that makes it possible to secure that what is in the version management system is also being rolled out.

Both the data set and hash totals ensure that what is in the version control system actually comes into production. The Scrum development team takes care of the roll-out of the development environment to the test environment. The management teams are responsible for the acceptance and production environment. There is no question of continuous delivery, but the manual tasks are 99% automated. Production disruptions are prevented by always going live in an inactive environment.

Service validation and testing
The testing of the care application is done on the basis of a risk analysis. No formal risk analysis is used. Different techniques are used, including peer review, regression tests and acceptance tests. The quality of the care application is further increased by the use of standards and guidelines, refactoring and modularity.

Service level management
The ICT organisation draws up the SLAs and agrees on the SLA norms with the customer. The SLA of the care application serves as input for the Scrum teams. The way in which the service is implemented and delivered is recorded in the service reference manual. This is and remains the responsibility of the management teams. The formal approval of the SLA and the service reference manual take place in the chain meeting by service teams and management teams. The SLA alignment is therefore not a responsibility of the product owner. Of course, the product owner is involved.

Service design processes
The Scrum teams are not responsible for the service design processes such as supplier management, availability management, capacity management etcetera. This is done by the service teams from the front office. However, design criteria of the service and management teams are taken into account during the design, construction and testing of the care application.

7.2.6 *Challenges and solutions*
The healthcare application has now been put on track and the initial project has stopped. The Scrum development team now only carries out maintenance on the healthcare application. No more themes are now recognized.

There is also no product roadmap more active. As a result, the Scrum development team has also been scaled down in terms of size. There is no longer a product owner. This role is fulfilled by the line manager who manages the care application Scrum teams. The composition of the Scrum development team and the job responsibilities has also been changed. This also gives them more "management tasks", broader assignment portfolio and smaller assignments. This makes it more difficult to focus in sprints.

7.3 Case #3

This case organisation is part of a financial institution in the Netherlands and is responsible for the entire lifecycle of financial applications. This case partly describes the functionality as it has been set up and partly the functionality that has yet to be set up.

7.3.1   Introduction

We have traditionally worked with a development organisation that worked on a project basis and a service management organisation that applied service management processes. The effectiveness and efficiency of this approach was not what was expected of it. The bureaucracy resulted in a loss of time without really controlling a lot of risks. In recent times the ship has turned around and Agile has been embraced. The purpose of this is to increase the speed of the production of operational software and the reduction of the overhead of the existing methodical approaches.

7.3.2   Organisation

The organisation has made a split between ALM and ILM. ALM is assigned to an ALM organisation and ILM is assigned to the ILM organisation.

ALM includes both the construction and the maintenance of applications that are subsequently rolled out and managed by the ALM organisation. The ILM organisation is only involved in case changes have to be made to the system software and to disruptions to the system software and the hardware.

7.3.3   Background

The ALM organisation traditionally worked with market standards such as PRINCE2 and ITIL. From the higher management came the awareness that giving substance to the realization of applications could take place better on the basis of Scrum. This top-down approach has quickly paid off. The PRINCE2 approach has been abandoned altogether and the ITIL processes are in second place. The layout of Scrum has been approached revolutionarily from the higher management and the content has been laid entirely on the work floor by means of the Caluwé green colour. Caluwé blue frameworks have been given by the management, but these are very minimal.

This case does not involve building applications but configuring applications in order to provide the information management department with financial information. This means that the deliverables are therefore not application components but configuration files with changes that have to be made in production. In this case it is not a single application but a chain of multi tenancy applications that together form an information processing chain.

7.3.4   Organisation model

Figure 7-3 gives an overview of the ALM organisation. Due to the size, a split has been made within the ALM organisation between the Front office and the Back office. The front office consists at strategic level of a product portfolio control by a number of architects, at tactical level a team of blueprint managers and at operational level a service desk and a team of service managers.

The back office consists of several ALM sub-areas, each of which is responsible for part of the product portfolio. An ALM sub-area consists of one or more Scrum teams. A specific role has been assigned to the generic service team. A special feature of this case is that many applications are focused on producing the same set of services. Thus, the various sub-areas often deliver together added value to the user organisation. The sub-areas can be seen as a production chain. The applications are mainly multi tenancy applications. This means that the applications must support different business models.

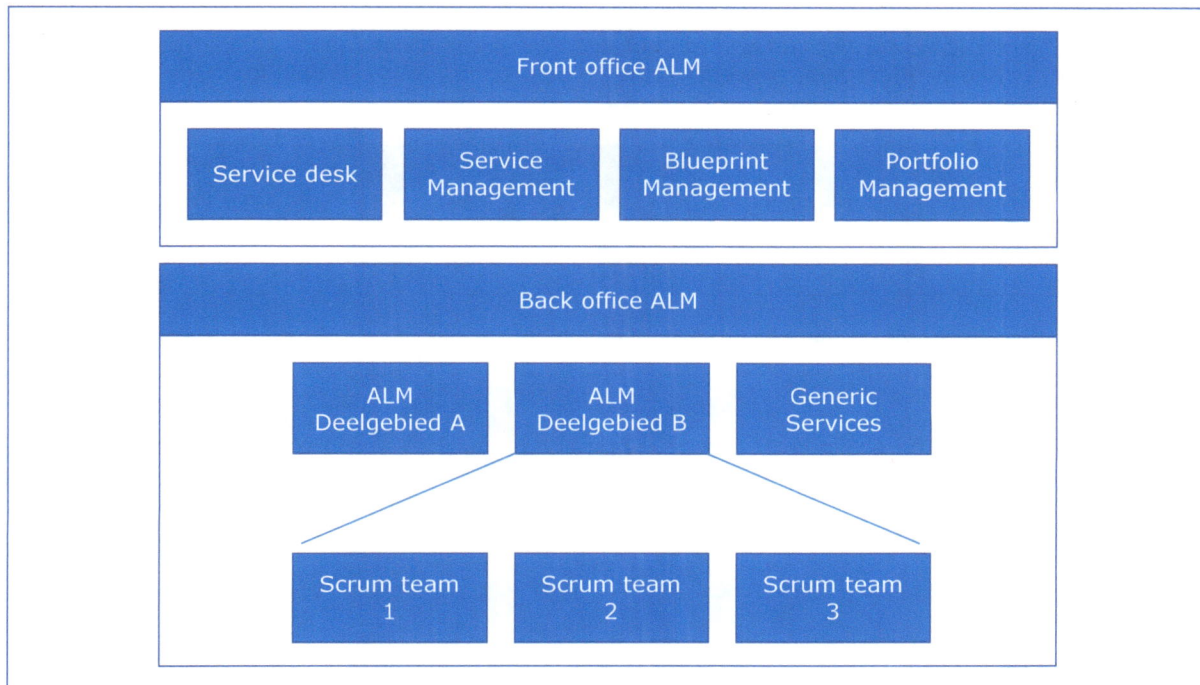

Figure 7-3, The ALM organisation.

Front-office ALM

The front office gives strategic direction to the product portfolio from an architectural perspective. Here the architecture scenarios are detailed into Themes. At the tactical level, the themes are being decomposed by the blueprint manager into features. Each feature is related to applications and involved components. On an operational level, the change manager distributes the features to the backlogs of the involved Scrum teams that are positioned in the back office. At the same time, the service desk is the SPOC for the end users at the operational level. The service desk receives the incidents and the feature requests. The service managers are responsible for monitoring the consistency of the distributed feature requests, incidents and problems across the entire chain of sub-areas. Herewith they each manage their own functional chain.

Back-office ALM

The front office directs the back office of ALM. The back office consists of sub-areas. Each sub-area consists of one or more Scrum teams. A special sub-area is the generic service team which, unlike the other sub-areas, does not produce a configuration of application software.

Sub area

A sub-area consists of one or more Scrum teams. The Scrum teams are managed by one product owner.

Scrum-team

A Scrum team consists of seven to ten dedicated employees who have been deployed in a multifunctional manner. Each Scrum team has a Scrum master. The Scrum team is responsible for the design, construction, testing and delivery of the configuration of software. The intention is that the distribution and implementation of the software is done by the Scrum team itself, but that is not yet the case. To this end, for the time being, the generic service team is being employed.

Generic services

Because the sub-areas make use of the same enabling services such as monitoring and scheduling, it has been decided to set up a generic team that fulfils this. However, this mainly concerns the generic fulfilment of these services but not the application-specific configuration. This is preferably done by the Scrum teams from the sub-areas. For the time being this is not the case.

Scope development process

Figure 7-3 shows the scope of the development process. A red cross means that at this level there is no relation to the development process. A green tick means that the development process does give substance to this.

Control level	Information Management	Application Management	Technical Management
Strategic	X	X	X
Tactical	X	X	X
Operational	X	V (2)	X
Innovation	V (1)	V (3)	X

Table 7-3, development process.

The first tick reflects the steering of the development process by the product owner. The second tick indicates that run processes are also performed in the development process, such as resolving incidents and handling access management change requests. The third tick indicates the actual execution of the development process.

7.3.5 Service management processes

SLAs
Generic and specific agreements are made with the owners of the applications. These agreements are made by the Front office service managers.

Service management processes
All management processes of ITIL are still being used. This involves both Front office and Back office staff.

Incident management
The incidents are reported at at the service desk. The service desk routes the incidents to the Scrum teams involved. Incidents also arise from the monitoring facility and batch processing. The incidents are picked up by the Scrum teams involved. The coordination and progress monitoring of the incidents is assigned to the service desk.

Problem management
The problems are handled with analogous to the incidents. It is only the Scrum teams that initiate a problem record because they have the related knowledge.

Change management
Adjustments in the application portfolio are called themes. The themes are discussed at the architectural level with the asset owners. On this basis, the courses are plotted on a broad basis. The first impact- and risk analysis also takes place at this level. The second level of impact and risk analysis takes place at the tactical level by specialists within the front office, called blueprint managers. They analyse the changes in the chain of applications and the involved application components and determine a theme in which way this can be realized. Based on this division, features are put together. For each feature, the change manager initially determines which stories should be put on the product backlog of which Scrum team The product owner of a Scrum team allows this allocation to be analysed by the involved specialists. For this purpose, these specialists are given a timebox. This analysis is the third level of the impact and risk analysis and concerns a low-level analysis such as the control of the impact of tables and columns, reporting data and business rule.

7.3.6 Challenges and solutions
Because the application architecture consists of a chain of multi tenancy applications, there are usually more sub areas involved in the realization of a feature and therefore more Scrum teams. The features are thus split horizontally into stories that are distributed over the Scrum teams involved.

The timely realization of a feature therefore requires a matching of the priority of the stories on the product backlogs that are related to this feature. To solve this tension, the product owners have a meeting about the prioritization. In addition, service managers have been appointed at the front office who are responsible for the monitoring of a functional area across the entire chain of the sub-areas and the involved Scrum teams.

In this way the accuracy, completeness and timeliness of the splitting of the features is monitored. To this end, the blueprint managers must regularly fine tune with the specialists in the Scrum teams. Timeboxes have been allocated for this purpose so that these meetings can take place regularly without disturbing the Scrum teams. The alternative to this problem is the assignment of functional areas to Scrum teams, which means that the features can be split vertically. This, however, means that several teams are working on the same application, which makes continuous integration and continuous delivery very complex.

7.4 Casus #4

This case organisation is part of an Independent Administrative Body in the Netherlands and is responsible for the entire lifecycle of six applications.

7.4.1 Introduction

Traditionally, this Independent Administrative Body has been working with a development organisation that works on a project basis and a service management organisation that applies the ITIL v2 management processes. The software development has been outsourced to an external agency. There was a need for better governance, closer cooperation and faster time-to-market for six applications. Two years ago, the ship turned around and the Agile Scrum was embraced. A lot of the old governance structure was left intact and only the development process was renewed. The employees of the external agency now work on location at the customer based on a Scrum development process. In the long term, the intention is also to work fully Agile for the inflow and the outflow of the development process. The usage of Agile for the intake is already at an advanced stage.

7.4.2 Organisation

The organisation has made a split between ALM and ILM. Both ALM and ILM are outsourced to suppliers. The Independent Administrative is therefore a control organisation. ALM covers both the development and the maintenance of applications that are then built and maintained by the ALM supplier. The ILM organisation is only involved in case changes have to be made to the system software and to disruptions to the system software and the hardware.

7.4.3 Background

The ALM organisation works with market standards such as PRINCE2 and ITIL v2. From the higher management came the awareness that Scrum makes a much closer cooperation with the supplier possible. This top-down approach has quickly paid off. The PRINCE2 approach and the ITIL v2 approach have been left intact and Scrum is Caluwé green shaped from a Caluwé blue framework. Thus, the implementation of Scrum has been approached evolutionarily from the higher management and the substance has partly been completed on the work floor.

This case concerns the construction and maintenance of six applications that link the information provision of the Independent Administrative Body to the outside world with the rest of the application landscape of the Independent Administrative Body. The six applications are based on a Service Oriented Architecture (SOA) structure and communicate via an Enterprise Service Bus (ESB) with the applications on the back.

7.4.4 The organisation

Figure 7-4 provides an overview of the ICT organisation. Due to its size, a split has been made between the Front office and the Back office. At the operational level, the front office consists of a service desk where the incident management and the problem management process are assigned. There is also a desk for submitting RFCs. The front office provides for the planning of the changes and projects on the tactical level. On a strategic level, the front office consists of product portfolio management and architecture.

The ALM organisation is part of the back office and is steered by the front office. In the ALM organisation, 5 Scrum teams have been recognized and 1 Kanban team. The 5 Scrum teams each have their own theme. The Kanban team provides the technical maintenance of all applications developed by the Scrum teams and taken into production by the management teams. The software developed by the external staff is tested in the acceptance environment and after approval taken into production by the maintenance teams.

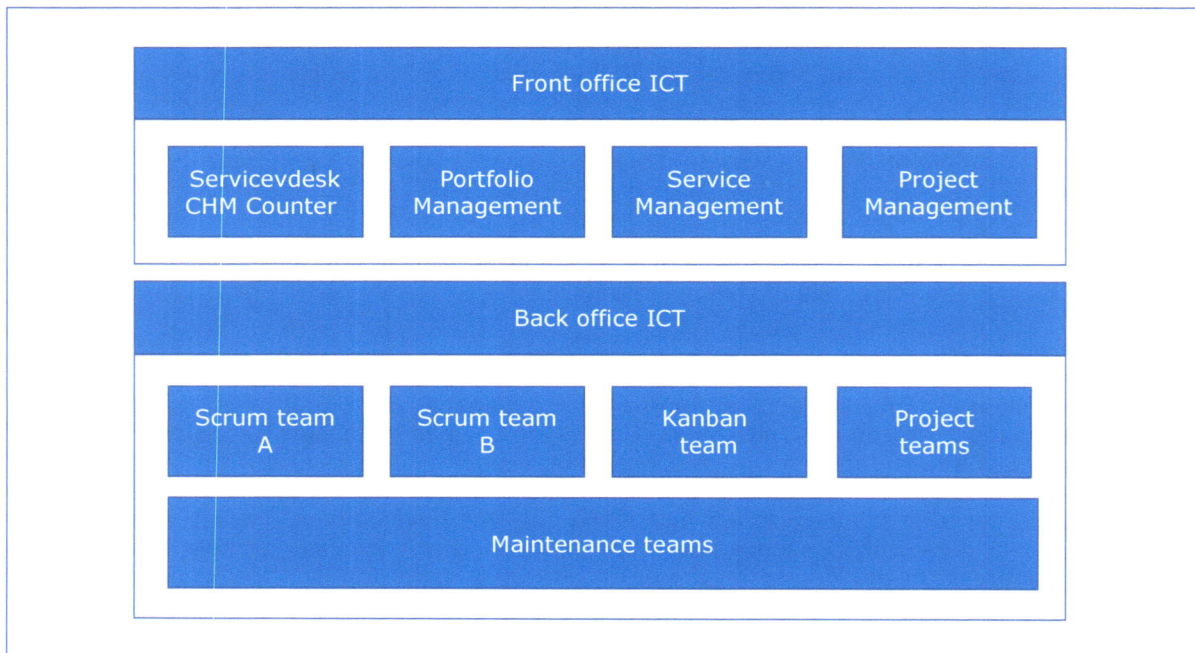

Figure 7-4, The ICT-organisation.

Front-office

The RFCs are submitted to a change management desk. These RFCs can vary from medium changes to projects. All RFCs go through the same steps of registration, assessment by the involved product group manager, impact analysis by specialists including architects, Scrummers and maintainers, decision making by CAB and specifying of an assignment. This last step is a bridgehead for the Scrum team working in the back office. The disruptions from production can be reported to the service desk. Resolving these incidents as well as small changes will be passed on to the Kanban team.

Back office ALM

The back office consists of 4 different types of teams: 5 Scrum teams, 1 Kanban team, various project teams and maintenance teams.

Scrum-teams

The 5 Scrum teams are divided into themes. These themes concern six applications that include the communication of the Independent Administrative Body with the outside world. These Scrum teams are steered by the front office based on changes for which an assignment has been specified. These assignments are divided into epics and user stories that are put on the product backlog concerned. A Scrum team is linked to a product owner and is facilitated by a Scrum master.

Kanban team

The Kanban team ensures that there is a quick solution for incidents and small changes from the production environment that originate from the application produced by the 5 Scrum teams. With a fast-lane approach (DevOps), incidents can be resolved quickly, even if adjustments to the application code are necessary. This team therefore works closely with the development team like branching of software that is adapted to solve incidents.

Project teams

The project teams (regular development) ensure that the six applications that are built and maintained by the Scrum teams via an ESB are linked to the applications in the underlying information supply chain of the Independent Administrative Body. These project teams are also responsible for the applications at the back of the ESB.

Maintenance teams

The Scrum teams, Kanban team and project teams are allowed to carry out the promotion from the development environment to the test environment. The promotion from the test environment to the acceptance environment and the promotion of the acceptance to the production environment is provided by the maintenance teams.

Scope development process

Table 7-4 shows the scope of the development process. A red cross means that at this level there is no relation to the development process. A green tick means that the development process does give substance to this.

Control level	Information Management	Application Management	Technical Management
Strategic	V (1)	X	V (8)
Tactical	V (2)	V (5)	V (9)
Operational	V (3)	V (6)	X
Innovation	V (4)	V (7)	X

Table 7-4, Scope development process.

The first and eighth tick reflect the imaging at strategic level of the change. This concerns architectural designs and the like. The ticks two, five and nine concern the planning of the change. The ticks three and six indicate the handling in the operation. Finally, the ticks four and seven indicate respectively the control and the execution of the development process.

7.4.5 The service management processes

SLAs

The SLAs are adjusted during respectively afterwards on the basis of the changed (non) functional requirements that have been collected from the production chain.

Scope Kanban service management process

Table 7-5 shows the scope of the Kanban management process. A red cross means that at this level there is no relation to the development process. A green tick means that the development process does give substance to this.

Control level	Information Management	Application Management	Technical Management
Strategic	X	X	X
Tactical	X	X	X
Operational	X	V (1)	V (3)
Innovation	X	V (2)	

Table 7-5, Scope service management process.

The first tick is the primary work area of the Kanban management process. The second tick only reflects the refactoring performed by the management team, which is why it is not shown bold. The third tick reflects the Ops part to be able to bring independently small changes to production.

Service management process
All management processes of ITIL are still being used. This involves both Front-office and Back-office staff.

Incidents
The incidents of users and the computer center are reported at at the service desk. The service desk routes the application incidents to the Kanban team. The coordination and progress monitoring of the incidents is assigned to the service desk.

Problems
The problems are dealt with analogously to the incidents. The execution of the problem management process is assigned to the service desk.

Changes
The RFCs are reported at at the service desk and all follow the same route. After registration, the adjustments must be approved by the product owners. They are responsible for the products in their portfolio. Then a global impact analysis is carried out by architects, employees of the Scrum teams and maintainers. Based on this information, decision-making takes place in the CAB or management team. Approved changes are elaborated in change specifications. A technical analysis is carried out, a risk analysis is performed, a preliminary calculation is made, and the assignment is assigned to the involved development team. This can be a Scrum team or a project, depending on the to be modified application. At this moment in time, a transfer takes place from the Independent Administrative Body to the external agency that takes care of the realization on the basis of a Scrum development process, under the supervision of the Independent Administrative Body.

A Scrum team then carries out the following steps:
- definition of the epic and user stories and helping the product owner to prepare the product backlog;
- realization in a three-weekly sprint of the desired functionality;
- integration of sprint with regression test.

If the software works in accordance with the specs, it will be transferred to the maintenance teams of the Independent Administrative Body who will place this software in the acceptance environment for acceptance. After a successful acceptance, the adjustments are taken into production.

7.4.6   Challenges and solutions
The Scrum teams build and maintain the applications that are part of the chain. Despite the fact that this takes place within the walls of the Independent Administrative Body, the integration of the development process is not yet complete.

For example, there is a split in tooling from the Independent Administrative Body organisation and that of the external agency. This means that there are breaks in the connection of the information provision that obscures the traceability.

The required traceability includes the following information flow:
- Front office
  - RFC (for a service / application) in the service management tool
  - CI in the CMDB in the service management tool
- Back office development
  - User story / epic
  - Requirement
  - Test case
  - Software CI
  - Baseline
  - Release built

- Back office maintenance
  - Deployment package
  - Object-ID in production

At this moment the Independent Administrative Body is working on improving and accelerating the development process through continuous integration, continuous delivery and regression testing. Therefore, the order of the above information flow is a precondition. To this end, the collaboration and integration of the various tools must be investigated further. Furthermore, the management of the development team on the basis of a service architecture (Business service, information service, information system service and technical service) as defined within IAF (TOGAF) has not yet been implemented. This means that the relationship to the business processes is still mapped at application level. Architecture addresses this aspect. The integration of service level management at the front of the change still needs to be addressed. This prevents surprises for the service level managers. There is also still a way to make the services that are generated by the development teams measurable, such as programming aspects that makes the handling of events and incidents flexible.

7.5 Case #5

This case organisation develops application software for financial institutions in the Netherlands. The software can be taken into production by customers themselves. A Software as a Service (SaaS) solution has also been put on the market by the case organisation. The part of this organisation described in this case is responsible for the maintenance of the software. In this case, this is called the case application.

7.5.1 Introduction

We have traditionally worked with a development organisation that was organized on a project basis. In recent years there has been an increasing need for productivity improvement, focus on essentials and time to market. There was also a need for a better understanding of what can be delivered.

7.5.2 Organisation

The organisation has made a split between ALM and ILM. The ILM organisation consists of an internal management team for the SaaS solution. In case the customer himself takes the case application into production, there is an external ILM organisation. The ALM organisation consists of several teams. The (further) development of the case application is done by four Scrum development teams. The management of the case application is assigned to a separate team that works on the basis of Kanban. There is also an integration team and a service desk team.

7.5.3 Background

The ALM organisation works with market standards such as ITIL. From the work floor came the awareness that the implementation of the realization of the case application could be better based on Scrum. During the formation of the teams the control was implemented Caluwé blue and the interpretation of the Scrum working process was to a limited extent Caluwé green.

7.5.4 The organisation

Table 7-5 provides an overview of the ALM organisation. Within the ALM organisation, a split has been made between the front office and the back office. At the operational level, the front office consists of a service desk that handles incidents and service requests. They also create problem records. The service desk is also responsible for part of the configuration management. Finally, the service desk is responsible for the publication of the case application on the portal where customers can download the case application.

On a tactical level, a service management team has been set up consisting of account managers and a financial staff for contract management and license management. At strategic level, there is steering from policy and architecture. This department is formed by the management and the architects who determine the application portfolio and compose the roadmaps. The ALM back office consists of four Scrum development teams. These teams develop the new releases of the case application.

These Scrum development teams are also responsible for managing the new release of the case application for six months. The Kanban management team then takes over the application management. The integration team is responsible for the daily build of the case application.

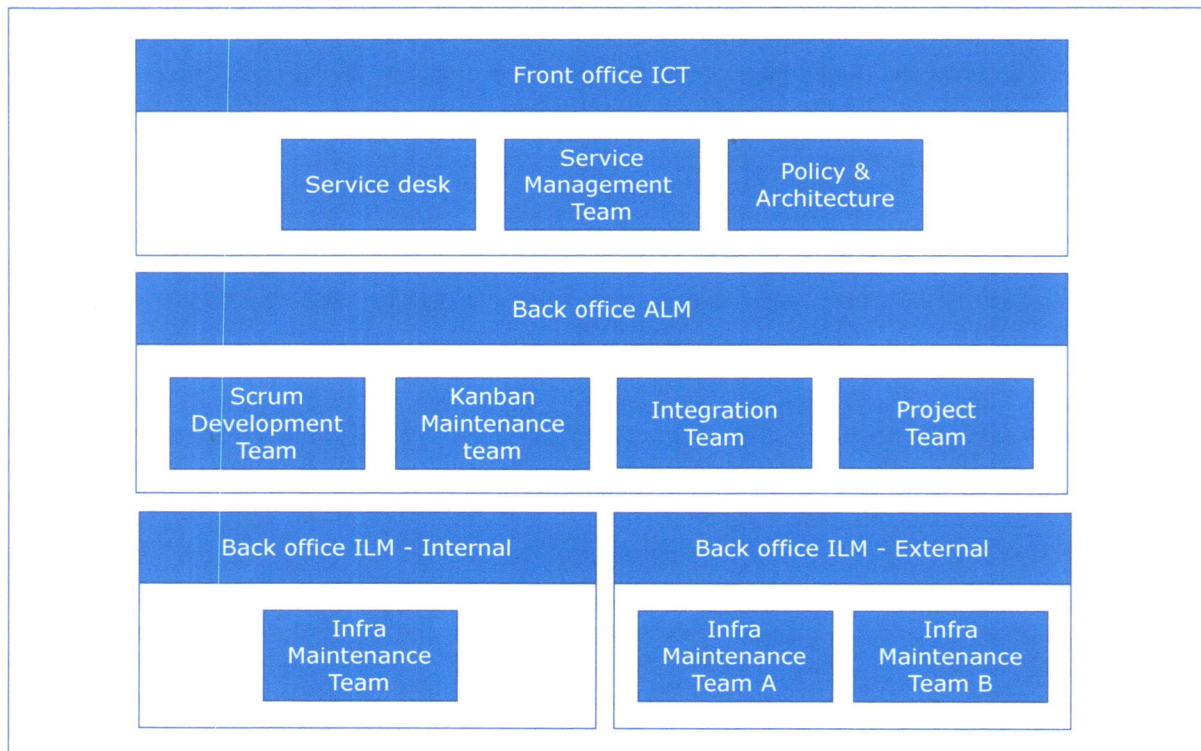

Figure 7-5, The ICT-organisation.

Front office ALM

The service desk is the (SPOC) for the end users of the case application. These end users are employees of the clients of the case organisation. The service desk receives the incidents and service requests and handles with them as much as possible themselves. Only if a reproducible incident cannot be closed within the set SLA norm it will be passed on to the Kanban maintenance team. A problem ticket is then created. From the other incidents, the team makes a Pareto analysis to identify problems and have them solved by the Kanban maintenance team. The service management team is responsible for customer contact at tactical level. The desired service level is agreed with the customers and recorded in an SLA. At this level, financial settlement also takes place on the basis of licenses purchased by the customer. The management gives substance to the policy. On that basis architecture establishes a target architecture. The target architecture results in a roadmap that forms the basis of the product backlog of the Scrum development teams.

Back office ALM

The front office directs the back office of ALM. The back office consists of an ALM domain and an ILM domain. Both domains consist of different teams. At the operational level, the service desk steers the Kanban management team. At tactical level, the account managers steer the product owners on the basis of the closed SLAs. And at the strategic level, the product owners are steered on the basis of the prepared roadmaps.

Scrum development team

There are four Scrum development teams. A Scrum development team consists of a product owner (1 FTE), a Scrum master (1 FTE) and an average of seven multifunctional developers and an integration tester. The product owner has been appointed dedicated. There is a back-up for the product owner in case the product owner is not available. A Scrum development team is responsible for the design, construction, testing and delivery of software to the integration team.

However, the distribution and implementation of the software is not done by the Scrum development team.

Kanban maintenance team

The Kanban maintenance team consists of a product owner (1 FTE), a Kanban master (1 FTE) and 16 multifunctional developers and integration testers. This team is split up into two Kanban teams, each with its own Kanban master and accountability area of the application. The Kanban teams are divided into the mid- and back-office areas. The Kanban master is a senior developer in the team. The Kanban maintenance team is responsible for maintaining the design, adjusting software, testing and delivering the software to the integration team. However, the distribution and implementation of the software is not done by the Kanban maintenance team.

Integration team

The integration team is responsible for the daily build and delivery of the software in the test and acceptance environment. This team also carries out the regression tests. Finally, this team is responsible for delivering a new release of the case application to the service desk. The service desk places the release on the portal where customers can download the software.

Service desk team

The service desk team consists of managers who form the first line for the service desk. They are responsible for the processes: incident management, problem management, configuration management (partly) and release management (partly).

Scope development and maintenance process

Table 7-6 shows the scope of the development process (Scrum development team) and the management process (Kanban maintenance team). A red cross means that at this level there is no relation to the development or management process. A green tick means that the development or management process does give substance to this.

Control level	Information Management	Application Management	Technical Management
Strategic	X	V (1)	X
Tactical	X	V (2)	X
Operational	X	V (3)	X
Innovation	X	V (4)	X

Table 7-6, Scope development process.

At strategic (first tick) and tactical level (second tick) the development process plays a role in the direction and planning. The actual core business of the development team is reflected by the realization of functionality (fourth check). The service management process is presented by the third tick.

7.5.5 *The service management processes*

SLAs

Specific agreements have been made for the application. There is a basic SLA for all customers. If customers wish, a golden SLA or platinum SLA can be purchased. The SLAs have no formal influence on the operation of the Kanban maintenance team. This is because the SLAs relate to the service desk. The Kanban maintenance team does, however, have KPIs and management controls on these KPI's. These KPIs are in line with the SLA norms.

Service management processes

All service management processes of ITIL are still used by the Kanban maintenance team. In that respect, the introduction of Scrum has made no changes.

Incidents

The incidents are reported at at the service desk.

The service desk checks whether the incident is reproducible and looks for a solution or a work around. For reproducible incidents that are not solvable within the SLA norm, a problem ticket is created. All problem tickets are offered to the Kanban maintenance team. Every week, the priority of incidents and problems is discussed by the service desk and the Kanban maintenance team.

Problems
The problem tickets are created by the service desk. All problem tickets go to the Kanban maintenance team. The Kanban maintenance team can also create problem tickets based on a Pareto analysis. The problems regarding software that was released less than six months ago are passed on to the concerned Scrum development team.

Changes
Adjustments in the application portfolio are decided on a strategic level. All changes are passed on to the Scrum development teams by means of a roadmap. They place user stories on the product backlog based on the roadmap. Change management or a CAB has not been organized for this. However, this was not the case before the introduction of Scrum.

In addition to the product owner, the Kanban maintenance team is one of the acceptors of the deliverables. They monitor the maintainability of the delivered software. To this end, the Kanban maintenance team participates in the focus sprint that will be carried out prior to a release. In this focus sprint, all teams involved in the lifecycle work together to make the case application production-ready. The integration team also ensures that the deliverables are installed in the acceptance and production environment on the basis of facilities provided by the ILM organisation.

The changes that the Kanban maintenance team implements to solve problems are registered in the service management tool. Due to the major overlap with the administration of the problem management process, it was decided to merge the problem management and change management process. The changes that the Kanban maintenance team implements are effected in the same development street as those of the Scrum development teams.

Release and deployment management
The Scrum development teams use a version management tool that contains the case application that is delivered. A sprint lasts three weeks and every three months a new release is delivered to the customer. For the Kanban maintenance team and the Scrum development teams, the same baseline is used that is compiled daily by the integration team into a new build. The modified code of both the Kanban maintenance team and the Scrum development teams is also checked by an external organisation for compliance with the agreed code standards.

After three development sprints / maintenance sprints, the code is bundled in the form of a new release and a focus sprint follows to make the release production-ready. The new releases are placed on the portal by the service desk. From there, a customer can download the new release and take it into production, whether or not supported by the project team. The new release of the case application is also included in the SaaS service by the internal ILM management team.

The Kanban maintenance team and the Scrum development teams use the same tooling for the administration of the requirements, user stories and test cases. This prevents disruptions due to version control problems. All objects are also tagged so that they are identifiable in every environment.

7.5.6   Challenges and solutions
In the beginning, working with Scrum was unaccustomed because a release had to be delivered at fixed times. Employees also had to work multifunctional. The challenges for the coming period are to further develop the tooling or to purchase other tools. Integration is an important issue here. The Scrum development teams must ensure that no focus release sprint is needed. This also saves workload on the Kanban maintenance team. Finally, the Kanban maintenance team needs to develop further.

7.6 Case #6

This case organisation develops application software for organisations in the Netherlands. The part of this organisation described in this case is responsible for the entire lifecycle of an application that is offered to government organisations as a SaaS solution. In this case it is called the case application.

7.6.1 Introduction

We have traditionally worked with a development organisation that was organized on a project basis. The need for faster delivery times has increased in recent years. There was also a need for a better connection of the customer's wishes to the realization.

7.6.2 Organisation

The organisation has made a split between ALM and ILM. The ILM organisation consists of two internal management teams and an external supplier for the hosting of the case application. The ALM organisation consists of a service team and a Scrum team. The Scrum team has been specially designed for the delivery and maintenance of the case application.

7.6.3 Background

The ALM organisation works with market standards such as ITIL. From the shop floor came the awareness that giving substance to the realization of applications could take place better on the basis of Scrum. This bottom-up choice of applying Scrum is still in an orientation phase in which the organisation is still looking for the best way to collaborate between information system development, information system maintenance and exploitation. The implementation of Scrum is therefore evolutionary. When the team was formed, the control is organized Caluwé blue and the implementation of the Scrum work process Caluwé green. What has helped a great deal here is that employees from the service team are involved in the Scrum team. This allows the interaction to be regulated very quickly.

7.6.4 The organisation

Figure 7-6 gives an overview of the ALM organisation. Within the ALM organisation, a split has been made between the front office and the back office. At the operational level, the front office consists of a service desk that handles incidents and service requests. They also create problem records. On a tactical level, a service management team has been set up consisting of service coordinators. The product owner of the Scrum development team also acts at this level to collect and align the requirements of the stakeholders. The service management team has various roles such as those of service level manager and availability management. At a strategic level, there is steering of the management of managed services. They determine the application portfolio and compile the roadmaps in collaboration with architects.

The ALM back office consists of a service team and a Scrum development team. The development team transfers the developed or changed application components to the service team. The service team ensures that these are implemented in the infrastructure, ILM facilitates but the service team does the deployment itself.

Front office ALM

The service desk is the SPOC for the end users of the information system. The service desk receives the incidents and the feature requests. The service management team is responsible for the tactical planning of the service. Management of the managed services is responsible for the product portfolio and the guidance of the ALM and ILM back office. An application architect and a technical architect are also working in this team.

Back office ALM

The front office directs the back office of ALM. The back office consists of an ALM domain and an ILM domain. Both domains consist of two teams.

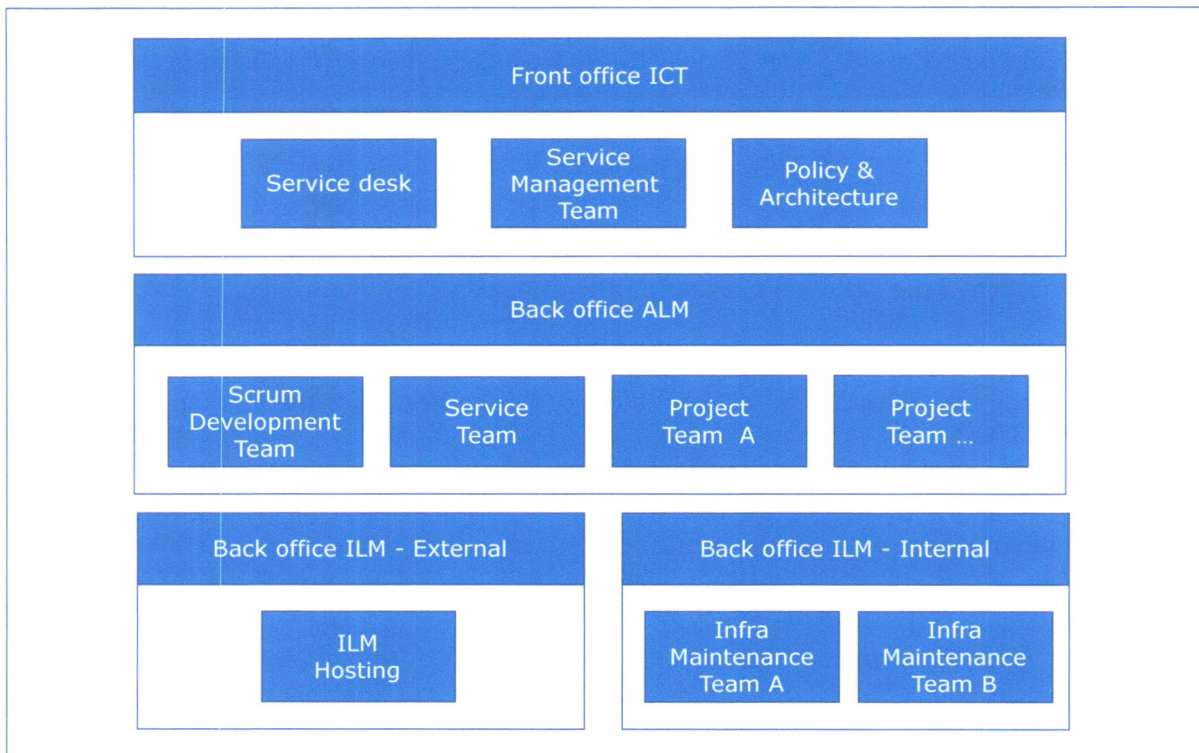

Figure 7-6, The ICT-organisation.

Scrum team

The Scrum team consists of a product owner (0.4 FTE), a Scrum master (0.3 FTE), two developers, a tester and an application specialist / application architect. The product owner has been appointed dedicated. There is a back-up for the product owner in case the product owner is not available. The Scrum team is responsible for the design, construction, testing and delivery of software. However, the distribution and implementation of the software is not done by the Scrum team The team members are not multifunctional. So, specialists have been assigned to specific tasks.

Service team

The service team consists of managers who form the 2nd line for the service desk. However, they also carry out changes to the applications delivered by the Scrum team If the size of the change is too large, it is put on the product backlog of the Scrum development team. There is no sharp ratio to distribute the workload. However, a limit of 300 hours has been set whereby the consideration must be made to redirect the change to the development team.

Scope development process

Figure 7-7 shows the scope of the development process. A red cross means that at this level there is no relation to the development process. A green tick means that the development process does give substance to this.

Control level	Information Management	Application Management	Technical Management
Strategic	X	V (3)	X
Tactical	X	V (4)	X
Operational	V (1)	V (5)	X
Innovation	V (2)	V (6)	X

Table 7-7, Scope development process.

The first tick shows the information management run-organisation processes that are executed by the Scrum team. The second tick is the operational management of the development process. At strategic (third level) and tactical level (fourth check) the development process plays a small role in the direction and planning; therefore, they are not shown bold. The actual core business is reflected by the realization of functionality (sixth tick) supplemented with the run-processes (tick five).

7.6.5 The service management processes

SLAs
Specific agreements have been made for the application.

Service management processes
All service management processes of ITIL are still used by the maintenance team. In that respect, the introduction of Scrum has made no changes.

Incidents
The incidents are reported at at the service desk. The service desk routes the incidents to the service team or to one of the two ILM teams. The incidents are picked up by the maintainers who work in the service team.

Problems
The problems can be initiated by the service desk. However, the solution is realized by the service team.

Changes
Adjustments in the application portfolio are decided on a strategic level. The roadmap in question is drawn up for each application. Not all changes are realized in an Agile Scrum manner. So, there is still waterfall and Agile Scrum development. In the case of the case application, the Agile Scrum development was chosen for the first time. Each time a release is delivered by using a miniature waterfall in a number of sprints. In addition to the product owner, the service team is one of the acceptors of the deliverables. They monitor the maintainability of the delivered software. The service team also ensures that the deliverables are installed in the acceptance and production environment on the basis of facilities provided by the ILM organisation.

Release and deployment management
The Scrum team uses a version management tool that contains the delivered software. With every release, the entire application is provided with a baseline tag and compiled. The service team is responsible for the installation and configuration in the acceptance and production environment. In the case of defects demonstrated in the acceptance environment, these must be resolved, and a new build must be transferred. Of course, this means that branching is necessary because the Scrum development team may already be making adjustments or expansions. But the service team must also adapt the code of existing functionality to remedy incidents.

7.6.6 Challenges and solutions
In the beginning, working with Scrum was unaccustomed because a release had to be delivered at fixed times. This did not always work because the employees involved could not be deployed full-time in the Scrum team. There is too much pressure from the organisation to justify this. Therefore, a release has not always been delivered. Furthermore, there were many discussions about who is responsible for what. There is a lot of commitment from the higher management of the organisation.

7.7 Case #7

This case organisation develops application software for organisations in, but especially outside the Netherlands. The application software is built around an engine developed by the case organisation itself. The engine is being developed further on the basis of a classic project approach. The application software is developed through Agile Scrum. This team is discussed in this case. In this case the different applications are called the case application.

7.7.1 Introduction
We have traditionally worked with a development organisation that was organized on a project basis. In 2014 the need for iterations increased because it helped to get a better grip on the end result (faster jump in the development process and less unnecessary things). The time-to-market was not a primary drive.

7.7.2 Organisation
The case organisation provides the engine and the case application as software products. The customer is responsible for the integration with their own applications and for the infrastructure to host the software. The ALM organisation is split into an engine team that works on a project basis (waterfall) and an application software team that works according to Agile Scrum. The Scrum team has been specially designed for the delivery and maintenance of the case application.

7.7.3 Background
The ALM organisation works with market standards such as ITIL. From the shop floor came the awareness that giving substance to the realization of applications could better take place on the basis of Scrum. During the formation of the team, a self-organizing team was chosen (Caluwé green). Because the team must ensure that the case application connects and continues to connect to the engine, agreements have been made about the use of tooling.

7.7.4 The organisation
An overview of the ALM organisation was given in Figure 7-7.

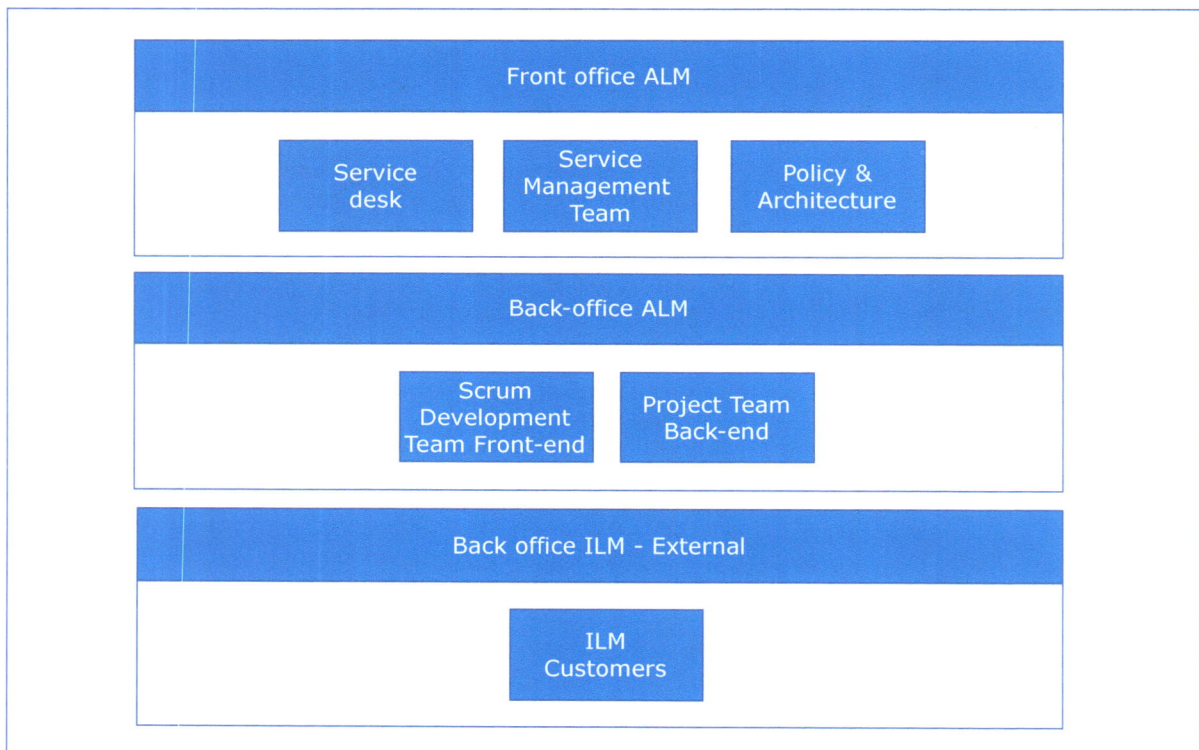

Figure 7-7, The ICT-organisation.

Within the ALM organisation, a split has been made between the front office and the back office. At the operational level, the front office consists of a service desk that handles incidents, service requests and feature requests. At the tactical level, SLAs are agreed with the customers who purchases the software. The product owner of the Scrum development team also acts at this level to collect and coordinate the requirements of the stakeholders. The management team and the architects are steering on the strategic level. They put together the application portfolio and also give substance to the roadmap per application.

The ALM back office consists of two development teams. Each development team is responsible for the entire lifecycle of their products. Both teams have complete control over the development and test environment. The integration tests of the engine and the application software take place in the acceptance environment. There is no production environment because the software is only in production at customers. A new release takes place once a year.

Front office ALM

The line manager of both development teams is the SPOC for the customer and acts as a service desk. This is possible because the products that operate worldwide are very stable and hardly cause disturbances or questions during use. The line manager receives the incidents, service requests and feature requests. The SLAs with the customer are agreed by the line manager. In addition to the service level manager, the service management team is formed by the participation of the architect and the designers during the initiation phase of a new product. They determine the high level non-functional requirements and indicate which measures must be taken to ensure that they comply with the SLA norms. The most important non-functional requirements are the resolution time of incidents and the performance of the software. Finally, policy & architecture is responsible for controlling the innovation. This gremium consists of the CIO, the product manager and the line managers of development and sales.

Back-office ALM

The front office directs the back office of ALM. The back office consists of two development teams.

Scrum-team

The Scrum team consists of a product owner (1 FTE), a Scrum master (1 FTE) and 5 developers. The product owner has been appointed dedicated. There is no back-up for the product owner in case the product owner is not available. The Scrum team is responsible for the design, construction, testing and delivery of software. However, the distribution and implementation of the software is not done by the Scrum team. The team members are partly multifunctional. So, specialists have been assigned to specific tasks. The Scrum team is also responsible for the maintenance of the software in terms of incidents and feature requests.

Scope development process

Table 7-8 shows the scope of the development process. A red cross means that at this level there is no relation to the development process. A green tick means that the development process does give substance to this.

Control level	Information Management	Application Management	Technical Management
Strategic	X	V (1)	X
Tactical	X	X	X
Operational	X	V (2)	X
Innovation	X	V (3)	X

Table 7-8, Scope development process.

The first tick indicates the compilation of the product portfolio by the product owner. The second tick indicates the operational task of the development team regarding incident management. The third and final tick concerns the actual work of the development team, being the development of new functionality.

7.7.5   The service management processes

SLAs

Specific agreements have been made for the application.

Service management processes

All service management processes of ITIL are still used after the introduction of Agile Scrum. In that respect, the introduction of Scrum has made no changes.

Incidents
The incidents are reported at at the service desk. The service desk routes the incidents to one of the two ALM teams.

Problems
No problem management process is used. There are too few incidents for this.

Changes
Adjustments in the application portfolio are decided on a strategic level. A related roadmap is drawn up for each application. The product owner is from that point responsible for filling the product backlog. In addition to the product owner, there is a CAB.
This CAB is formed by the same members as the policy & architecture team. They monitor the maintainability of the delivered software on based the results of the acceptance tests.

Release and deployment management
The Scrum team uses a version management tool that contains the software that is delivered. With every change in the version management tool, a build is automatically created by the build server. Branching is rare, at most in the event of an incident that needs to be solved at customers in production.

7.7.6   Challenges and solutions
The current set-up of the Scrum team is good. In the future, it will still be necessary to examine to what extent the service management processes have to be further formalized. However, with the current workload, this is not really necessary.

7.8 Case #8
This case organisation provides financial services in the Netherlands. The part of this organisation described in this case is responsible for the entire lifecycle of a portal application.

7.8.1   Introduction
We have traditionally worked with a development organisation that was organized on a project basis. In recent years the need for faster time to market and less procedural overhead has increased, and a start has been made with the introduction of Scrum.

7.8.2   Organisation
The organisation has made a split between ALM and ILM. ILM has been outsourced to two suppliers. One ILM organisation maintains the server park and the branch network. The other supplier maintains the portal. The ALM organisation consists of a front office and a back office.

7.8.3   Background
The ALM organisation works with market standards such as ITIL. From the business the need arose to succeed in creating a faster time to market. Here a Kanban approach has been chosen. This business-driven approach to apply Kanban is still in an orientation phase in which the organisation is still looking for the best way of working together between the service transition & service operations team on the one hand and the application management team on the other. During the formation of the team, the control was organized Caluwé green.

7.8.4   The organisation
Figure 7-8 gives an overview of the ICT organisation. Within the ALM organisation, a split has been made between the front office and the back office. At the operational level, the front office consists of a service desk that handles incidents and service requests. They also create problem records. On a tactical level, a service management team has been set up consisting of service coordinators. They have various roles such as those of service level manager and availability management. At the strategic level, there are two architects who give direction to the change in the back office and the suppliers.

The ALM back offices consist of a Kanban development team, a service team, project team and application management teams.

The development team can take certain deliveries into production themselves. Other deliveries require the assistance of the ILM internet provider. Where there are connections with the back-office applications, there is coordination with them.

Front office ALM

The service desk is the SPOC for the end users of the portal service. The service desk receives the incidents and feature requests and registers them in the service management tool. At a tactical level, the service coordinator of the service management team directs the back-office teams, as well as the external ILM suppliers.

Back office ALM

The back office consists internally of an ALM domain and externally of an ILM domain. There is one Kanban development team and a number of project development teams. The project development teams work in accordance with the waterfall model. The service team works in accordance with the ITIL management model. The back-office application maintenance teams are responsible for the lifecycle management of a suite of applications.

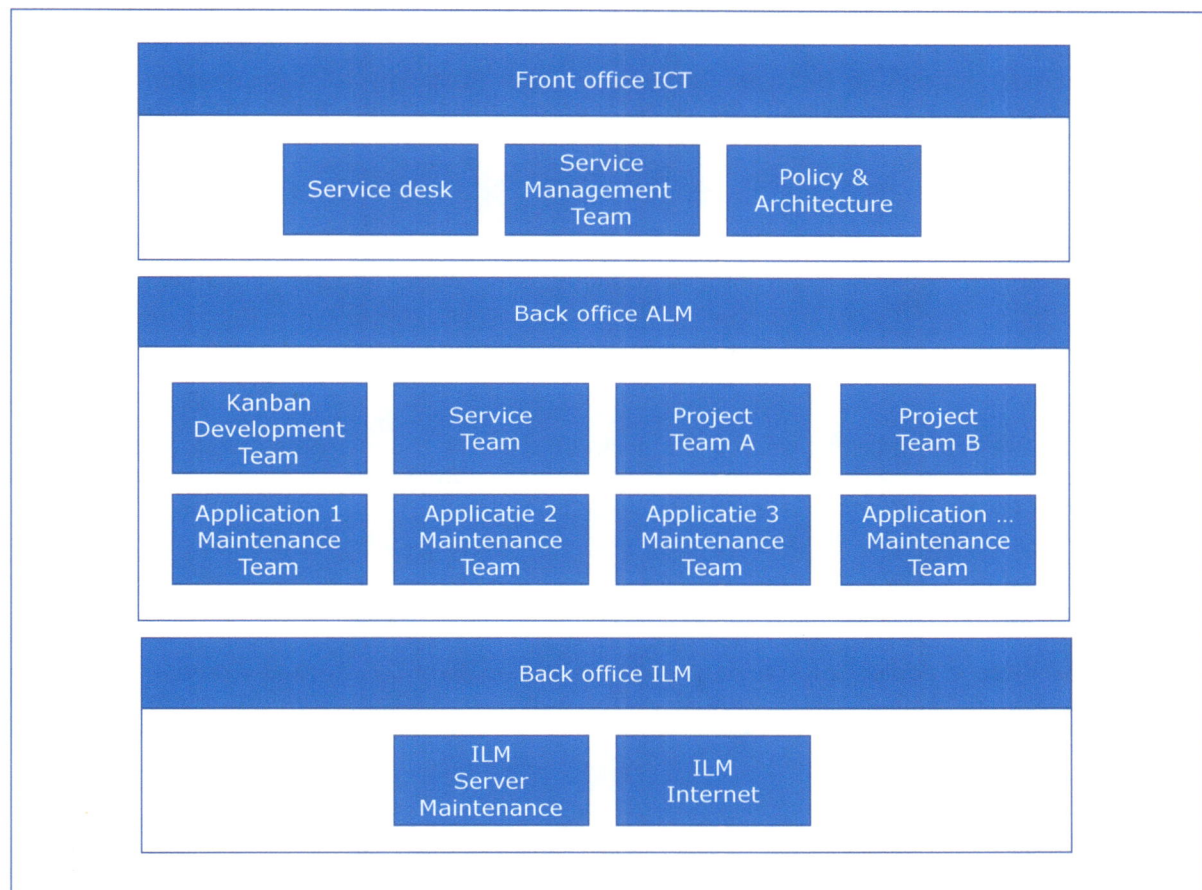

Figure 7-8, The ICT-organisation.

Kanban team

The Kanban team consists of a product owner (1 FTE), a Scrum master (0.5 FTE) and 17 people who work part-time in the Scrum team 7 employees work on extensions (additive management) and 10 employees on perfective management.

The Scrum team is responsible for the design, construction, configuration, testing and delivery of the (CMS) that forms the basis for the portal. The construction of the CMS takes place at the ILM internet provider.

Service team
The service team is not involved in the Kanban team in terms of service management processes. There are meetings to exchange information.

Scope development process
Table 7-9 shows the scope of the development process. A red cross means that at this level there is no relation to the development process. A green tick means that the development process does give substance to this.

Control level	Information Management	Application Management	Technical Management
Strategic	X	X	X
Tactical	X	X	X
Operational	X	V (1)	X
Innovation	X	**V (2)**	X

Table 7-9, Scope development process.

The development process in this case organisation is limited only to the development of new functionality, as the second tick shows. Some operational activities are still being performed as indicated by the first tick, which is why it is not shown bold.

7.8.5 The service management processes

SLAs
SLAs have been agreed between the internal customer (marketing) and the Kanban team.

Service management processes
Only the incident management process and the request fulfilment of ITIL are used.

Incidents
The incidents are reported at at the service desk. This routes the incidents to the Kanban team. Most incidents are immediately resolved and closed in Clientele. The others are included in the Leankit tool of the Kanban team.

Problems
Are not used.

Changes
From the back-office application management teams, it is carefully checked whether there is an impact of a change on the portal. This also takes place in the Kanban team. But there is no other change administration than the epics and features of the Kanban team that are recorded in the Kanban tool.

Release and deployment management
The CMS requires changes at various levels. At the content level, the customer can make changes to the CMS himself. Where the structure of the CMS needs to be worked on to implement a change, the Kanban team is used. The ILM internet provider builds these and distributes these. Where links are with back-office applications, these are coordinated with the involved application management teams.

7.8.6 Challenges and solutions
The current method is well applicable for the portal function. However, as soon as it develops further, it is important to increase governance and structure. A reorganisation plan is being written for this purpose.

7.9 Case #9

This case organisation develops software components for internal customers. The part of this organisation described in this case is responsible for the entire lifecycle of the software components. The components are designed by a separate Scrum team. The components are built by another Scrum team. The components supplied are used by a configuration team that configures the components and has them taken into production.

7.9.1 Introduction

We have traditionally worked with a development organisation that was organized on a project basis. In recent years the need increased to respond flexibly to the demand. The production of the software had to become more predictable.

7.9.2 Organisation

The organisation has made a split between ALM and ILM. The ILM organisation consists of various maintenance teams. The ALM organisation consists of a change and run teams. The change teams apply Scrum.

7.9.3 Background

The ALM organisation works with market standards such as ITIL. From the shop floor came the awareness that giving substance to the realization of applications could be done better on the basis of Scrum. This bottom-up choice of applying Scrum has already quite far been implemented. When the teams were formed, the control is organized Caluwé blue and the implementation of the Scrum work process Caluwé green.

7.9.4 The organisation

In Figure 7-9 an overview is given of the ALM organisation.

Within the ALM organisation, a split has been made between the front office and the back office. At the operational level, the front office consists of a service desk that handles incidents, service requests and changes. The service desk is also responsible for implementing the problem management process and the service asset & configuration management process. On a tactical level, a service management team has been set up, consisting of service coordinators. Here the planning of the service provision takes place and the SLA, OLA's and underpinning contracts are drawn up.

The product owners are line managers in the information management organisation. The product owner also acts on the tactical level to collect and align the requirements of the stakeholders. The service management team has various roles such as those of service level manager and availability management. At a strategic level, there is steering of policy and architecture.

The ALM back office consists of a software component factory. Four different types of Scrum teams have been identified, namely the component design teams, the construction teams, the back-end application teams and finally the teams that configure the components to use them for the ICT services to be offered. This case concerns the description of the Scrum team that builds a new component.

Front office ALM

The service desk is the SPOC for the end users of the information system. The service desk receives the incidents, service requests and changes.
The service management team is responsible for the tactical planning of the service provisioning. Policy & Architecture is responsible for indicating the direction on the basis of a portfolio and defining a target architecture.

Back office ALM - Change

The front office directs the back office of ALM. The back office consists of an ALM domain and an ILM domain. Only the ALM domain works on the basis of Scrum. The ALM domain is split into a change subdomain and a run subdomain. A subdomain consists of a number of Scrum teams.

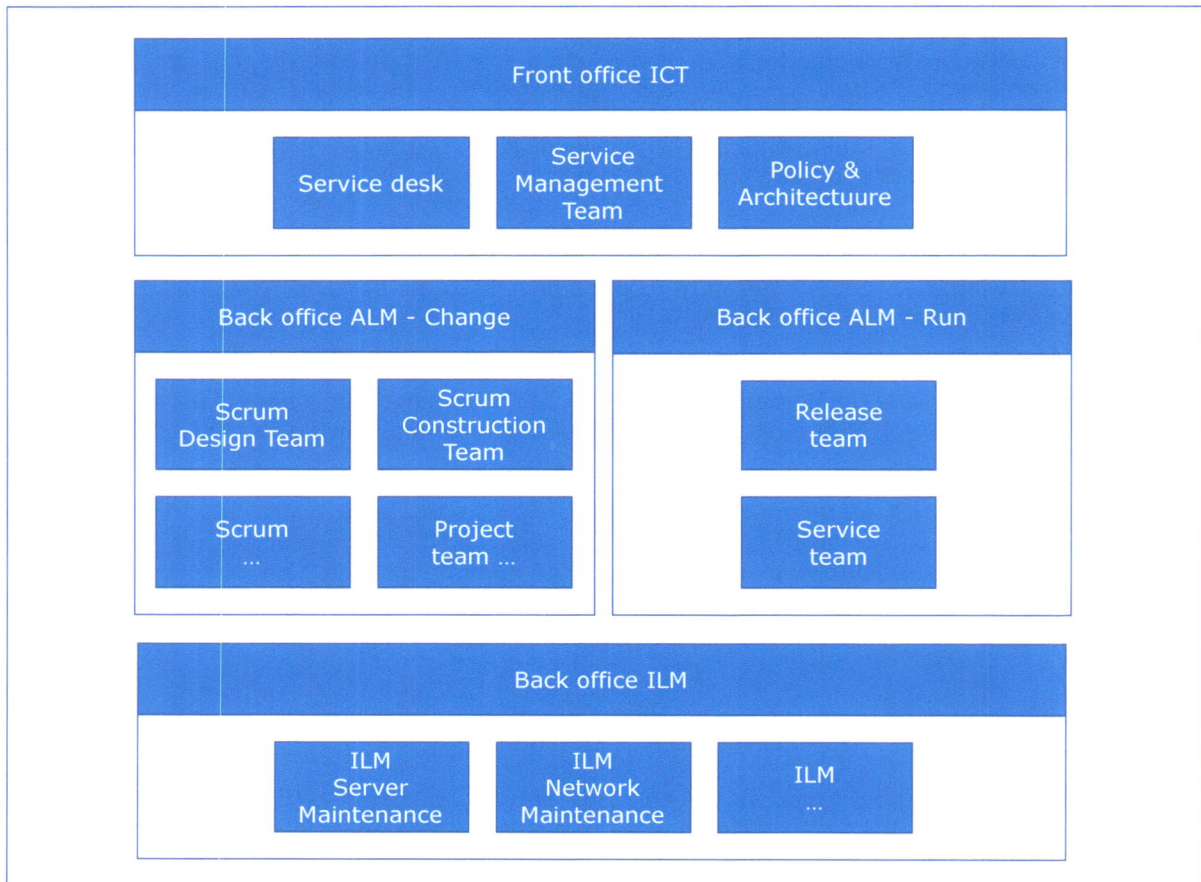

Figure 7-9, The ICT-organisation.

Scrum team

For the realization of a component, a design team and a construction team are required. The backlog is controlled by (1) delegated product owner. Each team is managed by (1) Scrum master. Together, the two teams consist of (2) testers, (11) developers and (1) application / infrastructure specialist. A delegated product owner has been appointed who is in contact with the product owner who communicates with the business. There is one product owner. There is a back-up for the delegated product owner. The Scrum building team is responsible for building, testing and delivering a complete component. However, the distribution and implementation of the software is not done by the Scrum team, but by the run organisation. The team members are not fully multifunctional. So, specialists have been assigned to specific tasks.

Back office ALM – Run

The run subdomain consists of a release team and a service team, as shown in Figure 7-9.

Release team

The release team is responsible for the distribution and implementation of software.

Service team

The service team consists of managers who form the 2nd line for the service desk. However, they do not make any changes to the application components that have been delivered by the Scrum team.

Scope development process

In Table 7-10 the scope of the development process is shown. A red cross means that at this level there is no relation to the development process. A green tick means that the development process does give substance to this.

Control level	Information Management	Application Management	Technical Management
Strategic	X	X	X
Tactical	V (1)	X	X
Operational	X	X	X
Innovation	X	**V (2)**	X

Table 7-10, Scope development process.

The first tick reflects the planning of the newly developed functionality. The second tick indicates the execution of the development process itself. The biggest effort of the development process is represented by the second tick; therefore, the first tick is not shown bold.

7.9.5   The service management processes

SLAs
Architectural designs are made for new services. Also, the design teams are requested to include the non-functional requirements. SLAs are prepared on this basis. However, the construction team no longer has to deal with NFRs per feature. However, requirements are set on the DoD for the performance of the entire component. These are tested by the run organisation in the acceptance environment.

Service management processes
All service management processes of ITIL are still used by the run organisation. The change organisation is part of a number of processes but does not work in a process-oriented manner.

Incidents
The incidents are reported at at the service desk. The service desk routes the incidents to the service team. The construction team has 10% of the time available for resolving incidents that the run organisation cannot resolve.

Problems
The problems can be initiated by the service desk. However, the solution is done by the service team. The root-cause analysis often takes place in the construction team.

Changes
Adjustments in the application portfolio are decided on a strategic level. The related roadmap of components is drawn up for each application. Not all changes are picked up in an Agile Scrum manner. So still waterfall development and Agile Scrum development are taking place. However, Agile Scrum development is used for the construction of components. Every two weeks a new build is delivered to the run organisation. The construction organisation is only responsible for the D-T environments. In addition to the product owner, the service team is one of the acceptors of the deliverables. They monitor the maintainability of the delivered software. The service team also ensures that the deliverables are installed in the acceptance and production environment on the basis of facilities provided by the ILM organisation.

Release and deployment management
The Scrum team uses a version management tool that contains the software that is delivered. With each release the entire component is provided with a baseline tag and compiled. The service team is responsible for the installation and configuration in the acceptance and production environment. In the event of defects demonstrated in the acceptance environment, these must be resolved, and a new build must be transferred.

7.9.6   Challenges and solutions
At this moment the organisation is looking at the introduction of continuous integration / continuous delivery.

7.10 Case #10

This case organisation is part of a group of financial organisations. The team described in this case is responsible for the entire lifecycle of an ESB.

7.10.1 Introduction

We have traditionally worked with a development organisation that uses standard project management tooling and a service management organisation that applies ITIL processes. In recent years, the need to get a better grip on the workflow has increased. There was also a need to further streamline the roll-out from development to acceptance and production.

7.10.2 Organisation

The organisation has made a split between ALM and ILM. ALM is assigned to an ALM organisation and ILM is assigned to the ILM organisation. ALM includes both the construction and the maintenance of applications that are then rolled out and maintained in collaboration with the ILM organisation.

7.10.3 Background

The ALM organisation works with market standards such as standard project management tooling and ITIL. From the work floor came the awareness that giving substance to the realization of applications can be done better on the basis of Scrum and / or Kanban. This bottom-up choice of applying Scrum has expanded over the past years and various departments are currently working with a combination of Scrum and Kanban. Standard project management tooling is still used for some projects. The implementation of Scrum is therefore evolutionary and can be characterized as Caluwé green on the work floor and Caluwé blue on management level.

7.10.4 The organisation

In Figure 7-10 an overview is given of the ALM organisation. Due to the size, a split has been made within the ALM organisation between the Front office and the Back office. At the operational level, the Front office consists of a Service Desk, at a tactical level it consists of a Service Management Team and at a strategic level it consists of a Policy and Architecture Team.

The back office consists of various Scrum teams that each (partly) serve a business department and are therefore responsible for a part of the product portfolio. There are also generic Scrum teams like those for the ESB. The ILM organisation is not based on Scrum or Kanban.

Front office ALM

The service desk is the SPOC for the end users. The service desk receives the incidents and the change requests. On a tactical level, the service management organisation recognizes the planning processes of ITIL. The policy & architecture team is responsible for the product portfolio and the steering of the back office.

Back office ALM

The front office directs the back office of ALM. The back office consists of several business departments. Each business department consists of one or more Scrum teams.

Scrum- / Kanban-teams

There is a product owner per team (usually from the business). A team is supervised by a Scrum master and an Agile coach. For the rest, a team consists of developers who take care of the design, construction and testing of applications. In principle, the teams are multifunctional.

For the ESB team, the product owner is the line manager. The ESB Scrum team delivers a new version of the ESB every three weeks on the basis of requests from projects that other Scrum teams carry out or on the basis of changes that come from the front office. In some cases, changes must be implemented to resolve incidents.

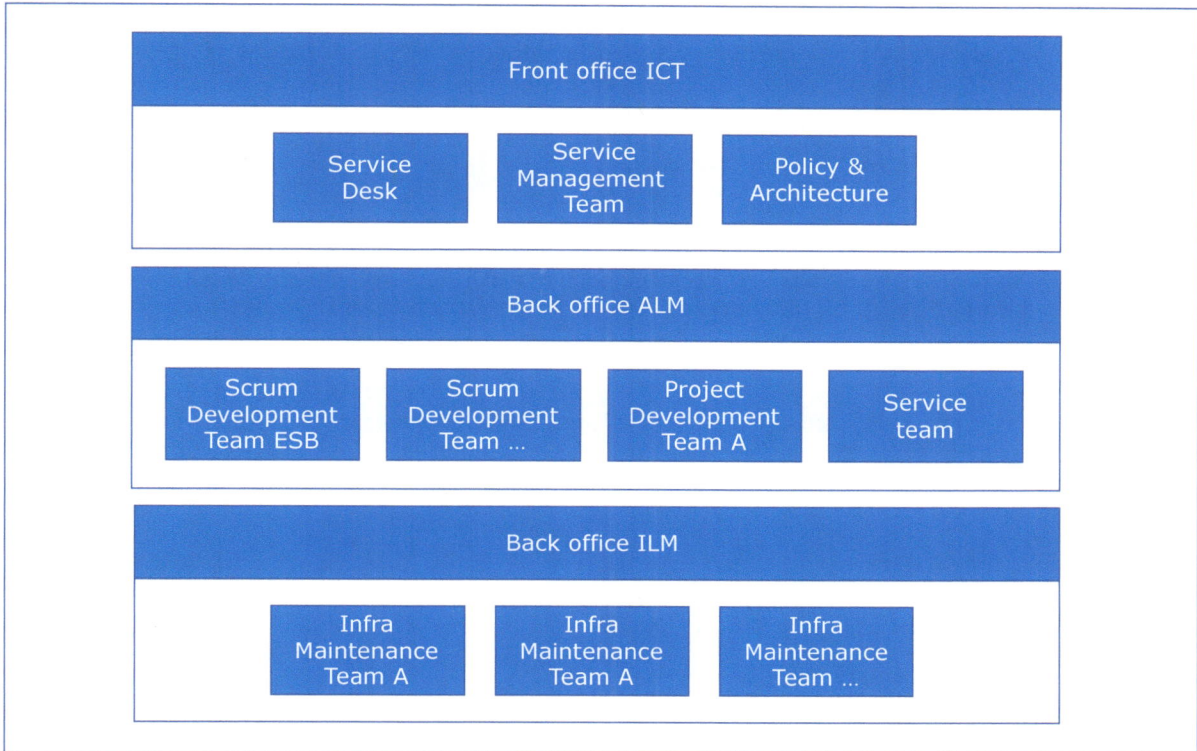

Figure 7-10, The ALM-organisation.

However, the distribution and implementation of the software is not done by the ESB Scrum team. The team members are not fully multifunctional. So, specialists have been assigned to specific tasks.

Scope development process
Table 7-11 shows the scope of the development process of the involved team in the research. A red cross means that at this level there is no relation to the development process. A green tick means that the development process does give substance to this. The first and third tick indicate the tactical direction on the development. The second and fourth ticks represent the development of the new functionality.

Control level	Information Management	Application Management	Technical Management
Strategic	X	X	X
Tactical	V (1)	V (3)	X
Operational	X	X	X
Innovation	V (2)	V (4)	X

Table 7-11, Scope development process.

7.10.5 The service management processes

SLAs
An SLA has been agreed with the business for ESB service provision. This is being agreed with the business by the service level manager of the service management organisation. OLAs and Underpinning Contracts (UC) have also been drawn up for the ESB service, but they are also drawn up by the service management organisation. With a new application and / or service, the high level NFR is initially looked at from an architecture perspective. Based on this, implementation choices are made, and a functional and technical design is drawn up.

The product owner has no real influence on the NFRs. These therefore do not affect the Scrum team. However, the SLA norms are monitored by component and End-to-End (E2E) monitoring.

Service management processes
All management processes of ITIL are still used by the service management team. In that respect, the introduction of Scrum has not brought any changes.

Incidents
The incidents are reported at at the service desk. The service desk routes the incidents to the Scrum teams involved. The incidents are backlogged and prioritized by the product owner. The incidents are then picked up by developers working in the Scrum teams. There is no question of a fast-lane approach.

Problems
The Scrum team does a regular check to determine which escaped defects recur and whether a SIP should be started for that. Furthermore, this is a management task that is performed by the service team.

Changes
Adjustments in the application portfolio are decided at policy & architecture level. The related roadmap drawn up for each application. The product owner is then responsible for the realization and maintenance.

7.10.6 Challenges and solutions
There are still many improvements to be made. We are currently looking at continuous integration / continuous delivery. This should help to speed up the transition of T / A and A / P. Herewith is also looked at a tooling that can support the entire lifecycle from wish to implementation. Portfolio management is now being worked on.

Appendices

Appendix A, Scrum self-assessment

1. Introduction

This appendix describes the self-assessment to determine the maturity of the Scrum development process. This chapter describes the scope, purpose, structure and operation of the self-assessment. The next chapter contains the assessment questions.

1.1 Scope

The successful organisation of a Scrum development process is mainly human work. The team organizes itself. Nevertheless, generic aspects can be recognized by such a Scrum process. The work performed by the team can be divided into maturity stages. Getting a Scrum development process in order is not a sinecure, especially when the Scrum teams need to share information with each other and therefore have to coordinate the implementation. It takes a lot of time and perseverance to get the team to an effective and efficient introduction and to hold on to it. The drafting of a plan of approach for the implementation of the Scrum development process is therefore an important tool.

A useful approach here is to divide the plan of action into a number of phase plans, each phase giving substance to a certain maturity level of the Scrum development process. To determine whether a level has been reached, a measuring rod of scales must be used. The self-assessment can be used for this purpose. This assessment contains a number of questions for each level of maturity, on the basis of which it can be determined to what extent the Scrum development process meets the maturity level.

The questionnaire can be used by the Scrum master in the form of a self-assessment and by an auditor in the form of an audit questionnaire. The structure of the questions is kept the same as the ITIL v2 self-assessment, as published on the OGC website [http: OGC]. However, the questions are more detailed, because they are provided with help questions.

2. Self-assessment questions

1.1 Level 1, Prerequisites

Q#	Question List	Y/N	M/O
Q1.0/1	Has a Scrum team been established that produces new information systems and / or changes to them in an Agile manner? Q1. Which Scrum teams are established? Q2. Which (type) of applications are involved?		M
Q1.0/2	Have you identified the customers for your development services? Q1. Which customer group do you recognize? Q2. Are all customers assigned to a product owner? Q3. Where are the services provided described?		O
Q1.0/3	Has the interface with the customer been identified? Q1. What can a customer request e.g. features / stories / service requests etcetera? Q2. Is this interface also identified e.g. the product owner or the service desk?		O

Q#	Question List	Y/N	M/O
	The minimum score to reach this level is: 'Y' for all ('M') questions plus one 'Y' for the ('O') questions.		**No**

Table A-1, Assessment level 1.

1.2 Level 1.5, Management intention

Q#	Question List	Y/N	M/O
Q1.5/1	Is the purpose and benefits of the Scrum development process disseminated in the organisation? Q1. How can this be proven?		M
Q1.5/2	Have control data been defined to make the Scrum process measurable? Q1. Is the backlog controlled by the product owner? Q2. What is the reliability of the planning of the entries on the product backlog?		O
Q1.5/3	Are there any agreements about the sprint lead time and the amount of story points that are processed in a sprint? Q1. How is it managed and reported?		O
	The minimum score to reach this level is: 'Y' for all ('M') questions plus one 'Y' for the ('O') questions.		**No**

Table A-2, Assessment level 1,5.

1.3 Level 2, Process functionality

Q#	Question List	Y/N	M/O
Q2.0/1	Are responsibilities assigned to the various Scrum development process activities (formally ratified) and is the organisation aware of this)? Q1. Who is the product owner and who is the Scrum master? Q2. Are the tasks, responsibilities and powers of these roles described?		M
Q2.0/2	Has the scope of the Scrum development process been established in terms of products and services? Q1. Which products are supported? Q2. Which services have been recognized?		M
Q2.0/3	Are there mechanisms for monitoring the lead time of entries on the product backlog and the sprint backlog? Q1. How does monitoring take place and how do you review this?		M
Q2.0/4	Are all feature requests from the customer verified for applicability and authorization? Q1. How do you determine what rights a customer has have?		M
Q2.0/5	Do you have a procedure for handling the feature request from request until implementation?		M

Q#	Question List	Y/N	M/O
Q2.0/6	Do you have a mechanism to improve the Scrum process (sprint retrospective at the end of a sprint)? Q1. How do you deal with this? Q2. Who controls them?		O
Q2.0/7	Do you have a mechanism for carrying out continuous integration, regression testing and continuous delivery? Q1. Which mechanism are used, for example, a DTAP environment? Q2. Has a complete flow been defined, for example integration, regression testing and deployment?		O
	The minimum score to reach this level is: 'Y' for all ('M') questions plus one 'Y' for the ('O') questions.	No	

Table A-3, Assessment level 2.

1.4 Level 2.5, Internal integration

Q#	Question List	Y/N	M/O
Q2.5/1	Do you compare the delivered deliverables with the originally (non) functional requirements? Q1. Do you register requirements, for example in the format of a user story?		M
Q2.5/2	Do you have a mechanism to reuse or update the (non) functional requirements regarding an application in case of a new increment? Q1. Do you determine the impact of a feature based on existing requirements?		M
Q2.5/3	Do you use regression tests based on the requirements to determine whether the functionality and quality that have not been changed still meet the requirements? Q1. Has a relationship been made between requirements on the one hand and acceptance criteria and test cases on the other? Q2. Is a check done in the DoD to determine whether the set requirements have been met?		O
	The minimum score to reach this level is: 'Y' for all ('M') questions plus one 'Y' for the ('O') questions.	No	

Table A-4, Assessment level 2,5.

1.5 Level 3, Products

Q#	Question List	Y/N	M/O
Q3.0/1	Are the standard acceptance reports regularly created and submitted to the stakeholders? Q1. Which acceptance test types are recognized (Functional Acceptance Test (FAT), User Acceptance Test (UAT) or Performance Stress Test (PST))?		M

Q#	Question List	Y/N	M/O
	Q2. Is this managed??		
Q3.0/2	Is the service provision of the Scrum team explicitly defined and agreed, including service levels and service norms? Q1. Where are these recorded and managed?		O
Q3.0/3	Are the products and services recorded in a CMDB? Q1. Is an administration kept of CIs in order to determine the impact and the risk of the requested feature requests?		O
	The minimum score to reach this level is: 'Y' for all ('M') questions plus one 'Y' for the ('O') questions.		No

Table A-5, Assessment level 3.

1.6 Level 3.5, Quality control

Q#	Question List	Y/N	M/O
Q3.5/1	Are the standards and other quality criteria applied by the Scrum team documented? Q1. Is there an establishment of the DoD?		M
Q3.5/2	Are the team members of the Scrum team adequately trained? Q1. Which employees? Q2. Which education?		M
Q3.5/3	Does the organisation set and review SMART goals for the Scrum development process and is there a steering on areas for improvement? Q1. Which goals are recognized (functionality, quality and maturity)?		O
Q3.5/4	Does the organisation use any tools to support the Scrum development process? Q1. Which tools for continuous integration? Q2. Which tools for continuous delivery? Q3. Which tools for the regression tests?		O
	The minimum score to reach this level is: 'Y' for all ('M') questions plus one 'Y' for the ('O') questions.		No

Table A-6, Assessment level 3,5.

1.7 Level 4, Management information

Q#	Question List	Y/N	M/O
Q4.0/1	Do you provide management with information about service goals and up-to-date performance? Q1. Which service norms have been recognized and what are you reporting on? Q2. How do you report on the progress of feature requests and (epic) user stories?		M

Q#	Question List	Y/N	M/O
	Q3. Are measures taken to correct service standard deviations? Q4. Can the product owner initiate organisational changes?		
Q4.0/2	Do you provide management with information about trends in velocity and service level shortcomings?		M
Q4.0/3	Do you provide management with information about the provision of standard services?		O
Q4.0/4	Do you provide management with information about number of requests for new services or changes to existing services?		O
	The minimum score to reach this level is: 'Y' for all ('M') questions plus one 'Y' for the ('O') questions.	No	

Table A-7, Assessment level 4.

1.8 Level 4.5, External integration

Q#	Question List	Y/N	M/O
Q4.5/1	Does the product owner actively involve the service level manager and availability manager when setting up service norms?		M
Q4.5/2	Does the product owner consult service delivery and support processes such as capacity management and financial management when negotiating on service levels and service norms?		M
Q4.5/3	Is there a central risk and impact analysis for heterogeneous features (more Scrum teams are involved) through a change management process?		O
	The minimum score to reach this level is: 'Y' for all ('M') questions plus one 'Y' for the ('O') questions.	NO	

Table A-8, Assessment level 4,5.

1.9 Level 5, Customer interface

Q#	Question List	Y/N	M/O
Q5.0/1	Do you check with the user whether the activities carried out by the Scrum team adequately meet the needs of the business?		M
Q5.0/2	Do you check with the users if they are satisfied with the offered services? Q1. How do you check this?		M
Q5.0/3	Do you actively monitor the trend in customer satisfaction?		M
Q5.0/4	Do you use the information from customer satisfaction surveys in your service improvement agenda? Q1. How do you use the information?		
Q5.0/5	Do you monitor the perception of the customer regarding the Services offered to them? Q1. How do you monitor the perception of the customer?		M

Q#	Question List	Y/N	M/O
	Minimum score to reach this level is: 'Y' for all ('M') questions.	**No**	

Table A-9, Assessment level 5.

Appendix B, Change management self-assessment

1. Introduction

The same method is used for this self-assessment as for the Scrum self-assessment. As a result, the maturity of these processes has become comparable.

2. Self-assessment questions

2.1 Level 1, Prerequisite

Q#	Question List	Y/N	M/O
Q1.0/1	Have there been any Change Management (CM) activities recognized in the organisation (are they present, and do you execute these), such as registering RFCs, RFC analyses, RFC schedules? Q1. How do you register them?		M
Q1.0/2	Are CHM activities assigned to specific individuals or functional areas? Q1. Which activities? Q2. Which activities are executed?		O
Q1.0/3	Is there a procedure for notifying an RFC? Q1. Which procedure ?		O
	The minimum score to reach this level is: 'Y' for all ('M') questions plus one 'Y' for the ('O') questions.	No	

Table B-1, Assessment level 1.

2.2 Level 1.5, Management intention

Q#	Question List	Y/N	M/O
Q1.5/1	Are the objectives and benefits of the Change Management process known in the organisation? ? Q1. How can this be proven, there are illegal changes, etcetera. Q2. How do you know that there are no illegal changes?		M
Q1.5/2	Has the scope of the Change Management process been determined within the organisation? Q1. What is inside and what is outside, has that been defined? For example, a subset of the portfolios (application and infrastructure). Q2. Also, in terms of products?		O
Q1.5/3	Does the organisation have standards for, among other things, quality criteria for notifying and registering changes? Q1. What must be registered?		O

Q#	Question List	Y/N	M/O
	The minimum score to reach this level is: 'Y' for all ('M') questions plus one 'Y' for the ('O') questions.	**No**	

Table B-2, Assessment level 1,5.

2.3 Level 2, Process functionality

Q#	Question List	Y/N	M/O
Q2.0/1	Are the responsibilities for the various Change Management activities assigned? Q1. Who may do what?		M
Q2.0/2	Are the procedures for initiating changes followed? Q1. How?		M
Q2.0/3	Is there a procedure for approving, verifying and planning of the RFCs?		M
Q2.0/4	Are business and technical impact analyses always carried out?		M
Q2.0/5	Is the progress of the RFC adequately monitored by Change Management?		M
Q2.0/6	Will the successful implementation of an RFC be confirmed by Change Management?		O
Q2.0/7	Is there a procedure for the review of all RFCs?		O
Q2.0/8	Are adequate Change Management reports produced?		O
	The minimum score to reach this level is: 'Y' for all ('M') questions plus one 'Y' for the ('O') questions.	**No**	

Table B-3, Assessment level 2.

2.4 Level 2.5, Internal integration

Q#	Question List	Y/N	M/O
Q2.5/1	Are all RFCs initiated by the agreed Change Management channel?		M
Q2.5/2	Are the RFCs planned and prioritized centrally or by general agreement? Q1. Are the changes passed to the ICT service desk?		M
Q2.5/3	Do the RFCs represent the actual status they have? Q1. Is the tool up-to-date, how do you know that? Q2. Is there a flow control? Q3. Which statuses are recognized?		O
Q2.5/4	Are the causes of the RFC failures explicitly recorded and evaluated? Q1. Are follow-up incidents checked?		O
Q2.5/5	Are the successful changes reviewed against the original needs of the business? Q1. How?		O

Q#	Question List		
	The minimum score to reach this level is: 'Y' for all ('M') questions plus one 'Y' for the ('O') questions.		No

Table B-4, Assessment level 2,5.

2.5 Level 3, Products

Q#	Question List	Y/N	M/O
Q3.0/1	Are the formal change records maintained?		M
Q3.0/2	Is a schedule of approved RFCs regularly drawn up?		O
Q3.0/3	Are regular standard reports about RFCs created?		O
Q3.0/4	Are standards used to document RFCs? Q1. Risk analysis, impact analysis planning?		O
	The minimum score to reach this level is: 'Y' for all ('M') questions plus one 'Y' for the ('O') questions.		No

Table B-5, Assessment level 3.

2.6 Level 3.5, Quality control

Q#	Question List	Y/N	M/O
Q3.5/1	Are standards for other quality criteria for documentation of RFCs made explicit and applied?		M
Q3.5/2	Are personal responsibilities for the Change Management activities appropriately trained?		M
Q3.5/3	Have organisational objectives for the Change Management process been established and reviewed?		O
Q3.5/4	Does the organisation use any tools to support the Change Management process?		O
	The minimum score to reach this level is: 'Y' for all ('M') questions plus one 'Y' for the ('O') questions.		No

Table B-6, Assessment level 3,5.

2.7 Level 4, Management information

Q#	Question List	Y/N	M/O
	Provides Change Management with relevant information concerning:		
Q4.0/1	- received RFCs?		M
Q4.0/2	- the planning of the RFC?		M
Q4.0/3	- number of RFCs?		O
Q4.0/4	- number of successful or failed RFCs?		O
Q4.0/5	- lead time per category?		O
Q4.0/6	- RFC delays (slippage)?		O
Q4.0/7	- number of RFCs initiated by problem records?		O

Q#	Question List	Y/N	M/O
	The minimum score to reach this level is: 'Y' for all ('M') questions plus one 'Y' for the ('O') questions.		**No**

Table B-7, Assessment level 4.

2.8 Level 4.5, External integration

Q#	Question List	Y/N	M/O
Q4.5/1	Do you regularly hold meetings with interested parties in which Change Management matters are discussed?		M
-	Exchange Change management information with Configuration Management regarding:		
Q4.5/2	progress of RFCs and RFC closures?		M
Q4.5/3	impact of RFC on configuration items?		M
-	Does Change Management exchange information with Problem Management regarding:		-
Q4.5/4	- required RFCs to solve problems and known errors?		M
Q4.5/5	- progress reporting and for receiving problem of escalation reports?		M
Q4.5/6	- obtaining problem information related to RFCs?		M
-	Does Change Management exchange information with Service Desk regarding:		-
Q4.5/7	- publish the progress of RFCs?		O
Q4.5/8	- announce the RFC planning?		O
Q4.5/9	- performing impact analysis of RFCs on the Service Desk support levels?		O
Q4.5/10	- obtaining information regarding incidents and calls related to RFCs?		O
-	Does Change Management exchange information with Release Management regarding:		-
Q4.5/11	- change implementations?		O
Q4.5/12	- announce and planning software releases?		O
-	Does Change Management exchange information with Service Level Management:		-
Q4.5/13	- the RFC planning?		O
Q4.5/14	- potential impact of RFCs on service level agreements?		O
-	Does Change Management exchange information with Business Continuity Management:		-
Q4.5/15	- announce the RFC planning?		O
Q4.5/16	- performing an impact analysis on the contingency plan?		O
-	Does Change Management exchange information with Capacity Management:		-
Q4.5/17	- performance and capacity matters related to RFCs?		O
	The minimum score to reach this level is: 'Y' for all ('M') questions plus one 'Y' for the ('O') questions.		**No**

Table B-8, Assessment level 4,5.

2.9 Level 5, Customer interface

Q#	Question List	Y/N	M/O
Q5.0/1	Do you verify with the customer whether the activities carried out by Change Management sufficiently support the business needs?		M
Q5.0/2	Do you verify with the customer that they are satisfied with the services offered?		M
Q5.0/3	Do you make trend analyzes of the customer satisfaction?		M
Q5.0/4	Do you use customer research information when drawing up your quality improvement agenda (service improvement agenda)?		
Q5.0/5	Do you measure the customer's satisfaction perception with regard to the services you offer?		M
	Minimum score to reach this level is: 'Y' for all ('M') questions.		**No**

Table B-9, Assessment level 5.

Appendix C, Literature list

Reference	Publication
Best 2011	B. de Best, "SLA best practices", Dutch language, Leonon Media 2011, ISBN13: 978 90 71501 456.
Best 2012	B. de Best, "Quality Control & Assurance", Dutch language, Leonon Media 2012, ISBN13: 978 90 71501 531.
Best 2014	B. de Best, "Acceptatiecriteria", Dutch language, Leonon Media, 2014, ISBN 13: 978 90 71501 784.
Best 2015b	B. de Best, "Ketenbeheer in de Praktijk", Dutch language, Leonon Media 2015, ISBN13: 978 90 71501 852.
Best 2017a	B. de Best, "Cloud SLA", English language, Leonon Media, 2017, ISBN13: 978 94 92618 009.
Best 2017b	B. de Best, "SLA Templates", English language, Leonon Media, ISBN13: 978 94 92618 030, 2017.
Best 2017c	B. de Best, "DevOps Best Practices", English language, Leonon Media, 2017, ISBN13: 978 94 92618 078.
Best 2017d	B. de Best, "Beheren onder Architectuur", Dutch language, Leonon Media, 2017, ISBN13: 978 90 71501 913.
Best 2018	B. de Best, "Agile Service Management with Scrum", English language, Leonon Media, 2018, ISBN13: 978 94 92618 085.
Caluwé 2011	L. de Caluwé en H. Vermaak, "Leren Veranderen", Kluwer, 2011, tweede druk, ISBN13: 978 90 1301 65 43.
Deming 2000	W. Edwards Deming, "*Out of the Crisis*. MIT Center for Advanced Engineering Study", 2000, ISBN13: 978 02 6254 11 52.
Galbraith 1973	Jay R. Galbraith, "Designing complex organisations", Addison-Wesley Longman Publishing Co., Inc. Boston, MA, USA, 1973, ISBN10: 02 01025 590.
Kaplan 2004	R. S. Kaplan en D. P. Norton, "Op kop met de Balanced Scorecard", 2004, Harvard Business School Press, ISBN13: 978 90 2542 30 32.
Layton 2012	Mark C. Layton, "Agile" Project Management for Dummies", Wiley Publishing Inc., 2012, ISBN 13: 978 1 118 02624 3.
Looijen 2011	M. Looijen, L. van Hemmen, "Beheer van Informatiesystemen", zevende druk, Academic Service, 2011, ISBN13: 978 90 12582 377.
Nimwegen 1992	prof. Drs. H. van Nimwegen R.A., "Praktijkgids De Controller & Informatiemanagement afl. 2 (augustus 1992)".
Nimwegen 1993	prof. Drs. H. van Nimwegen R.A., "Administratieve processen vastleggen, verbeteren en ontwikkelen", Kluwer Bedrijfswetenschappen, Deventer, 1993, ISBN13: 978 90 2671 68 81.
OGC 2011 CSI	OGC, "Continual Service Improvement", ISBN13: 978 01 13313 082.
OGC 2011 SD	OGC, "Service Design", ISBN13: 978 01 13313 051.
OGC 2011 SO	OGC, "Service Operation", ISBN13: 978 01 13313 075.
OGC 2011 SS	OGC, "Service Strategy", ISBN13: 978 01 13313 044.
OGC 2011 ST	OGC, "Service Transition", ISBN13: 978 01 13313 068.

Reference	Publication
Pols 2009	R. Van de Pols, "ASL 2 - Een framework voor applicatiemanagement", Van Haren Publishing, 2009, ISBN13: 978 90 87533 120.
Pols 2011	R. Van der Pols, "BiSL - Een framework voor Functioneel Beheer en Informatiemanagement", Van Haren Publishing, 2011, ISBN13: 978 90 87536 879.
Shalloway 2011	A. Shalloway, "Demystifying Kanban", Net Objectives Press, www.netobjectives.com/system/fils/Demystifying-Kanban_0.pdf.
Thiadens 1999	T. Thiadens, "Beheer van ICT-voorzieningen", Academic Services, derde herziene uitgave, ISBN13: 978 90 3951 39 03.

Table B-1, Literature list.

Appendix D, Glossary

In the glossary, words in the explanation text are underlined if they appear as a defined term.

Term	Explanation
ASL	ASL is a framework for application management. This model describes how application management can be implemented based on operational, tactical and strategic management processes.
Balanced scorecard	The balanced scorecard is a control model depicting critical success factors and performance indicators in four perspectives, namely: the financial perspective, internal perspective, innovation perspective and customer perspective. This control model is used by many companies to monitor the chosen strategy.
BiSL	Business information Services Library, is the first and only public standard for functional management and information management. BiSL explains the processes and activities necessary to send information from user and business options. It is a coherent framework, focusing on both operational, tactical and strategic processes, as well as mutual relationships (definition www.ITSMF.nl).
CAB	The Change Advisory Board is an advisory body within the Change Management process. In the CAB, change requests are authorized, scheduled and released for production.
CFIA	The Component Failure Impact Analysis is an analysis technique that links an ICT service to the ICT components involved. On the basis of this, weak spots in the ICT infrastructure can be found and countermeasures can be taken.
Change Management	Change management is the implementation of changes in the ICT infrastructure in such a manner that disturbances in ICT services as a result of changes are prevented or minimized.
CRAMM-analysis	A CRAMM analysis is performed to determine the risks of a product or service. The threats and vulnerabilities are based on the product or service concerned. A countermeasure must be devised of any identified risk.
Critical success factor	A critical success factor is a factor that affects the extent to which the goal of a process is achieved.
Daily Scrum	Every day a sprint begins with a meeting in which the participants of the Scrum team meet and review the status of the previous day and discuss the activities of the present day. The impediments are also mentioned.
Definition of Done	The Definition of Done (DoD) states which acceptance criteria a product must meet in order for it to be finalized. The acceptance criteria in the DoD usually apply to all PBIs, as opposed to the acceptance criteria that apply to a specific user story. The DoD can include activities that need to be completed, such as an executed code review, described and successful unit tests, a created and checked baseline, and an event-updated event catalogue. The DoD is primarily intended as quality control of the development process. Optionally, an entry may be included as a Functional Acceptance Test (FAT), but checking whether a FAT has taken place is a quality aspect of the process.
Development team	The development team consists of different disciplines, namely requirement analysts, designers, builders and testers. Important to mention is that in principle any team member can perform any activity.

Term	Explanation
	A development team usually consists of seven plus or minus two people who organize themselves. This means that they themselves define the Scrum process according to their own requirements. The final result of a sprint is a workable product for the end user. The development team often only performs the Scrum development process. However, the development of the potential shippable products can also be done by the development team. Otherwise, a deployment team has to be in place.
DTAP street	Development, Test, Acceptance and Production street
Epic	An epic basically describes a business function or product function that is complete and provides added value. An epic can be detailed into a number of features. An epic ranges between twenty to one hundred working days.
Escaped defect	This is an error (defect) in the software that is detected by the user. Within service management this is defined as an incident. This error should have been noted during the (acceptance) testing.
Feature	A feature describes a part of a high-level product. Features describe the new functionality of a product that a user wants to receive.
Generic Acceptance Criteria	Generic acceptance criteria are the requirements that the service management organisation imposes on the ICT products and ICT services to be used. The generic acceptance criteria are based on the critical success factors of the service management organisation's service management processes. These acceptance criteria are called "Generic Acceptance Criteria" because they are information system independently defined. They can even be defined organisation independently by choosing a commonly used reference model like ITIL.
Impediment	An impediment is an obstacle for being productive, for example lack of tooling, disruption by management requests, lack of knowledge or customer, etcetera.
ITIL	ITIL is a set of best practices focused on managing ICT infrastructures.
Measurement requirements	An acceptance criterion should indicate how to determine whether the information system complies with the acceptance criterion.
Performance indicator	A performance indicator is a means that makes a critical success factor measurable. A performance indicator must be able to assign a norm and a measurement unit.
Product backlog	This is a prioritized list of items needed to realize a project. An item is also called a Product Backlog Item.
Product backlog item	A Product Backlog Item (PBI) may be of different size and meaning. Common PBIs are themes, epics and features, bugs and chores. A priority is given to each PBI. Bugs are the work that needs to be done to solve defects and chores include work that needs to be done, but that does not have immediate added value for the business.
Product owner	The product owner is the owner of the product to be developed. A product may be an information system or a service. The product owner is also called asset owner. Generally, a product owner will be a delegated asset owner. This means that the product owner acts in the name of a manager higher in the line organisation. The product owner acts as a customer who has the budget for producing the product by the development team. He proposes priorities for the work to be carried out. This is also called refining. The list of activities to be performed is called product backlog.
Project team	A project team consists of a Scrum team plus the stakeholders.

Term	Explanation		
RACI	Responsible, Accountable, Consulted and Informed (RACI) is a way of making tasks, responsibilities and powers of a process clear. This is also called RASCI, with the 'S' for Supportive '.		
Refactoring	Re-create, develop or program a particular component to make it better (maintainable) without changing the functionality or behaviour of the component.		
Refining	Epics are too big to be used in a sprint. At the time that an epic is at the top of the product backlog, it must be broken down into smaller parts (features) so that they can be included taken in the sprint. Refining requirements on the product backlog so that they are sufficiently decomposed and clear in terms of definition is also referred to as grooming. During the backlog refinement session, the effort and priority of the PBIs are also determined.		
Review	The term has two meanings in this book: • a way of accepting; • a way to verify whether a process is correct implemented and performed.		
RFC	A Request For Change (RFC) is a change request to get a new configuration item or change an existing one.		
Scrum master	Each team is supervised by a Scrum master who accompanies the team. The Scrum master ensures that the correct Scrum process is followed, arranges meetings, manages facility issues including the necessary hardware and software. The Scrum master also manages any necessary training. Important to recognize is that the Scrum master is not a project manager. He is therefore not responsible for the delivery of results in accordance with time, money and quality requirements. He is also not responsible for human resource management such as recruitment & selection, appointment of people, ratings and rewards and redundancies. However, the Scrum master is responsible for ensuring that the team can focus on the agreed sprint goal, for example, by ensuring that the team does not have to spend time on third-party efforts such as inadequate capacity or extra requirements. The Scrum master is also responsible for any necessary contracting of Scrum team suppliers, such as the required tooling.		
Scrum team	A Scrum team consists of the product owner, the Scrum master and the development team.		
SLA	A Service Level Agreement (SLA) is an agreement between a customer and the ICT service provider about the ICT services to deliver in terms of quantity, quality and cost.		
SMART	Specific	A concrete and clear target with described results.	
	Measurable	The desired results are measurable in terms of, for example, time, cost and / or other quantitative criteria.	
	Acceptable	The goal is acceptable and achievable in both the eyes of the one who determines the target as the one who has to achieve the target. The 'A' also stands for 'Accountable', someone must be responsible for the intended purpose.	
	Realistic	The target is realistic (achievable) and relevant given the environment / circumstances within which the goal is to be achieved.	
	Time-bound	The goal is to measure progress towards the goal in terms of milestones and time.	

Term	Explanation
Specific Acceptance Criteria	Specific acceptance criteria are the requirements that the user organisation imposes on the ICT products and ICT services to be used. The specific acceptance criteria are based on the critical success factors of the user organisation's business processes. These acceptance criteria are called "Specific Acceptance Criteria" because they need to be determined by organisation and even by product.
SPOF	A Single Point of Failure is component in a system that is causing potential disturbance. The intended solution of a SPOF is to double the relevant component. A SPOF analysis therefore includes the analysis of single-run components in a system.
Sprint	In a sprint, the tasks of the sprint backlog are realized. A sprint is usually performed within one to four weeks. Scrum is working with the time box principle.
Sprint backlog	In analogy with the product backlog, the sprint backlog indicates which tasks should be performed within a sprint.
Sprint backlog planning session	The planning of a sprint is performed during the sprint backlog planning session. The product owner, the scrum master and the development team are attending this session. In this session, a selection is made of the PBIs to be realized in the next sprint. The selected PBIs are broken down into tasks. A task is scheduled for hours. A task may not cost more than twelve hours to realize. It is a best practice to choose a task size of less than a day.
Sprint burndown chart	During a sprint, daily progress is tracked in a graph. This is called the sprint burndown chart. This graph consists of two axes where the X axis is the time that expires. This is usually noted in units of days. The Y-axis shows what the team has achieved. There are several possible units that can be used. A unit that provides a fairly reliable picture of progression is the number of story points. The Y-axis then indicates how many story points are awarded to the sprint and the X-axis at which time in the sprint which part is realized.
Story point	A story point is an arbitrary measurement unit used by a Scrum team to determine how much work (effort) needs to be done to realize a feature. Important to mention is that a story point is not related to hours but to a baseline feature that the team uses as a reference. Thus, a feature of the same size can get a different number of story points within different development teams, while actually giving the same effort estimate to realize the feature. This in contrast to, for example, function points from the function-point analysis method.
Test case	A test case describes what needs to be tested. Both logical and physical test cases are recognized. The logical test case describes 'what' to be tested, the physical describes 'how to be tested'.
Test scenario	A collection of test cases that are related to each other. For example, a test scenario that is defined for a use case.
Theme	A theme is set of epics.
User story	A user story is the format to describe a feature or epic of a theme. A user story is a statement that describes the user's requirements in common business language. It includes the terms "who", "what" and "why".
Velocity	Velocity is a performance indicator that indicates the productivity of the development team. Productivity is the work that the team can deliver during one sprint. The velocity can be calculated based on already realized PBIs in previous sprints.

Term	Explanation
	The velocity is measured in the same units as the PBIs are estimated. These can be story points, days, or hours. The velocity is a guideline for the team and the environment to properly estimate how much one can do and what one can expect.

Table D-1, Glossary.

Appendix E, Abbreviations

Abbreviation	Meaning
ALM	Application Lifecycle Management
API	Application Programming Interface
ASL	Application Services Library
BI	Business Intelligence
BiSL	Business information Services Library
BSM	Business Solution Manager
BUM	Business Unit Manager
CAB	Change Advisory Board
CCCQ	ClearCase ClearQuest
CCTA	Central Computer Telecommunications Agency
CDB	Change Decision Board
CEMLI	Configuration, Extension, Modification, Localisation, Integration
CFIA	Component Failure Impact Analysis
CI	Configuration Item
CIA	Confidentiality, Integrity and Availability / Accessibility
CIO	Chief Information Officer
CMDB	Configuration Management DataBase
CMM	Capability Maturity Model
CMMi	Capability Maturity Model Integration
CMS	Configuration Management System
CMS	Content Management System
CRAMM	CCTA Risk Analysis and Management Method
CRC	Cyclic Redundancy Check
CSI	Continual Service Improvement
CSF	Critical Success Factor
DAP	Dossier Agreements and Procedures
DDD	Detailed Design Document
DevOps	Development & Operations
DML	Definitive Media Library
DoD	Definition of Done
DoQ	Definition of Quality
DoR	Definition of Ready
DRP	Disaster Recovery Plan
DSDM	Dynamic Systems Development Method
DTAP	Development-, Test-, Acceptance- and Production environment
E2E	End-to-End
EPD	Electronic Patient Dossier

Abbreviation	Meaning
ESB	Enterprise Service Buss
ETL	Extract Transform Load
EVO	Evolutionary Project Management
FAT	Functional Acceptance Test
FiFo	First in First Out
FTA	Fault Tree Analysis
FTE	FullTime-Equivalent
FTR	First Time Right
GIT	Global Information Tracker
GSA	Generic & Specific Acceptance criteria
GTA	Global Tooling Architecture
GUI	Graphical UserInterface
HP ALM	HP Application Lifecycle Management
HP QC	HP Quality Center
HP SC	HP Service Center
I&A	Information & Automation
ICT	Information & Communication Technology
ID	IDentification
ILM	Infrastructure Lifecycle Management
IP	Internet Protocol
IPMA	International Project Management Association
ISO	International Standardisation Organisation
IT	Information Technology
ITIL	Information Technology Infrastructure Library
KPI	Key Performance Indicator
LCM	LifeCycle Management
LTC	Logical Test Case
MCC	Monitoring and Control Centre
MRM	Microsoft Release Manager
MSCC	MicroSoft Competence Center
MSI	MicroSoft Installer
MT	Management Team
NFR	Non-Functional Requirement
OGC	UK Office of Government Commerce
OLA	Operational Level Agreement
Ops	Operations
OSI	Open Systems Interconnection
PBA	Patterns of Business Activity
PBI	Product Backlog Item
PEN test	Penetration-test

Abbreviation	Meaning
PID	Project Initiation Document
PRA	Product Risk Analysis
PRINCE2	PRojects IN Controlled Environments
PST	Performance StressTest
QA	Quality Assurance
QoS	Quality of Service
RACI	Responsible, Accountable, Consulted and Informed
RASCI	Responsible, Accountable, Consulted, Supportive and Informed
RFC	Request For Change
ROI	Return On Investment
RPO	Return Point Objective
RTO	Return Time Objective
RtV	Route to Value
S-CMDB	Software Configuration Management DataBase
SaaS	Software as a Service
SAD	Software Architecture Design
SAFe	Scaled Agile Framework
SCCM	System Center Configuration Manager
SCM	Software Configuration Management
SDL	Secure Development Lifecycle
SIG	Software Improvement Group
SIP	Service Improvement Plan / Service Improvement Programme
SIT	System Integration Test
SKMS	Service Knowledge Management System
SLA	Service Level Agreement
SMART	Specific, Measurable, Realistic, Accountable / Acceptable and Timely
SNMP	Simple Network Management Protocol
SOA	Service Oriented Architecture
S-CI	Software Configuration Item
SOP	Standard Operating Procedure
SPOC	Single Point Of Contact
SPOF	Single Point Of Failure
SQL	Structured Query Language
SQP	Service Quality Plan
SRG	Standards, Rules & Guidelines
SSD	Secure Software Development
SSL	Secure Socket Layer
SVN	SubVersioN
TAD	Technical Architecture Document
TCO	Total Cost of Ownership

Abbreviation	Meaning
TDD	Test Driven Development
TFS	Team Foundation Server
TOM	Target Operating model
UAT	User Acceptance Test
UC	Underpinning Contract
UP	User Profile
URL	Uniform Resource Locator
VP-sales	Vice President of Sales
VSM	Value Stream Mapping
WIP	Work In Progress
WSP	Windows SharePoint
XP	eXtreme Programming

Table D-1, Abbreviations.

Appendix F, Tools

This appendix describes the tools that are used by the case organisations. Due to the long names of these tools, only shortened names for these tools have been used in this book. In Table F-1 the short and long name are related to each other. For each tool it is indicated on which website more information about this tool can be found.

Short name	Long name	Website
#define	issue-tracker	(proprietary)
Bamboo	Bamboo	www.atlassian.com
CCCQ	IBM® Rational® ClearCase® ClearQuest	www.ibm.com
Cherwell	Cherwell Software	www.cherwell.com
ClearCase	IBM® Rational® ClearCase	www.ibm.com
Clientele	Mproof Clientele IT Service Management	www.mproof.com
Enterprise Architect	Sparx Systems Enterprise Architect	www.sparxsystems.com
FitNesse	FitNesse	www.fitness.org
GIT	Global Information Tracker	www.git-scm.com
HP ALM	HP Application Lifecycle Management	www8.hp.com
HP QC	HP Quality Center	www8.hp.com
HP SC	HP ServiceCenter Software	H10076.www1.hp.com
HP Service Manager	HP Service Manager	www8.hp.com
IBM Tivoli Service Management Suite	IBM Tivoli Service Management Suite	www-01.ibm.com
Ice-Scrum	Ice-Scrum	www.icescrum.org
Installshield	Installshield	www.installshield.com
IT Service Management	IT Service Management (Mexon)	www.mexontechnology.com
Jenkins	Jenkins	www.jenkins-ci.org
Jira	Jira	www.atlassian.com
JMeter	Apache JMeter™	jmeter.apache.org
LeanKit	LeanKit™	www.Leankit.com
Maven	Apache Maven Project	maven.apache.corg
Mavim	Mavim	www.mavim.com
McAfee	McAfee®	www.mcafee.com
MRM	Microsoft Release Manager	www.ibm.com/software
MS Excel	MicroSoft Excel	www.microsoft.com
MSI	MicroSoft Installer	msdn.microsoft.com
MTM	Microsoft Test Manager	msdn.microsoft.com
Nexus	Nexus	www.ichrome.com/solutions/nexus
NPS	Net Promoter Score	www.netpromoter.com
Octopus Deploy	Octopus Deploy	www.octopusdeploy.com
Omnitracker	Omnitracker	www.omnitracker.com
OTRS	Open source Ticket Request System	www.otrs.org

Short name	Long name	Website
Powershell	Automated Powershell script	microsoft.com/powershell
ReportServer	SQL Server Reporting Services (SSRS)	msdn.microsoft.com
Robot Framework	Robot Framework	www.robotframework.org
ROSS	RepliWeb Operations Suite for SharePoint	www.repliweb.com
ScrumWise	ScrumWise	www.scrumwise.com
Selenium	Selenium	docs.seleniumhq.org
Serena Dimensions	Serena Dimensions	www.serena.com
SOAtest	Parasoft SOAtest	www.parasoft.com
SonarQube	SonarQube™	www.sonarSource.org
Subversion	Apache SubVersioN (SNV)	subversion.apache.org
TestComplete	TestComplete	SmartBear Software
TFS	Team Foundation Server	msdn.microsoft.com
TOPdesk	TOPdesk	www.topdesk.nl
Twist	Twist	www.thoughtworks.com
WinMerge	winMerge	www.winmerge.com

Table F-1, Tools.

Appendix G, Usage of tools

The case organisations have indicated in this book for which purpose certain tools have been used. In Figure G-1 an overview is given of the tools and the use of these tools in this book. This does not mean that these tools do not give substance to the other topics. It is also important to recognize that the use of tools is changing rapidly. Figure G-1 is therefore a snapshot.

Tool	Agile Project Management								Test Mngt.				Service Management									Totals
	Feature / User story admin	Sprint backlog	Dashboard	Software configuration management	Code repository	Code review	Version control / Baselining	Continuous Integration	Issue tracking	Test cases / Test scripts	Test automation	Regression testing	Security management	Incident management	Problem management	Change Management	Configuration management	Release & deployment management	Continuous Delivery	DTAP	Reporting	
#define	1					1		1	1	1	1									1		7
Bamboo								1														1
CCCQ				1	1	1	1						1		1		1					7
Cherwell														1	1	1						3
ClearCase				2	1	1	1										1					6
ClearQuest						1			1				1		1		1					5
Clientele									1				2	1		1	1	1				7
Enterprise Architect	2	1															1					4
FitNesse										1												1
GIT				1	2		2	1														6
HP ALM	1								2	3	2	3		1			1					13
HP SC													1	1	1	1	1	1				6
HP Service Manager													1	1	1	1						4
IBM Tivoli Service Management													1	1								2
Ice-Scrum	1																					1
Installshield																		1				1
Jenkins								5												1	1	7
Jira	3	4	3			1			2						1							14
JMeter											2	4										6
Leankit	2	1	1										1		1							6
Maven				1				2			1									1	1	6
Mavim								1														1
McAfee																			1			1
Mediawiki															1							1
MS Excel									1								1	1				3
MSI				1	1	1	1	1						1	1		1			1	1	10
MTM										1	1	1										3
Nexus					1		1															2
NPS			1																			1
Octopus Deploy								1														1
Omnitracker													1	1	1		1					4
OTRS									1				1									2
Other																			1			1
Powershell																				1	1	2
ReportServer			1														1					2
Robot Framework												1										1
ROSS																		1		1	1	3
ScrumWise	1	1	1																			3
Selenium										1	4	4										9
Serena Dimensions				1																		1
SOAtest										2	1	2										5
Sonar				2			2															4
Subversion					2	2	2	1														7
TestComplete										1	1	1										3
TFS	2	2	2	1	2	2	3	1	1	1	1	1			1		1	1		1	1	24
TOPdesk													1	1	3	1	1	1				8
Twist											1	1										2
Totals	13	9	9	10	10	10	13	15	10	11	15	18	11	9	14	5	13	7	2	7	6	

Figure G-1, Use of tools by the case organisations.

Appendix H, Websites

Reference	URL
htpp Dialogueincubator	http://www.dialoguesincubator.nl/wp-content/uploads/2011 /06 /Scrum.pdf
http Blog	http://blog.coryfoy.com/2011/07/recreating-Scrum_using-Kanban-and-explicit-policies/
http Blogspot	http://abcdsliithswkprojects.blogspot.nl/2013_08_01_archive.html
http Fastlane	https://blog.codecentric.de/en/2014/07/DevOps-product-ownership/#more-23866
http IBM	http://www.ibm.com
http Netobjectives	http://www.netobjectives.com/blogs/real-differences-between-Kanban-and-Scrum.
http OGC	http://www.cabinetoffice.gov/
http Onion	https://myagilemind.wordpress.com/2011/10/28/what-does-the-planning-onion-mean-to-you/
http Scrumallicance	http://www.Scrumalliance.org/why-Scrum
http Wiki	https://nl.wikipedia.org/wiki/Agile-softwareontwikkeling#Agile-methoden

Table H-1, Websites.

Appendix I, Index

#

#define · 181

A

acceptance · 172
acceptance criteria · 3, 19, 20, 55, 72, 73, 74, 86, 87, 90, 96, 159, 169, 171, 172, 174
acceptance test · 20, 24, 35, 72, 79, 81, 87, 96, 103, 119, 129, 146
adapter operations · 21
adaptive application management · 60, 61
additive application management · 60, 61
administrator · 1
affinity estimation · 37
Agile · 179
 - approach · 2
 - architecture · 44
 - development process · 1, 2, 5, 6, 7, 11, 13, 24, 37, 38, 44, 59, 115, 116, 123
 - method · 2, 45, 121
 - service management · 115
 - system development · 1, 3, 10, 11
 - team · 28, 29, 31
 - term · 37
 - tool · 55
agreement · 16, 31, 35, 43, 52, 69, 70, 74, 76, 80, 83, 101, 119, 125, 132, 139, 143, 144, 145, 158, 166
ALM · 25, 56, 93, 123, 124, 130, 131, 133, 134, 137, 138, 141, 144, 145, 146, 147, 149, 150, 152, 153, 177
ALM organisation · 131, 153
Apache SubVersioN · *See* SVN
API · 177
application
 - component · 92, 126, 130, 132, 141, 150
 - maintainer · 77, 82, 85, 88, 112
 - maintenance · 70
 - maintenance team · 89
 - management · 1, 7, 60, 61, 62, 83, 84, 89, 92, 125, 126, 128, 132, 135, 138, 139, 142, 145, 146, 148, 151, 153, 171
 - management process · 1
 - manager · 26, 75, 76, 80, 109, 124
Application Lifecycle Management · *See* ALM
Application Programming Interface · *See* API
Application Services Library · *See* ASL
appointment · 173

architect · 1, 11, 48, 72, 86, 118, 126, 130, 134, 136, 137, 141, 144, 146
architecture roadmap · 50
ASL · 4, 62, 115, 116, 117, 119, 120, 170, 171, 177, 185
assessment level · 163
asset owner · 172
audit · 71
auditor · 2, 90, 91
automate · 106
automated testing · 18, 20, 91
availability · 8, 23, 25, 59, 73, 78, 79, 81, 104, 112, 129, 141, 146, 149, 161
availability management · 23, 78
availability manager · 23, 78, 79, 161
awareness training · 44

B

backlog · 15, 16, 17, 20, 22, 25, 29, 50, 55, 56, 84, 85, 88, 93, 98, 119, 150, 158, 173, 174
backlog management · 56
balanced scorecard · 171
Bamboo · 22, 181
baseline · 18, 71, 82, 90, 93, 94, 97, 101, 104, 136, 140, 143, 151, 171, 174
baselining · 55
batch processing · 70, 73, 132
behaviour · 173
BI · 45, 177
BiSL · 4, 115, 116, 117, 120, 170, 171, 177
BizTalk · 14, 76, 89, 106
black box · 73
black-list · 105, 106
blueprint expert · 49
blueprint manager · 131
Board of Directors · 15
brainstorming session · 89, 95
branche · 45, 103
branching · 102, 103, 134, 143
BSM · 70, 177
bug · 172
builder · 171
building block · 21, 67, 72, 79, 80, 90, 95, 96
BUM · 177
burndown chart · 15, 17, 37, 174
business · 2, 17, 23, 35, 39, 48, 67, 81, 103, 118, 167
 - alignment · 65
 - case · 41
 - language · 174
 - owner · 18

L

LCM · 178
LCM change · 10, 102
lead architect · 27, 77
lead time · 17, 110, 158, 165
Lean · 24
Leankit · 55, 57, 76, 88, 148, 181
license · 119, 138
lifecycle change · 53, 54, 55, 102
LifeCycle Management · *See* LCM
line manager · 2, 85, 145, 149
line organisation · 172
load balancer · 81
load test · 19, 20, 81
log file · 73, 106
Logical Test Case · *See* LTC
logical test case document · 95
loosely coupled · 42
LTC · 178

M

main contractor · 60
maintainability · 8, 79, 80, 140, 143, 146,
  151
maintainable · 173
maintenance · 17, 21, 23, 41, 46, 61, 67,
  69, 72, 73, 74, 78, 87, 98, 99, 101, 103,
  104, 105, 106, 107, 113, 116, 117, 119,
  120, 123, 127, 129, 130, 133, 134, 137,
  141, 144, 145, 152, 154
  - change · 84, 126
  - control · 19
  - costs · 67
  - deliverable · 53, 87
  - department · 67, 70
  - domain · 57
  - organisation · 69, 85, 86, 99
  - phase · 49
  - process · 55, 139
  - request · 17
  - service · 17
  - sprint · 140
  - team · 60, 69, 72, 78, 80, 85, 86, 92, 93,
    98, 107, 108, 109, 110, 111, 112, 119,
    123, 124, 125, 135, 136, 143, 147, 149
management · 158, 163
management information · 160
Management Team · *See* MT
mandator · 48
mandatory field · 31
master test plan · 21, 53, 90, 95, 96
maturity · 1, 2, 5, 6, 11, 13, 19, 21, 24, 25,
  32, 44, 120, 157, 160, 163
maturity level · 2
Maven · 181

Mavim · 55, 181
McAfee · 181
MCC · 26, 29, 178
measurable · 173
message queue · 81
Mexon · 29, 31, 53, 88, 93, 107, 181
Microsoft Competence Center · *See* MSCC
MicroSoft Installer · *See* MSI
Microsoft Release Manager · *See* MRM
Microsoft Test Manager · *See* MTM
mindset · 45
miniature waterfall · 143
minor change · 47
mock up · 19, 80
modularity · 79, 129
monitor facility · 79
monitor function · 82
Monitoring and Control Center · *See* MCC
MRM · 22, 178, 181
MS Excel · 21, 22, 35, 55, 56, 181
MSCC · 47, 57, 178
MSI · 93, 95, 101, 102, 178, 181
MSI package · 93, 101, 102
MT · 15, 22, 25, 27, 38, 41, 46, 47, 57, 75,
  84, 89, 95, 99, 112, 117, 119, 125, 128,
  129, 135, 136, 137, 138, 140, 141, 144,
  145, 146, 147, 149, 154, 178
MTM · 22, 181
multi tenancy · 42
multidisciplinary · 44
multidisciplinary design team · 65
multifunctional · 48, 138, 139, 140, 150, 152

N

Net Promoter Score · 24, *See* NPS
Nexus · 22, 55, 56, 99, 100, 101, 181
NFR · 8, 19, 31, 65, 66, 70, 71, 72, 73, 74,
  81, 82, 86, 128, 145, 151, 153, 154, 178
Niko-Niko chart · 37
Non Functional Requirement · *See* NFR
NPS · 181

O

object-ID · 137
Octopus Deploy · 22, 181
OGC · 2, 157, 169, 178, 185
OLA · 68, 69, 70, 71, 72, 149, 153, 178
Omnitracker · 32, 57, 88, 106, 181
onbeschikbaarheid · 79
Open source Ticket Request System · *See*
  OTRS
Open Systems Interconnection · *See* OSI
operating system · 60

R

RACI · 173, 179
radiator · 38
RASCI · 179
reconciliation · 77
recurring defect · 98
recurring incident · 9, 112
refactoring · 38, 67, 68, 79, 80, 82, 83, 87, 89, 111, 129, 135
reference architecture · 73, 88, 105, 106
reference framework · 2
refining · 38, 173
registration · 107
regression test · 9, 11, 18, 19, 20, 21, 22, 26, 38, 41, 53, 54, 56, 79, 81, 82, 87, 95, 96, 97, 98, 103, 117, 129, 136, 137, 139, 159, 160
regression test script · 56
regular feature · 54, 89
release
  - and deployment management · 10, 129, 140, 143, 146, 148, 151
  - built · 136
  - cycle · 72
  - frequency · 41, 63
  - management · 19, 21, 24, 28, 29, 34, 59, 63, 73, 93, 116, 117, 139
  - manager · 25, 27, 34, 48, 85
  - notes · 53
  - plan · 51
  - planning · 38, 49, 117, 125
  - sprint · 50
  - team · 46
reliability · 15, 16, 39, 79, 158
reliable · 40
renewal · 84, 126
renovation · 67, 83
RepliWeb Operations Suite for SharePoint · See ROSS
reporting method · 22
ReportServer · 21, 182
repository · 100
request · 172
Request For Change · See RFC
request fulfilment · 62, 64, 110, 148
requirement · 14, 15, 16, 19, 20, 25, 30, 31, 40, 41, 44, 45, 52, 53, 54, 55, 63, 66, 69, 71, 72, 74, 76, 77, 78, 88, 90, 91, 96, 98, 117, 120, 125, 135, 136, 140, 141, 144, 145, 149, 151, 159, 172, 173, 174
requirement analyst · 171
requirement management · 41
research · XVII, 1, 2, 3, 5, 7, 11, 47, 55, 59, 116, 121, 153, 167
resilience · 81
resilient · 80
responsibility · 16

Responsible Accountable Consulted Informed · See RACI
Responsible Accountable Consulted Supportive Informed · See RASCI
retrospective · 16, 17, 18, 21, 23, 37, 159
Retrospective meeting · 18
Return On Investment · See ROI
Return Point Objective · See RPO
Return Time Objective · See RTO
review · 54, 173
RFC · 15, 25, 26, 27, 28, 29, 30, 31, 32, 33, 34, 53, 64, 71, 74, 80, 84, 85, 86, 87, 88, 98, 117, 118, 120, 128, 133, 134, 136, 163, 164, 165, 166, 173, 179
  - planning · 34
risk · XVII, 1, 2, 5, 7, 9, 10, 11, 40, 59, 77, 85, 86, 89, 95, 96, 104, 105, 130, 171
  - analysis · 31, 90, 95, 96, 129, 132, 136
  - appetite · 2
  - management · 2, 5, 7, 9, 59, 86, 101, 118, 120, 121
roadmap · 23, 42, 44, 49, 50, 86, 117, 138, 140, 143, 144, 146, 151, 154
roadmap team · 50
Robot Framework · 56, 182
ROI · 179
role · 47
root-cause analysis · 113, 151
ROSS · 56, 182
Route to Value · See RtV
RPO · 76, 77, 179
RTO · 76, 77, 179
RtV · 179

S

SaaS · 179
SaaS solution · 137, 141
SAD · 19, 20, 179
SAFe · 51, 179
SAP service · 47
Scaled Agile Framework · See SAFe
SCCM · 179
SCCM package · 33
S-CI · 93, 136, 179
SCM · 57, 179
S-CMDB · 179
Scrum · 46, 63
  - assessment · 15, 16, 19, 22, 23
  - demo · 15, 22
  - development process · 1, 2, 3, 13, 23, 25, 44, 45, 47, 53, 62, 63, 64, 133, 136, 157, 158, 160
  - handbook · 16
  - master · 1, 16, 18, 19, 21, 22, 37, 38, 44, 45, 48, 50, 73, 75, 78, 124, 127,

Epilogue

My experience is that the ideas I capture in an article or a book continue to evolve. In case you work with Scrum in relation to management in your own service management organisation, then I advise you to contact me. Perhaps there are additional articles or experiences in this area that I can share with you. This also applies inversely proportional. If you have certain experiences that complement what is described in this book, I invite you to share this with me. Perhaps they can be shared with others through this book. You can contact me via my e-mail address bartb@dbmetrics.nl.

About the author

Drs. Ing. B. de Best RI has been active in ICT since 1985. He worked primarily with the top 100 of Dutch business and government organisations. He has acquired experience in different roles within all aspects of system development, including operations for 12 years. After that, he focused on the subject of service management. Currently, as a consultant, he is active in all aspects of the knowledge management cycle of service management, such as training ICT managers and service managers, advising service management organisations, improving service management processes and outsourcing (parts of) service management organisations. He graduated at both the HTS and University level in the management field.

Other books by this author

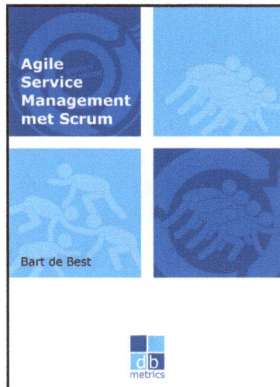

Agile Service Management with Scrum
On the way to a healthy balance between the dynamics of developing and the stability of managing the information provision

Using Agile software development is taking off. The terms Scrum and Kanban are already common to many organisations. Agile software development needs different requirements for the management of software. Many organisations are mastering this new challenge.

In particular, the interaction between the Scrum development process and the support of the software that the Scrum development process has produced, is an important aspect. This book specifically discusses this interaction.

Examples of topics that are discussed here are the service portfolio, SLAs and the handling of incident and change requests. This book first defines the risk areas when implementing Scrum and Kanban. Next the various Agile terms and concepts are discussed. The content of Agile service management is described both at the organisational- as the process level. The relevant risks are specified for each of the service management processes. In addition, the implementation of each process within the context of Scrum is indicated. This book is just one of the best practices reads of best practices that have been published by this author in a series of publications.

Author   : Bart de Best
Publisher   : Leonon Media, 2018
ISBN   : 978 94 92618 085

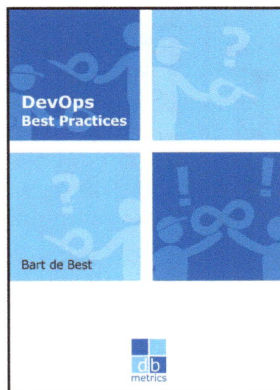

DevOps Best Practices
Best Practices for DevOps

In recent years, many organisations have experienced the benefits of using Agile approaches such as Scrum and Kanban. The software is delivered faster whilst quality increases and costs decrease. The fact that many organisations that applied the Agile approach did not take into account the traditional service management techniques, in terms of information management, application management and infrastructure management, is a major disadvantage. The solution to this problem has been found in the Dev (Development) Ops (Operations) approach. Both worlds are merged into one team, thus sharing the knowledge and skills. This book is about sharing knowledge on how DevOps teams work together.

For each aspect of the DevOps process best practices are given in 30 separate articles. The covered aspects are: Plan, Code, Build, Test, Release, Deploy, Operate and Monitor. Each article starts with the definition of the specifically used terms and one or more concepts. The body of each article is kept simple, short and easy to read.

Author   : Bart de Best
Publisher   : Leonon Media, 2017
ISBN   : 978 94 92618 078

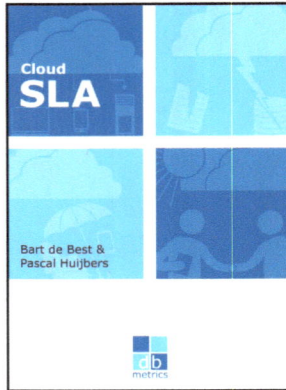

Cloud SLA
The best practices of cloud service level agreements

More and more organisations choose to replace traditional ICT services by cloud services.

Setting up effective SLAs for traditional ICT services is a real challenge for many organisations. With the arrival of cloud services, this seems to be much simpler at first, but soon the hard questions come up like data ownership, information links and security. This book describes what cloud services are. The risks involved in entering into contracts and SLAs are discussed. Based on a long list of risks and countermeasures, this book also provides recommendations for the design and content of the various service level management documents for cloud services.

This book first defines cloud and then describes various aspects like cloud patterns and the role of a cloud broker. The core of the book is the discussion of contract aspects, service documents, service design, risks, SLAs and cloud governance. In order to allow readers to get started with Cloud SLAs, the book also includes checklists of the following documents: Underpinning Contract (UC), Service Level Agreement (SLA), Document Financial Agreements (DFA), Document Agreement and Procedures (DAP), External Spec Sheets (ESS) and Internal Spec Sheets (ISS).

Author   : Bart de Best
Publisher   : Leonon Media, 2017
ISBN   : 978 94 92618 009

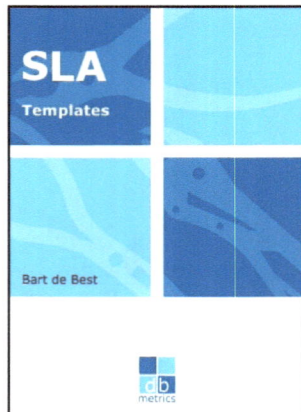

SLA Templates
A complete set of SLA templates

The most important thing in providing a service Is that the customer is satisfied with the delivered performance. With this satisfaction, the supplier gets re-purchasing's, promotions in the market and is the continuity of the company ensured. Perhaps the most important aspect of this customer satisfaction for a supplier is that the employees in question get a drive to further develop their own knowledge and skills to satisfy even more customers. This book describes the templates for Service Level Agreements in order to agree with the customer on the required service levels. This book gives both a template and an explanation for this template for all common service level management documents.

The following templates are included in this book:
- Service Level Agreement (SLA)
- Underpinning Contract (UC)
- Operational Level Agreement (OLA)
- Document Agreement and Procedures (DAP)
- Document Financial Agreements (DFA)
- Service Catalogue
- External Spec Sheet (ESS)
- Internal Spec Sheet (ISS)
- Service Quality Plan (SQP)
- Service Improvement Program (SIP)

Author   : Bart de Best
Publisher   : Leonon Media, 2017
ISBN   : 978 94 92618 030

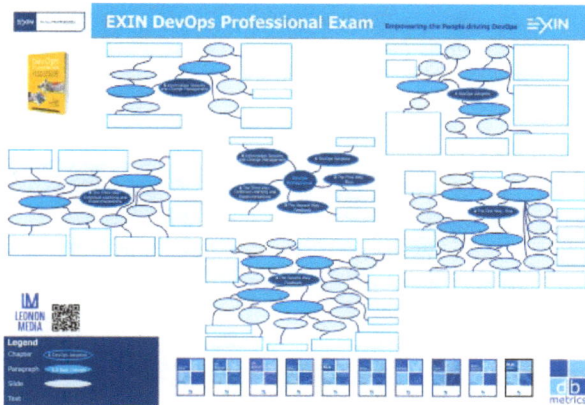

Author : Bart de Best
Publisher : Leonon Media, 2018
Ordering : info@leonon.nl

DevOps Poster
DevOps Professional Exam Poster
This poster lists all the DevOps terms that a student must learn in order to pass the exam of DevOps Professional of Exin. This poster can be ordered at info@leonon.nl.

The subjects on the poster are based on the basic training material of Exin. Since there are many terms to be learned, this poster will help to learn them by reviewing them all at once daily.

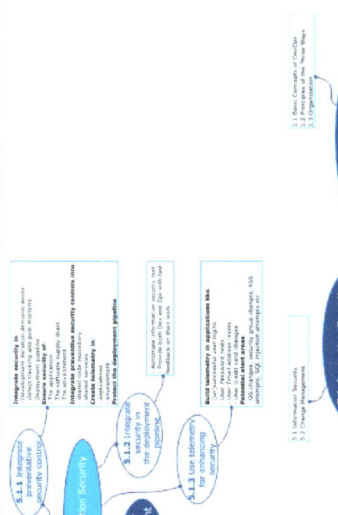

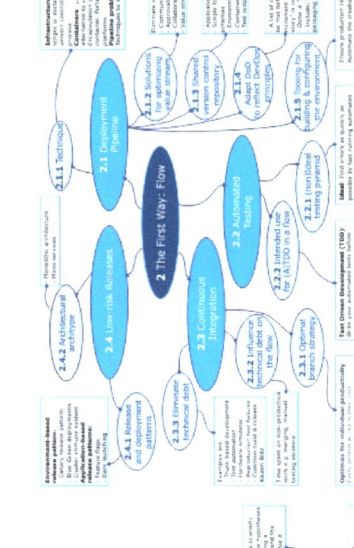
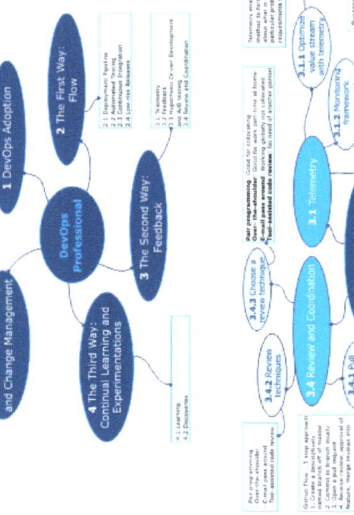
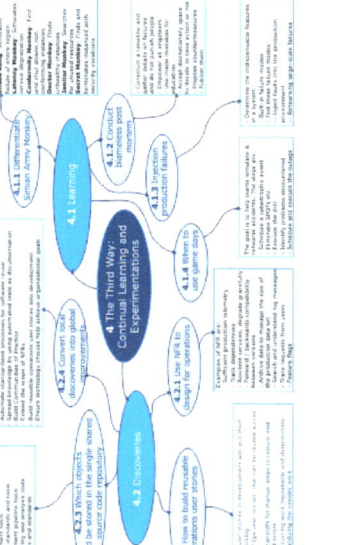
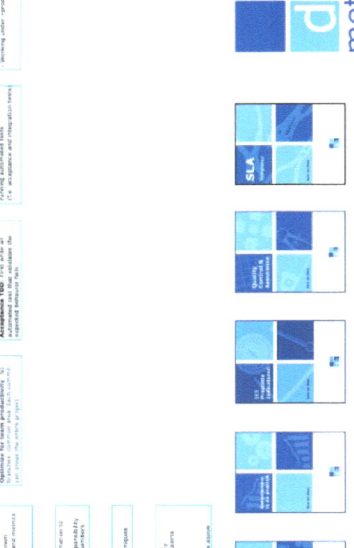
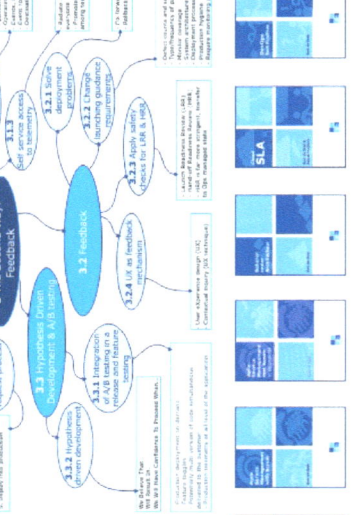

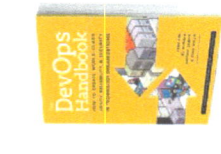

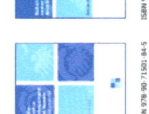

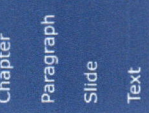

www.ingramcontent.com/pod-product-compliance
Lightning Source LLC
Chambersburg PA
CBHW050839220326
41598CB00006B/405